Sherwood M. Nelson

June, 1975

PHILOSOPHY AND THE NOVEL

PHILOSOPHY AND THE NOVEL

Philosophical aspects of

Middlemarch   *Anna Karenina*   *The Brothers Karamazov*
A la recherche du temps perdu

and of the methods of criticism

by

PETER JONES

CLARENDON PRESS · OXFORD
1975

Oxford University Press, Ely House, London W. 1

GLASGOW NEW YORK TORONTO MELBOURNE WELLINGTON
CAPE TOWN IBADAN NAIROBI DAR ES SALAAM LUSAKA ADDIS ABABA
DELHI BOMBAY CALCUTTA MADRAS KARACHI LAHORE DACCA
KUALA LUMPUR SINGAPORE HONG KONG TOKYO

CASEBOUND ISBN 0 19 824526 2
PAPERBACK ISBN 0 19 824533 5

*Printed in Great Britain by
Richard Clay (The Chaucer Press) Ltd.,
Bungay, Suffolk*

the doubtful illustration of principles still more doubtful?

Middlemarch, Chapter 48

ACKNOWLEDGEMENTS

WITH the exception of the chapter on *The Brothers Karamazov* this book was first delivered in lecture form as part of a course given in 1967–8 to students of Philosophy and Literature in the University of Edinburgh. I thank Naomi Diamond, Charles P. Bigger, Stanley Jones, M. J. Scott-Taggart, and W. H. Walsh for commenting on individual chapters and for their encouragement. I have profited from sustained argument with many of my students, and my debt to them is greater than they will believe. The essays on *Anna Karenina* and *A la recherche du temps perdu* first appeared in *Forum for Modern Language Studies*, 1969 and 1971; I am grateful to the General Editor for permission to reprint them here in an extended and revised form. In the last chapter I have used extracts from articles which were published in *The British Journal of Aesthetics*, 1969 and 1971; I am grateful to the Editor for permission to use this material in a revised form. My greatest debt, however, is to my wife. I dedicate the book to her.

CONTENTS

INTRODUCTION

THIS book consists of essays on four novels, and an outline of the theory of interpretation applied in the essays. The phrase 'philosophical aspects' in the sub-title of the book refers to the viewpoint I adopt, properties of the novels I discuss, and, using an old sense of 'aspect', to the act of consideration. I have tried to show some of the respects in which four novels commonly described as 'philosophical' do, in fact, merit that description. In addition, I have tried to show how an interest in philosophical matters can be sustained by reflection upon particular novels. I must stress that I have not sought to impose a common theme on the novels, although I have applied the same method of interpretation to each of them. The mere juxtaposition of the first four chapters shows parallels between the four novels that need no further emphasis, especially when it is remembered that Tolstoy greatly admired the work of George Eliot, and Proust greatly admired the work of George Eliot, Tolstoy, and Dostoevsky. Two underlying assumptions of my approach may be mentioned. First, great novels demand and reward the closest scrutiny of which we are capable; second, literary criticism is most fruitful when it indicates how it may be challenged. Thus I have given textual references for all my claims about the novels. It is part of my theory of interpretation that, in an important sense, the end justifies the means; in particular, that the rewards of an interpretation justify it. One consequence of my interpretations is that an orthodox view of each novel is displaced: for example, I show that it is false that one can find in *Middlemarch* only a few general philosophical commonplaces; that it is false that the narrator in Proust's novel believes that knowledge is unattainable; that it is misleading to represent the views in *The Brothers Karamazov* as merely existentialist; that it is untenable to take the views of Levin as providing criteria by which other characters in *Anna Karenina* should be judged. I hope that two other consequences will follow from my essays: first, that readers will re-examine the text of each novel and, second, that they will re-examine their own critical methods and assumptions.

The book is designed for readers who are already familiar with the four novels, but my essays may be read independently of each other. Philosophically inclined readers may prefer to read first the theoretical chapter at the end of the book. In that chapter I claim that what a text means for a given reader—I use the term 'significance'—in a sense is the creation of that reader. It is in the light of my emphasis upon the creative role of the interpreter that a feature of my vocabulary is to be understood. My frequent references in the first two chapters to 'inferences' that may be drawn from the texts may inadvertently emphasize the inductive elements in interpretation at the expense of what might be called 'immediate perception'; for some implications may strike a reader without the apparent mediation of inference. I preferred to risk such over-emphasis, however, in order to avoid the parallel danger of historically-oriented enquiry encouraged by talk of the text 'showing' a reader certain things—an expression I have used only occasionally. For it must be made clear that I do not aim to establish a particular author's intentions in or for his novel, nor his own preferred interpretation of it; my own historical discussion of George Eliot's views is designed to parallel but in no way to legitimize my creative interpretation of *Middlemarch*.

The elements of a text which each reader decides are worthy of attention are governed by his knowledge, interests, and aims, but these determinants do not covertly make all interpretation historical, any more than they force a reader to foist his own ideas on to a text. But, again, anyone who feels that I concern myself with what a particular text *could* mean, at the expense of what it *does* mean, should consult the last chapter. It will be realized that philosophical assumptions underlie my own interpretations of the novels, and that they condition my acceptance or rejection of the various views I infer from the novels. I have displayed, but rarely stated, these assumptions in what can be called the rhetoric of my presentation. A remark by Wittgenstein is appropriate in this context, although I do not claim that his own contextual use of it sanctions mine: 'a perspicuous representation produces just that understanding which consists in "seeing connections"' (*Philosophical Investigations*, paragraph 122). I believe that a creative critic provides a perspicuous representation of the texts he discusses, in the light of which readers can reflect on connections between their own situation and the situations presented in the novels. For a perspicuous representation captures the way we look at things.

It should not be necessary to stress that my comments on the novels represent only one type of criticism, or to point out that the theory of interpretation I outline in the final chapter has profound consequences. As a result of these consequences the theory requires more detailed analysis than I have here provided, and I hope to undertake it on another occasion.

SUMMARY OF THE ARGUMENT

In outline, the argument of my first chapter is simple. In *Middlemarch* a particular theory of knowledge is presupposed by the two distinguishable types of egoism we are shown, and textual evidence supports the claim that imagination is the central concept in that theory.

Indeed, once we have noticed the prevalence of imagination-vocabulary in *Middlemarch*, the numerous references to images and imagining, to conjectures, inclination, preconceiving, foreseeing, fashioning, and fancying, we discover that other prominent notions are subsumable under the concept of imagination—notions such as possibilities and plans, conscience and consciousness, even power and providence. If we then distinguish three roles of imagination, a picture emerges which illuminates the whole novel. As a presupposition of perception, imagination provides us with concepts for the purposes of making sense, in even the simplest way, of our most basic experiences; secondly, imagination alone enables us to get beyond our immediate experience, by allowing us to postulate the consequences and implications of our experience—features which, by definition, are not present to consciousness at the time. Imagination thus frees a man both from the past and the present, but unfortunately, it is subject to his brute psychological nature, in particular to his desires. These psychological states loosen a man's control over his imagination, such that he mistakes the mere possibilities he is able to imagine for the actual world. I claim that all the major characters in *Middlemarch* can be taken to make these mistakes. The third role of imagination is in the sympathetic understanding of other men; such understanding cannot be reached by men who are exclusively concerned with themselves, for it depends on the use of imagination to interpret the outward signs of other men's inner lives. I show that there is an occasional tension in the novel between the view that we receive information passively from the external world, without any necessary processing on our part, and the view that we are engaged in some sort of interpretation even at the most fundamental levels of experience, whatever those levels are. When the former, passive, theory is assumed one of the moral injunctions detectable in the novel becomes clearer, and more persuasive. On this analysis the implicit injunction is to determine the nature of our experiences, and the first step is to ensure that we have perceived phenomena correctly; further, whatever account we give of perception, we can establish that correctness only by comparing our descriptions with those of other people who, for the sake of the argument, are assumed to have had analogous experiences.

In contrast to my concentration on the recurrent vocabulary of imagination in *Middlemarch*, in *Anna Karenina* I focus upon the recurrence of two questions asked by all the major characters. In order to explain the significance of those questions, however, and of other elements in the text with which they may be associated, I introduce a pair of my own terms, *actio* and *passio*, to characterize the difference between an active and a passive response to a situation. The two questions are: 'What is to be done?' and 'What is the meaning or significance of the situation in which I find myself, and in which I have to act?' I show that much of the novel is concerned with the various obstacles which prevent the characters from answering these questions. I claim that when a character explicitly asks 'What is to be done?' the question emphasizes the moments of decision which explain subsequent deeds, and the points at which change might have been consciously initiated; on a deeper level, however, the question is related to the problem of what it is to be a human agent. Agency, in the fullest sense, is essential not only for self-respect, but ultimately for sanity, and it is for this reason that doing becomes equated with living. Most of the main characters, finding no acceptable answer to the question in their particular context, do nothing, and allow themselves to be passive precisely when action is called for. All the characters hope that things will right themselves so that no action from them will be required. Sometimes they ascribe to the situation an elemental force opposing them, which justifies their failure to act, but we are shown that there are other factors which explain inaction, such as the operation of egoistic desires and specious reasoning. Another factor is role-playing. I claim that the explicit adoption of a role in the novel is always an indication of a character's special needs, although the precise nature of the need cannot always be inferred from the role adopted. Self-conscious role-playing is to be contrasted with what a man would naturally and spontaneously do, other constraints notwithstanding. Where the demands of a role are allowed to subdue duties attached to his nature, a man is responsible for having denied himself agency. Indeed, we can infer the view that there can be no answer to the question 'What is to be done?' in terms of either roles or rules. Only the voice of conscience can give the correct answer. All the major characters are said to hear the voice of conscience, although for various reasons they fail to recognize or heed it; and it is important to note the implication that conscience furnishes a man with both non-moral knowledge of the facts, as well as with verdicts of what is right and wrong.

The Brothers Karamazov differs from the other novels I discuss in that it contains the statement of an explicit moral doctrine. In Chapter 4 I begin by outlining that doctrine, and claim that it provides the focus for both understanding and assessing everything that happens in the novel.

The doctrine itself is simple. Man cannot achieve salvation without unconditional and unconditioned faith in God and in immortality. On the basis of such faith man must pursue the practical moral policy of 'actively loving others'. By so doing, a man will be able to refrain from judging his neighbours and thereby avoid asserting himself at their expense and causing their humiliation; in addition he will be able to understand them, fulfil himself, and achieve self-knowledge. In the absence of faith and the practical policy, man is dominated by his pride. A proud man is an essentially passive man, who succumbs to both willed states such as self-punishment, and unwilled states such as shame, resentment, despair. The intellect is a mere tool, possessing no motive power of its own; when controlled by a man's pride, it seduces him into the belief that he is the measure of all things and that he himself is a god. In the novel there are several occasions when characters make inappropriate demands for proof, or limit the kinds of evidence they are willing to consider, because pride has command of their minds. Men suffer mental or spiritual crises when their inner voice of conscience claims to be heard in the face of the verdicts of pride. But although a man must seek to control his intellect, making it play a proper role in the service of faith and morality, he must not ignore his mind altogether; self-fulfilment can be achieved neither by self-indulgence in one faculty at the expense of others, nor by avoiding faculties it may be hard to control. True freedom consists in loving others and accepting responsibility for all men; such love, however, is hard to acquire and to sustain, but by means of such love the divine mystery of things, as well as their meaning, become apparent. Only by turning outwards can man satisfy the inner needs he constantly, and unwittingly, reveals—the need, above all, for others. A man who is bound up with himself satisfies his needs by indulging in self-punishment, vice, cruelty; he causes others to suffer, and succumbs to despair himself. The mind and body of man must be subservient to his soul; with this recognition faith can operate, and man can learn to respect his neighbour. From such faith and such respect for others, man's self-respect follows; it is self-deception to suppose that one had better fulfil oneself before one attends to others.

The attack on egoism that we saw in *Middlemarch* thus becomes a fully-fledged religious and moral doctrine in *The Brothers Karamazov*. And the doctrine of actively living for others as the only means to combat the passivity of self-concern clearly develops the position we discovered in *Anna Karenina*. In *The Brothers Karamazov* there is little indication, however, of the ways and senses in which a man may be said to acquire knowledge—the strictures on scientific and legal procedures give fewer clues than one might hope for. On the other hand in *Middlemarch* and *Anna Karenina* we see how desires can distort the operations of imagination, and thus prevent the acquisition of knowledge. And these views, together with emphasis on the effects of egoism and habit, reappear in *A la recherche du temps perdu*.

The philosophical remarks in Proust's novel are more evidently interrelated than they are in the other three novels. I concentrate exclusively on the narrator's views about the nature of knowledge. He believes we have three faculties: our senses, our imagination, and our intellect. We attain knowledge when we successfully use our intellect to elicit the true nature of the data provided by our senses; we fail to attain knowledge, and suffer illusion, when our imagination and intellect, unknown to us, operate to prevent an accurate examination of this data. From the fact that we invariably misinterpret our first impressions of anything, it follows that our knowledge is of the past; for by the time we have rectified our first interpretation, the impressions we then had no longer accord with the present state of the object.

The narrator attaches some importance to first impressions. As the basic constituent of knowledge they serve, essentially, to determine the accuracy with which our impressions reflect their objects. Further, it is only in virtue of his present impressions that a man can reassure himself of his self-identity; we fully exist, the narrator holds, only to the extent that we grasp the nature of the initial impressions. Several factors, I claim, are shown to operate as barriers to knowledge: egoism, desire, imagination, memory, intellect, habit, and time. The narrator believes these barriers can be surmounted, but he does not hold that life as we know it would be possible in their absence; rather he takes them as features of life to be recognized for what they are. It should be noted that all the obstacles to knowledge are alleged to have a good side, the goodness being entirely utilitarian. For example, the good side of imagination is that by it alone may one grasp the individuality of phenomena; and the good side of habit is that it secures us against perpetual bewilderment in the face of new experiences. The obstacles also provide the ultimate justification for art, since art alone is said to show us their presence and their defects.

The narrator believes, therefore, that knowledge is possible, in spite of the obstacles, but it will be always knowledge of the past; and the display of knowledge will be as difficult as its attainment. The synoptic view necessary for this display will require careful comparison and contrast between particular cases.

In the final chapter I adumbrate a theory of interpretation with which I believe the preceding chapters conform. The main tenets of the theory are as follows: the primary referent in each discussion of the novels is the text. Texts are publicly available, and are independent of the creator and their subsequent readers. Interpretation is the business of making sense of a text, of rendering it, in some way, coherent. The coherence or significance of a text is, so to say, a variable property, dependent upon the contextual knowledge, interests and viewpoint of a particular reader. We have to assume the purposiveness of a text before we can interpret it in any way at all. Creative interpretation is remarkable because of the freedom a reader has in postulating possible purposes, which enable him to create interpretations he finds rewarding. Several otherwise seemingly intractable problems are largely solved, if we recognize both the existence and nature of creative interpretation.

The notion of understanding a novel cannot be defined in terms of jointly necessary and sufficient conditions, but it can be characterized in terms of criteria. Here, the behaviour of the reader, and how he interacts with his peers, are central matters. The criteria for understanding human creations, such as novels, are in some ways analogous to those for understanding human beings themselves.

CHAPTER 1

Imagination and Egoism in Middlemarch

THE portrayal in *Middlemarch* of different sorts of egoism rests upon a particular theory of knowledge. The moral views espoused in the novel are grounded in the same theory. I shall show how imagination is the focal concept in that theory.

Western philosophers since Aristotle have generally held imagination to be a faculty separate from, and intermediate between, mere sensing and any concept-forming faculty. Its data were derived from one's experience, but it possessed the freedom to transform sense-impressions directly into ideas suitable for the intellect, or to fabricate new complex ideas by amalgamating otherwise unrelated impressions—in the latter way one could imagine a chimera or satyr. Until the eighteenth century most philosophers believed that the mind received data passively from their various sources; on such a view, imagination begins to operate on the data after they have been received. Kant, however, following unsystematic hints by previous philosophers, such as Bacon and Hume, urged that the mind is active and controlling in the very act of perceiving. On this view imagination functions in the initial selection and sorting of sense-experience, as well as subsequently when preparing that data for intellect. There are many difficulties in both views, and we shall see that in *Middlemarch* there is an occasional tension between the view that the mind is passive in its initial perceptions, and the view that it is active. Above all, we shall find that although imagination is held to be an essential tool for the acquisition of knowledge, it is also held to function as an obstacle. We can infer from the novel the view that a proper control over our imagination is a necessary condition of moral action, and a proper exercise of its many powers a necessary condition of knowledge. We can also infer the view that imagination governs perception, but that desires govern imagination; so that, ultimately, desires govern perception. In a later chapter we shall see how Proust's narrator accords a central place in his theory of knowledge to these same views.

The view I infer from *Middlemarch* postulates certain relations between knowledge and morality. In the first part of this chapter I set out various roles assigned to imagination in those alleged relations. In the second part of the chapter I shall consider briefly some of the philosophical remarks in George Eliot's letters and essays, and their possible sources. My purpose is to provide comparison with the preceding discussion of *Middlemarch*; it is not to attempt to legitimize my interpretation of the novel by reference to the author's intentions or independently known views. Some theoretical aspects of these points are raised in the final chapter.

It will be convenient to begin by assembling reminders of the types and degrees of egoism which are to be illuminated by the concept of imagination.

I

EGOISM

'All conceit is not the same conceit' (15.111)[1] because it varies in its dimensions and its aetiology; but one may be an egoist, apparently, in either or both of two senses. On the one hand, egoism is deemed to be logically unavoidable because it is held that each man's knowledge is founded, ultimately, on his sensory-experience alone—a familiar, but troublesome, view on which I shall comment in a moment. I shall call this egoism 'epistemological egoism'. It is held that 'the world' of each individual is essentially mediated by his perceptions or 'feelings'—in a wide sense of that term which we shall encounter again in Proust's novel—and that this 'world' may be said to be a function of his viewpoint, psychology, and knowledge. In this way each man's world is different. Secondly, however, there is moral egoism: selfishness and self-centredness at the expense of others. In what follows I shall

---

[1] All chapter and page references to *Middlemarch*, are to the Riverside Edition, edited by Gordon S. Haight, Boston, 1956.

use 'egoism' to denote moral egoism, because we may infer from *Middlemarch* the view that moral egoism is rooted in epistemological egoism, and that moral egoism can be avoided only when the logically unavoidable epistemological egoism is seen for what it is, and in a manner transcended. For although 'the world' of each individual is unique to him, there must be 'a world', nevertheless, in which all individuals live together and communicate, and which is assumed to be the common source of all the perceptions that go to make up every private world. *Of what*, otherwise, would a man's private perceptions *be* perceptions? This problem, which comes to the fore in Proust's novel, is in the background of *Middlemarch*, but is no less important; in both novels there is talk of characters 'constructing' worlds.

Wittgenstein and other recent philosophers have argued that there can be no coherent account of knowledge in terms of 'constructing' an external world from internal, private sensations accessible only to their owner. For such a view is unable to explain how concepts could be taught or learned, or how communication could be possible. The absence of concepts entails the absence of procedures for making claims and establishing their truth, and for enabling a man even to pick out his inner states. We should hardly expect a novel to discuss, in the manner of a philosophical treatise, what it means to found knowledge on sensory experience; but we should notice that the emphasis in *Middlemarch* on epistemological egoism arises from a concern to determine the origin and nature of moral concepts. An essential feature of the account we may infer from the novel is that as *concepts*, moral concepts have to be learned in the same way as other concepts, and not by some special means such as divine inspiration. Nevertheless, as *moral* concepts they are accorded some unique privileges, and we shall find that several unexplained assumptions are made in order to avoid difficulties that are sensed in the general picture of concept-acquisition. When the possibility of moral action seems to be threatened, for example, the scepticism that is constitutive of epistemological egoism is dismissed as 'irrelevant'; but, at that point, there must be doubt whether epistemological egoism ever had anything to do with moral egoism, and if it did not, then we may be deprived of the original explanation of the nature of moral concepts. In *Middlemarch*, as in *Anna Karenina* and *The Brothers Karamazov*, special moves are made in order to give moral knowledge-claims something like the status traditionally reserved for *a priori* truths and denied to empirical claims; and the unreliability of man's intellect as a guide to properly moral action is explained as partly due to the essential corrigibility of empirical claims about the world in which he has to act. The association of corrigibility with unreliability, and then with doubt, encourages an almost imperceptible slide from holding that in our empirical claims we might, on a given occasion, turn out to be wrong, to holding that we might always be wrong, and thus might never be right. In this way, the very condition of the possibility of empirical judgements gets transformed into a condition of their impossibility, and their glory becomes their shame.

In *Middlemarch* the interpretation given by each character of the world he confronts is governed by two factors; the knowledge he already possesses, in terms of which he tries to classify his new experience, and his passions and desires, themselves the product of various but usually unspecified egencies. Of these two factors, passions and desires are the most powerful. We are told that 'there is no human being who having both passions and thoughts does not think in consequence of his passions (47.343). But the operation of either of these factors tends to isolate an individual from the world he is trying to interpret, since he perceives only what his passions and previous knowledge permit. Dorothea's initial judgement on Casaubon was governed by her principal source of knowledge, books, and a tendency to wish-fulfilment: 'everything I see in him corresponds to his pamphlet on Biblical Cosmology' (2.15); here was a man whose 'learning almost amounted to a proof of whatever he believed'. The union which attracted her was one which would 'deliver her from her girlish subjection to her own ignorance' (3.21); but her own self-absorption did nothing to diminish Casaubon's (5.37), and the fact that her heart had been little fed 'from the living beings around her' (22.164) blinded her to the parallel lack in him. Casaubon 'had been the mere occasion which had set alight the fine inflammable material of her youthful illusions' (10.62) and the real future only replaced the imaginary when the minutiae of actual experience forced themselves upon her consciousness (20.144). The overthrow of illusions and preconceptions may be so disorienting that the real world seems dreamlike, as both Rome and her return to Lowick seemed to Dorothea; at first, in this state, she felt able to respond only to the two-dimensional miniature portrait of Aunt Julia, Will's grandmother (28.203. See also the dream imagery in the account of Bulstrode's disorientation, 61.450; 68.504; 69.511). The ardour in terms of which Dorothea is so prominently characterized (e.g. 20.146; 22.162; 54.394; 62.462; 72.537; 76.558), and to which most of her faults are assigned (77.565) revealed itself in the passionate search for objects to satisfy her energy; she longed for objects who could be dear to her (48.348; cf. 77.568). Like Anna Karenina, as we shall see, her unconsumed energy brought loneliness (34.238) and a marriage which was a perpetual struggle of energy with fear (39.285). Although admirable in itself, her energy in fact combined with her egoism to enforce her blindness to whatever did not lie in her own purpose, such as her husband's relations to others (37.273), and led her to confident, but mistaken, interpretations of people's behaviour, for example, Will's (55.399; 77.565). She reached the view, which is not entirely clear, that knowledge based upon experience undistorted by one's imagination, enables one to understand others and to act aright; in such cases the course of action becomes self-evident, as if it were 'chosen for' the agent (80.577). It needs to be noted that this would be an essentially passive aspect of knowledge; and also that the central notion of experience is unclear.

Since what she 'saw' was primarily a construction of her imagination, it is not surprising that Dorothea found Casaubon 'all she had at first imagined him to be'; the egoism in virtue of which he talked only of what he was interested in (3.24) found approval because of her own egoism. Even his assertion that she exemplified a 'preconceived' fitness to supply a need in his life (5.31) enhanced her own pride that 'she was chosen by the man whom her admiration had chosen.' Apt to think others were 'providentially' made for him, he was shocked to find marriage more of a 'subjection' than he had been able to imagine (10.62; 20.150). Whereas Dorothea initially saw the world in the light of her imagined world, Casaubon somehow recognized that the actual world fell short of his own *a priori* expectations about it; but after recognizing that neither Dorothea, nor anything else in the external circumstances, accounted for 'the moderation of his abandonment' (7.47; 10.63) he failed to examine himself. His self-imposed isolation, shrinking from pity (10.63; 29.206; 42.305), was intensified by his refusal or inability to confess it. Casaubon had consciously mapped out for himself a life devoid of spontaneity and feeling (29.207), had avoided clerical duties that might call for at least the display of feeling, such as burials (34.237), and thus a capacity needing careful nurture became atrophied. Even at the end of his life he knew little of Dorothea's inner life (43.312). We all indulge in make-believe, it is suggested, even if it is not of a 'flashy' variety (20.145); Casaubon had computed in his imagination the rewards due to his studious bachelorhood (10.63). Ignorant of the gap between his self-estimate and that of others, partly because his 'proud reticence' diminished the possibility of full self-consciousness (37.276), he nevertheless sought to acquit himself in the public eye and to elicit favourable judgement of his behaviour (e.g. 20.146; 29.205). Such approval would serve as a prop, and in the end a substitute, for his private estimate of his achievements. But here self-deception merely extended its influence; for public judgement on his 'unimpeachable' conduct carried none of the desired implications about the quality of his mind or intellectual achievement. And yet how soothing it would be to have a companion who would neither determine nor judge the extent of his failure (42.307). But knowledge of oneself is dependent upon knowledge of others, and Casaubon had effectively denied himself both; even if he did not actively create illusions about himself, he did not actively seek to avoid creating them (20.145); in the end, ironically, he deceived himself more than he deceived others. We generally ascribe self-deception to a man when there is a gap between 'the report of his own consciousness about his doings' (10.62) and what he actually does; but it is implied that we should temper our judgement because those reports express the psychological needs which control his search for self-identity.

Like Casaubon, Lydgate walked more by habit than self-critic-ism, and took a wife to adorn the remaining quadrant of his life, assuming that it would be one of her functions to admire his pre-eminence 'without too precise a knowledge of what it consisted in' (11.70; 58.425; 27.197). Although he discovered early on that he apparently had two selves, emotional and rational (15.113), he failed to guard against the dominance of the former in his every-day life; the 'primitive tissue' of Rosamond quite escaped him, and the virtues he ascribed to her were ideal constructions of his imagination (27.200). Passionate, energetic, idealistic, and 'ambi-tious of a wider effect' (15.108) Lydgate came to realize, like Dorothea with whom he shared these traits, that life must be taken up on a lower level of expectation (64.477) but that, never-theless, the real wife still had claims upon him. He was able to recover some semblance of his original self wherein he had free energy for spontaneous research, only when he experienced the uninhibited trust and reassurance of Dorothea (63.473; 66.489; 76.558).

Rosamond is the most extreme egoist in *Middlemarch*. She seemed to learn almost nothing from her experiences, and conse-quently hardly changes in the course of the novel. Like Casaubon she was concerned that her behaviour be judged irreproachable and blameless (11.73; 12.86; 58.433; 64.482; 65.487); and like Anna Karenina her excessive self-concern led to ennui (59.439; 64.484; 75.552; 77.564). Sharing one trait with Casaubon and Dorothea, she was little used to 'imagining other people's states of mind except as material cut into shape by her own wishes' (78.569). Initially she had been concerned only with Lydgate's relation to her, not with him as a person (16.124), and we are told that her discontent with marriage 'was due to the conditions of marriage itself, to its demands for self-suppression and tolerance, and not to the nature of her husband' (75.552). Like her uncle Bulstrode, Rosamond succeeded in managing almost everybody (36.252); but unlike him, her sense of walking in an unknown world (81.583) seemed not long sustained.

To gain as much general power as possible Bulstrode engaged in much inward argument to adjust his motives (13.95; 16.116); sin was to him a question of doctrine and the bearing of his deeds a matter of private vision (53.384). When he discovered that he was carrying on two distinct lives, associated with religion and business respectively, he argued himself into feeling their compatibility (61.451); whereas Lydgate declined to use his intellect when indulging his passions, Bulstrode used his intellect to provide a specious justification for his indulgence. For example, reflecting on his past, he was able to break down the facts into little sequences each of which he could justify by reasons which seemed to prove them righteous (61.452). The point is not that analysis of complex phenomena is irrelevant, but that a man's intellect can be bent by his passions into mistaken analyses, ignoring, for example, many of the less obvious causal factors which have operated in the fulfilment of his desires (68.503). Only 'direct fellow-feeling with individual fellow-men' (61.453) can check the undermining effects of a man's desires on his morality, and can clear the way for an active conscience and a full consciousness of what he is doing. Egoists such as Bulstrode and Rosamond are quick to grasp and accept truths that are in their own interest (53.381; 58.427); other truths are ignored or suppressed.

Differences in the aims and circumstances in which characters find themselves, explain differences in their egoisms. In all cases, however, egoism is supposed to prevent a character from attaining knowledge of himself and his situation, and make fully moral action impossible. Because of the dominance of her fanciful constructions Dorothea failed to see the facts obvious to everybody else (4.27; 37.273), particularly with respect to Casaubon; intent on her own improvement she failed to consider that in every personal relationship there are two sides. Casaubon became uneasily aware that his *a priori* theories seemed not to fit the world they were purportedly about; he examined neither himself nor the nature of the patterns he tried to impose on the facts. Lydgate believed that the rigour applicable to scientific discovery was not needed in human relations; that his passionate nature could easily be accommodated to his intellectual aims; and that the effort to understand both others and himself did not require his full capacities or special effort. Bulstrode, like Casaubon and Lydgate, looked upon a wife as an uncritical prop for his own activities; confusing the intention with the deed, like Casaubon, he used his intellect to endorse his desires for as much power as possible over people— Lydgate's desire was for power over the forces of nature. It is implied that an egoist characteristically assumes that other men use of him those descriptions he would prefer them to use, to foist, in his imagination, his private estimate of himself on to others; anxiety reveals itself when he becomes concerned, as do Casaubon, Bulstrode, and Rosamond, with public estimates of his behaviour. Thus Bulstrode was shocked that Will Ladislaw should not see the offer of money as a 'striking piece of scrupulosity' and 'a penitential act in the eyes of God' (61.456).

Against this background sketch of some of the features of egoism portrayed in *Middlemarch*, it is now appropriate to turn to the various activities of imagination shown in the novel, and the different roles assigned to that portmanteau concept.

IMAGINATION AND INTERPRETATION

We can infer from *Middlemarch* the view that imagination functions in three related but distinguishable ways: firstly, as a presupposition of all perception; secondly, as a constructive agency; thirdly, as a foundation of sympathetic understanding and thus, of morality. It is not clear how the first and second functions are related; it may be that we should say constructive imagination operates both before and after perception, rather than postulate its function as a presupposition of perception.

Considered as a presupposition of perception it is logically impossible for imagination not to operate if a man is aware of anything at all; because in this role imagination is held to provide concepts for the purposes of recognizing and sorting the un-connected images which constitute a man's sensory data. How it does this, and how the concepts themselves are to be characterized, are among the issues that remain unclear. Nevertheless, on the doubtful assumption that the elements of experience are atomistic, unconnected, and evanescent in character, imagination is held to enable a man to impose some coherent pattern on his experience— a view which can be held independently of the assumption. But a man is able to think both of the continuity of his experience, and of the continuity of anything external to him (the world), which may be causally related to his experience. Here again imagination operates, enabling him to bridge not only the gaps in his sensory images, but also the gaps between those images and things external to them.

It may be argued that this last operation requires the construc-tion of hypotheses, and that this activity specifically belongs to the second principal role of imagination. For in the second role imagi-nation is essentially constructive in its operation; its 'proper' objects, in the Aristotelian term, are possibilities. The mind is somehow able to blend into new complex ideas various sensory images not so combined upon their original reception by the mind; thus one can construct a composite image of a satyr. The essential feature here is that imagination enables a man to escape bondage to his actual experience, and thus to the past, and to create a new world, a mental world, separate from the physical world to which it is ultimately, however indirectly, related. Con-structive imagination is thus associated with fancy, fantasy, and fiction; but also with aims and plans, and in connection with these, with desires, hopes, and wishes. Should it not therefore be avoided? On the contrary; for, according to the theory we are considering, constructive imagination alone enables a man to postulate causal connections between phenomena, to formulate explanatory hypotheses, to construct probable conjectures about the future and unobserved phenomena, to offer and compare in-terpretations of what is assumed to be only indirect evidence. It is necessary, in this last way, for understanding our fellow beings;

for we have to interpret the manifestations of their inner lives which are only indirectly available for our inspection.

It will be evident, therefore, that even if imagination in its first role is a logical presupposition of perception, it is also essential in the second role if that perception is to be usefully interpreted. But it is precisely the freedom of imagination in its creative role which can either prevent or ensure knowledge of our world and of other men. In both of the first two roles, imagination supplements sense-experience. Firstly, by supplying concepts which enable us to order our experience, and thus to construct, recognize, identify (these otherwise different notions seem intimately related in this context) a perception *as* a perception; secondly, by enabling us to postulate phenomena other than our perceptions—in the first place, an independently existing world, and then causal connections with it and within it. Comparisons, parallels, analogies, metaphors, are all the work of constructive imagination (cf. 61.451).

The third role of imagination in the view inferred from *Middlemarch* could be regarded as a special case of the second role, hypothetical or constructive imagination. It is 'the exercise of imagination on other people's needs' that Fred avoided (24.183), and is the foundation of sympathetic understanding of other people, and hence, of morality. Intelligible communication between men, it is supposed, rests on the assumption that their private sense-experiences are roughly similar in situations assumed to be similar. With respect to the privacy of his own experience, every man must be 'the centre of his own world' (10.62); but mutual understanding, and the moral life dependent on it, requires the assumption by constructive imagination of what we might call *the shared privacy* of experience. The need for such an assumption is denied by those who argue that knowledge cannot be constructed out of essentially *private* items. A 'wide difference . . . is manifest (in our own sensations) between ourselves and others' (58.429); a moral life consists, in part, in the constant effort to counteract this built-in bias of our experience. Morality depends as much on the recognition of the similarities between men (cf. 18.139), as on

remembrance of their individuality. This point is emphasized in
Middlemarch by the portrayal of similar responses by otherwise
very dissimilar people. Since we shall note this device in *Anna
Karenina* it is worth remarking upon the number of occasions on
which different characters have analogous experiences, or behave
in similar fashion. Mary Garth and Dorothea are equally incredu-
lous to learn that Farebrother and Ladislaw, respectively, are in
love with them (52.380; 50.360); Will and Dorothea misunderstand each other in ways analogous to those in which Lydgate and
Rosamond misunderstand each other (Chs. 62, 64); Dorothea,
Casaubon, Lydgate, and Bulstrode all experience a feeling of help-
lessness or powerlessness over some other person (48.348; 42.306;
58.427; 53.388); Dorothea and Mrs. Bulstrode both symbolically
change their clothes in recognition of a new emotional perspective
(80.578; 74.550), and their respective husbands, Casaubon and
Bulstrode, each fear that their wives have judged them (42.306;
68.504). Lydgate, Casaubon, and Bulstrode, who all wanted subservient wives, were driven to secrecy in their troubles, and denied
themselves any spontaneous support.

In our internal dialogues, as much as in our external communi-
cations, we assume certain repeated patterns or samenesses in our
experience which permit us to use the concepts we do. If we
expect others to understand us, we must assume they have some
basis of similar experiences in order to render our remarks intelligible; and the very same assumption provides a foundation for
morality. We shall see later that such assumptions presuppose the
use of concepts. Mrs. Cadwallader's warning to Dorothea has a
greater significance than might at first appear: 'We have all got to
exert ourselves a little to keep sane, and call things by the same
names as other people call them by' (54.391). In the context of
utterance, and as an expression of the speaker's own attitudes, the
remark is false. But a reader, although able to see that it is false for
the speaker, nevertheless can use the remark as the expression of a
deeper truth. The exertion can be taken to refer to the necessity of
publicly expressing at least some of our internal states; for only in
this way can we both establish the intelligibility of our own

account, and create a bond of understanding with other people, through shared knowledge. Casaubon's mind, both literally and metaphorically, was 'weighted with unpublished matter' (20.147); unable to 'thrill out of self-consciousness' (29.206) he could find no 'impulse needed to draw him out of himself' (66.489). He acquired no 'sense of fellowship deep enough to make all efforts at isolation seem mean and petty instead of exalting' (42.306); his failure to 'confess' his suspicions gave them a greater hold; he behaved like 'mortals generally' who make no 'attempt at exactness in the representation to themselves of what did not come under their own senses', or even of what did (15.114).

Reference should now be made to some of the passages which can be taken as illustrating the two interpretative roles of imagination—within and after perception. When Dorothea first looked into Casaubon's mind she saw 'reflected there in vague labyrinthine extension every quality she herself brought' (3.17); similarly when Fred considered Featherstone's intentions, 'half what he saw ... was no more than the reflex of his own inclinations' (12.89). Antecedent desires and expectations condition what one perceives; 'what believer sees a disturbing omission?' (5.37). Both cognitive factors and emotional states make 'a sort of background against which' we see events and people (77.567). This is a very general feature of perception; Celia was aware of the 'strange coloured lamps by which Dodo habitually saw' (84.600), but was not aware of their parallels in herself. On this view, there is no such thing as a purely passive and reliable perception of the external world; there is rather an interaction between us and the world. But the imagination operates yet again after our initial perceptions, completing the gaps in our perceptions and extrapolating from them. Thus Dorothea 'filled up all the blanks with unmanifested perfections, interpreting him as she interpreted the works of Providence' (9.55); her acquaintance with Casaubon was founded on 'the brief entrances and exits of a few imaginative weeks called courtship', where 'everything is regarded as provisional and preliminary'; and 'supported by her faith in their future', any 'imperfect coherence' in his behaviour 'seemed due to the brokenness of their intercourse' (20.145). Rosamond was equally constructive upon fragmentary data with respect to Lydgate; her initial postulate enabled her both to 'recognize' the data and to fill in any gaps in it: 'Rosamond, whose basis for her structure had the usual airy slightness, was of remarkably detailed and realistic imagination when the foundation had been once presupposed'; 'the construction seemed to demand that he should somehow be related to a baronet', and Lydgate was certainly 'better than any fancied "might-be" such as she was in the habit of opposing to the actual' (12.88).

It is common to find that 'we have been making up our world entirely without' a fact which has 'perhaps been staring at us' (35.243); but even with the incorporation of such facts, we must not forget the sense in which our world remains a construction. It is reasonable to infer from the novel the common, if not entirely clear, view that our knowledge is limited to our experience, and experience is itself limited both in extent and by the various factors which distort its interpretation. 'Intuition', 'conviction', 'opinion' are often the only evidence we can adduce for our assertions (15.105). The strongest determinants, even of the imaginative concepts which function as the presupposition of perception, are a man's psychological states; 'desires make their way into the imagination', and the images which form our controlling concepts 'are the brood of desire' (70.519; 34.237—it should be noted that 'images' are accorded a primary place in the activity of thinking, in *Middlemarch*). Bulstrode was dominated by 'images of the events he desired' in connection with Raffles; his images and conjectures 'were a language to his hopes and fears' (70.516; 69.511). Our moods help to condition the aspects of things which appear to us; aspects change with viewpoint, and metaphorically, the notion of viewpoint covers one's internal states. Necessarily our knowledge is a function of our viewpoints, and it is often useful to vary them (50.359; 40.292) in order to minimize self-interested elements in them. 'Perception of facts' on such a view, would thus refer not to an impossible ideal, wherein one is devoid of viewpoint and presuppositions of perception; it would refer to the self-conscious avoidance of partiality (37.267). It is a matter of contingent fact that we often best succeed only when the events do not touch us personally or are antecedently believed to be such that we have 'little expectation' of gain (35.243) from them. Mary Garth's 'attention had taken a new attitude' when she became aware of new interpretations of Farebrother's behaviour towards her (57.423); that is, forarmed with a new set of concepts for describing the phenomena—assumed to be independently existent —she noticed features not covered by the old concepts. Reference to making 'the mind flexible with constant comparison' and avoidance of seeing phenomena in terms of 'a set of box-like partitions' (22.157) can be taken to have a double significance. Firstly, there is no reason to suppose that any one description of an event or thing is both exhaustive and timelessly accurate; by comparing our descriptions of one thing we become more flexible in our attitudes and less blindly dogmatic about our own temporary viewpoint. Secondly, by comparing descriptions of different things we establish relations between them, and by securing reciprocal illumination extend our awareness. It is precisely with recognition of such relativism that scepticism rears its head; but it is 'irrelevant scepticism' (70.516). It should be noticed that no logical reasons have been adduced against scepticism; it is dismissed for purely pragmatic reasons. But the attempt to limit the domain of scepticism in such an apparently arbitrary way might be taken as an implicit acknowledgement of its invincibility. Now the facts have to be brought under concepts; the concepts we have reflect our needs, interests, and previous knowledge. The very use of concepts, reapplicable as they are in contexts other than the present, implies the possibility of reference beyond the present. When Rosamond 'registered every look and word, and estimated them as the opening incidents of a preconceived romance' with Lydgate (16.123) it should be remembered that imagination operated in the very 'registration' of the looks, as well as in the subsequent interpretation of them. According to the view we are discussing, there are no theory–neutral descriptions, and phenomena do not present themselves to us with ready-made labels.

We have to form hypotheses about the present which must be verifiable in the future; and the greatest obstacle to fruitful hypotheses, because the most powerful determinant of perception, is desire.

There may seem to be a minor puzzle at this stage. Even if alleged descriptions are essentially tied to viewpoints, does it not make sense to talk of brute facts? Casaubon felt, for example, that 'against certain facts he was helpless' (42.306). Two observations are pertinent. Nothing said threatens the stability of facts; however much our descriptions are relative to our interests, we are quite entitled to postulate an independent and stable referent of those descriptions. Secondly, there are passages in *Middlemarch* in which something like a passive theory of perception is espoused, in opposition to the active, interpretative theory we have been discussing. 'Acquired knowledge asserts itself and will not let us see as we saw in the day of our ignorance' (80.577); there is a 'directness of sense' (21.157) which is a guarantee of veracity. There need be no contradiction here, however. The reference in these cases is mainly to the conviction induced in us by some of the descriptions which we have applied, perhaps spontaneously and unselfconsciously, to a state of affairs; there is no implication of events carrying their own labels, of our descriptions being exhaustive or unamendable, and no implication, either, of these descriptions being free from the operations of imagination. The claim, in other words, is not that we all have some experience which *cannot* be misinterpreted, but that we all have some experience of which it is permissible to say that it *is* not misinterpreted; and that our criterion for recognizing this experience is something like conviction or 'immediacy'. The criterion, however, is not foolproof; it was reliable for Garth (cf. 40.300), for example, but not for Rosamond. And the reason, of course, is obvious. Because of her egoism, Rosamond was unable to distinguish between the conviction attendant upon her self-interested interpretations, and that attendant upon her disinterested ones. We would have to learn that an inner conviction was reliable, by testing our interpretations for reliability; we would have no rational ground for supposing such a feeling reliable in advance of such testing. In this context it is worth contrasting the clichés uttered by Garth and Rosamond. Firstly, Garth's were founded on particular events, and were the outcome of first-hand experience; secondly, they were testable by subsequent experience. Rosamond's commonplaces were learned as the dogmas of her education; as such they were not testable, and even when true, they could not be claimed as 'true for her', because they were not founded on experience.

Before proceeding with further discussion of the interpretative operations of perception, we may take our bearings. Since antiquity it has been held that man is both a thinking and a feeling being. If we associate imagination with his thinking side, we may say that in *Middlemarch* we are shown how the feeling side can dominate the thinking side. Desires, passions, and other psychological states prevent the proper operation of imagination, both within and subsequent to perception. Fancy is free to construct upon the data available to it, but it possesses no built-in filter which excludes already biased material. We shall later refer to cases in which characters lived in a world of make-believe precisely because their constructive imagination worked at the behest of their egoistic desires. On those occasions they tend to tamper with their existing knowledge, especially of the causal principle. For example, the imagined realization of their desires would require either exemption from causal sequences at present in operation, or a special and highly improbable divergence or interruption of that sequence; alternatively, it would require the desire itself to be a sufficiently dominating causal factor to ensure its fulfilment. When recognition of other causal factors is unavoidable, we find characters imagining the operation of 'chance'; but, as Hume observed, 'chance has no place, on any hypothesis'.[1]

At this stage reference should be made to an important passage which, at first, may seem to imply that no imagination is presupposed by perception, but that, on the contrary, one can have reliable passive perceptions.

[1] D. Hume, *Dialogues Concerning Natural Religion* (pub. 1779), Part VI: 'Chance has no place, on any hypothesis, sceptical or religious.'

An eminent philosopher among my friends, who can dignify even your ugly furniture by lifting it into the serene light of science, has shown me this pregnant little fact. Your pier-glass or extensive surface of polished steel made to be rubbed by a housemaid, will be minutely and multitudinously scratched in all directions; but place now against it a lighted candle as a centre of illumination, and lo! the scratches will seem to arrange themselves in a fine series of concentric circles around that little sun. It is demonstrable that the scratches are going everywhere impartially, and it is only your candle which produces the flattering illusion of a concentric arrangement, its light falling with an exclusive optical selection. These things are a parable. The scratches are events, and the candle is the egoism of any person now absent—of Miss Vincy, for example. (27.195)

Granting that this is a parable, there are issues to be unravelled. What are the differences between the conditions under which it is possible to know that the scratches go everywhere impartially, and those under which they appear in concentric rings? In the latter case, a person's egoism inclines him to impose a pattern upon patternless phenomena, and, moreover, a pattern which is a function of his interests and viewpoint; he projects himself as the focus of the events. In the former case, however, it seems possible both to illuminate the phenomena, and to adopt a viewpoint with respect to them, which avoid the private interests of the observer. But surely in both cases what the observer claims to observe will be a function of his perceptions and his viewpoint—backgrounds and foregrounds are relative to position and interest (34.238); and if imagination is an inalienable aspect of all perception, then the observer is offering an interpretation of phenomena even when he judges it patternless. We are told, as we shall see in the next long quotation, that the scientific method consists in framing critical hypotheses that are testable by the facts; but how are the facts themselves designated which will constitute the test—by means of further hypotheses? In the light of the preceding discussion we can avoid the apparent dilemma here. Even if imagination provides us with concepts in our original perceptions, and even if they may subsequently be amended, the primary purpose of the concepts is

to enable us to pick out the referent of our attention; their function is distinct from that of hypothesis, which is specifically the
role of constructive imagination, because in this latter role an
attempt is made to go beyond actual experience. The facts that
will test an explicit hypothesis will thus be designated by any
descriptions which serve on that occasion to pick them out. It
follows that only by determining its role and function in its context can we tell whether a particular utterance is operating as an
initial individuating expression, or as an hypothesis based on such
prior expressions. There are residual problems in this area which I
shall leave aside. I should emphasize that it is not necessary for
George Eliot to discuss these philosophical problems in her novel;
but it is important for a reader to recognize the difficulties here,
especially as they pinpoint the tension, discernible also in Proust's
novel, between the account of the evidence available to the
characters in the novel, and the account of what they actually
knew. The omniscient author appears immune from precisely
those obstacles to knowledge encountered by her characters, and
to which we are all alleged to be subject in everyday life. It may
be urged, of course, that such a move is not only permissible, but
essential, for any novelist concerned to draw attention to universal
characteristics; and that it explains why a moral fable rather than
a factual history is a preferable mode of presenting these truths.
The author operates in an imagined world of hypotheses or possibilities over which she exercises absolute control; in such a world
she is exempt from the barriers to knowledge to which she would
be subject if she were to tell a factual tale.

The intellectual procedures of Casaubon and Lydgate afford us
a clear view of the interpretative functions of imagination. Casaubon characterized himself in this way: 'My mind is something like
the ghost of an ancient, wandering about the world and trying
mentally to construct it as it used to be, in spite of ruin and confusing changes'—we should note the irony of the next sentence—
'But I find it necessary to use the utmost caution about my eyesight' (2.13). Of course, being an *a priori* theory, there was a sense
in which no eyesight had ever been necessary. This aside, the

reference to 'wandering about the world' carries an implication of an undirected search, and a willing subscription to a passive theory of perception. The following account bears out this interpretation.

Mr. Casaubon's theory of the elements which made the seed of all tradition was not likely to bruise itself unawares against discoveries: it floated among flexible conjectures no more solid than those etymologies which seemed strong because of likeness in sound, until it was shown that likeness in sound made them impossible: it was a method of interpretation which was not tested by the necessity of forming anything which had sharper collisions than an elaborate notion of Gog and Magog: it was as free from interruption as a plan for threading the stars together. (48.351)

Casaubon's method contrasts with Dorothea's youthful eagerness to turn all her small allowance of knowledge into principles (20.143), and with Bulstrode's doctrinal conviction that his deeds could be tested by 'theoretic phrases' (53.386). In extreme contrast, Lydgate framed testable hypotheses about the phenomena to be investigated (in the next section we shall discover the care needed in the contemplation of possibilities, and also that Lydgate did not carry his self-critical scientific method into his social life (58.431)):

He went home and read far into the smallest hour, bringing a much more testing vision of details and relations into this pathological study than he had ever thought it necessary to apply to the complexities of love and marriage, these being subjects on which he felt himself amply informed by literature, and that traditional wisdom which is handed down in the genial conversation of men. Whereas Fever had obscure conditions, and gave him that delightful labour of the imagination which is not mere arbitrariness, but the exercise of disciplined power— combining and constructing with the clearest eye for probabilities and the fullest obedience to knowledge; and then, in yet more energetic alliance with impartial Nature, standing aloof to invent tests by which to try its own work.

Many men have been praised as vividly imaginative on the strength of their profuseness in indifferent drawing or cheap narration:— ... But these kinds of inspiration Lydgate regarded as rather vulgar and

vinous compared with the imagination that reveals subtle actions inaccessible by any sort of lens, but tracked in that outer darkness through
long pathways of necessary sequence by the inward light which is the
last refinement of Energy, capable of bathing even the ethereal atoms in
its ideally illuminated space. He for his part had tossed away all cheap
inventions where ignorance finds itself able and at ease: he was enam-
oured of that arduous invention which is the very eye of research,
provisionally framing its object and correcting it to more and more
exactness of relation; he wanted to pierce the obscurity of those minute
processes which prepare human misery and joy, those invisible tho-
roughfares which are the first lurkingplaces of anguish, mania, and
crime, that delicate poise and transition which determine the growth of
happy or unhappy consciousness. (16.122)

Imagination must be used, therefore, on this view, to interpret
our experience; and if the concepts used are derived from egoistic
fancy, incomprehension and bewilderment ensue. Put in this way,
it is obscure how concepts for the purposes of interpretation can
be derived from egoistic fancy, which itself, so to say, is on the
same level as, or is an aspect of, interpretation. Rosamond and
Lydgate each imagined the other to have properties they in fact
lacked; each lived in a world of which the other knew nothing
(16.123). Rosamond interpreted his initial behaviour towards her
'as the opening incidents of a preconceived romance—incidents
which gather from the foreseen development and climax'; his
behaviour meant more to her because she cared more for it. The
meaning we attach to words, as a speaker or listener, depends on
our feelings (22.164; 27.197): '"What can *I* do, Tertius?" said
Rosamond, turning her eyes on him again. That little speech of
four words, like so many in all languages, is capable by varied
vocal inflexions of expressing all states of mind from helpless dim-
ness to exhaustive argumentative perception, from the completest
self-devoting fellowship to the most neutral aloofness' (58.434).
'Signs are small measurable things, but interpretations are illimit-
able' (3.18) precisely because they are influenced by our interests
and feelings. The very fragmentariness of the information that we
have encourages us to be constructive in imagination (22.157).

Lydgate had interpreted Rosamond's sylph-like frame as a sign of her intelligent sensitiveness (58.432) because such an interpretation conformed to his wishes. Even when the phenomena are accurately described, which can happen accidentally (3.18), the significance that may be inferred from them invariably reflects the interest of the interpreter. 'A man may be puffed and belauded, envied, ridiculed, counted upon as a tool and fallen in love with, or at least selected as a future husband, and yet remain virtually unknown—known merely as a cluster of signs for his neighbours' false suppositions' (15.105). The Lydgate with whom Rosamond had been in love 'had been a group of airy conditions for her, most of which had disappeared, while their place had been taken by everyday details which must be lived slowly from hour to hour, not floated through with a rapid selection of favourable aspects' (64.484). Rosamond had been occupied not with Lydgate 'as he was in himself, but with his relation to her' (16.124) and she did not consider it necessary to imagine his inner life, since she was 'sure of being admired by someone worth captivating' (27.197). Sympathy, we may infer, enables a man correctly to interpret otherwise overlooked signs (29.207; 55.399; 78.570) and such sympathy is not always reciprocated; Dorothea began to read the signs of Casaubon's moods, and Lydgate, Rosamond's. Between Lydgate and Rosamond there was 'that total missing of each other's mental track, which is too evidently possible even between persons who are continually thinking of each other' (58.428); the result was similar in the relation between Casaubon and Dorothea, because Casaubon failed to give anything of himself 'so that the past life of each could be included in their mutual knowledge and affection' (20.147).[1] It is unclear whether sympathy is supposed to

---

[1] Max Scheler was later to argue, in very similar vein, that 'egocentricity' was the illusion of taking one's own environment to be the world itself, and that this sort of solipsism led to egoism of character and attitude in volition and action. Sympathy and love, he held, could destroy the 'metaphysical delusion' of relative solipsism, just as they destroy the ethical evil of selfishness. 'Identification' at the 'organic' level, and learning at the intellectual level, enable a man to smooth out gradually the private idiosyncrasies and limitations that beset everyone. See Max Scheler, *The Nature of Sympathy* (pub. 1913), London, 1954.

be a special sort of imagination, and how it operates if it belongs
to a different level from interpretative imagination.

Constructive imagination is necessary not only for the recognition of causal connections between phenomena (68.503; 77.564),
but also for recognition of the many factors that may act as causes.
We are shown a wide variety of such causes. Other people, social
conditions, financial pressures and memories may all act as causal
determinants of a man's actions (36.252; 18.133; 37.272; 61.450);
so too may habit, ennui and the 'vague exactingness of egoism'
(60.441; 66.492; 59.439). Unknown but potent psychological
factors often operate, as in the case of Mrs. Cadwallader's match-
making (6.44). Indirect causes are no less effective than direct
causes, and it should be remembered that 'a human being . . . is a
slow creation of long interchanging influences' (40.300); the con-
vergence of the lives of Lydgate and Dorothea shows the 'slow
preparation of effects from one life to another' (11.70). Among the
most powerful determinants of action are a person's needs. Dorothea's great mental need was to make her life effective and to
escape the social bonds of her upbringing (3.20; 37.266); gradually she realized that not only Casaubon, but also everyone else,
has needs (21.156; 76.557)—Bulstrode, for example, had an immense need of being important (61.453). It is not clear, however,
whether a man is in a position to control his needs, even when he
recognizes them. If character is a process and an unfolding (of
what?), not something solid and unalterable (15.111; 72.538), how
much freedom is a man presumed to have? It should be observed
that both Casaubon and Garth are said to have unalterable traits
(20.147; 24.178), in each case dominating ones, and it is unclear
how much weight should be attached to the notion of changing
character; nor is the force of the epigraph to Chapter 70 at all
evident: 'what we have been makes us what we are.'

Garth's assertion that 'things hang together' (40.297—compare
Brooke's disingenuous 'We're all one family' 51.367) merely
draws attention to the web-like relations between people and
events so clearly displayed in the novel. The reader is told that
living bodies, and the expression is metaphorical, referring not

only to people but to institutions and morality itself, should be studied as webs (hence the structure of the novel); because any life is bound both by its own acts and traits, and by a 'zone of dependence' on others (15.110; 61.450): Will failed to recognize the extent of his dependence on Brooke, just as Lydgate failed to recognize his own dependence upon Bulstrode. The web should not be constructed from imagined properties, however, as may happen with two people in love (36.253). Only constant comparison keeps the mind flexible, ensures the avoidance of box-like partitions for our knowledge, and reveals that each of us is only a part of things as a whole (22.157; 42.306; 80.577). It is common for men to fail to compare the numerous strands of experience they have (58.429) and thus to deprive themselves of knowledge when they have all the evidence to hand. Perhaps conscience is supposed to operate here, as some guarantor of knowledge. Bulstrode failed to consider that the consequences he had long ago initiated were themselves causal factors from whose influence he was not immune: 'the train of causes' in which he had locked himself, went on (61.451). To Lydgate, in contrast, all his previous actions seemed, in retrospect, preparatory to his present disaster (73.540), but in this he was mistaken; nothing in the evidence entitled him to suppose that multiple causes necessarily issue in only one dominating effect; the set of effects one picks out is influenced by one's interests.

One other feature of constructive imagination may be noted. Dorothea is initially characterized as self-consciously self-denying (22.163; 50.359); she questioned the purity of her sensuous delight in jewellery and in riding (1.11), and Will Ladislaw remonstrated with her 'want of sturdy neutral delight in things as they were' (30.215). The point is here not simply her search for 'principles' (20.143); it is rather that constructive imagination may encourage a person to think more about an imagined world, whether or not it is set up as a religious ideal or goal, than about the actual world. In this respect Dorothea's 'theoretic' nature resembled Casaubon's search for an *a priori* explanation of mythology.

POSSIBILITIES AND PLANS

In common parlance, and in *Middlemarch*, there is a sense in which 'imagining' refers only to what a man does not know. Everything imagined, in this sense, has the status of an hypothesis or possibility. All the major characters in the novel fail, on occasion, to recognize that what they imagine are only possibilities in this sense; hypotheses fashioned by desire in the absence of knowledge or in the face of counter-evidence. Men are led astray when their fanciful constructions infect the working of imagination in its fundamental perceptual role, for then they see only what they desire to see, and inextricably confuse the possible with the actual. We should note that in its hypothetical role, imagination has a forward-looking aspect, since attempts to confirm or verify our suppositions lie in the future; and the projection into the future itself relies upon the principle of induction which supposes that laws assumed to have operated in the past will operate in the future.

Dorothea's 'favourite fad' was to draw plans (4.27). This should be associated both with her disinclination to see facts and with her impatience with those who did not do what she liked (9.61); further, as Will pointed out, it manifested a concern for the future at the expense of the present. Above all it exhibited her desire for power, albeit in a fairly harmless way. At the planning stage of a project a man exercises maximum control over his ideas; moreover, it is often *only* at this stage that he retains such control. The possibilities we imagine have all and only the properties we ascribe to them in imagining them; they are entirely our creations. But this total freedom is dangerous; for while it may pander to our egoistic desires for dictatorship, it discourages recognition of what the actual world is like, and may induce a man to surrender completely to his imagined world. Dorothea's assertion that she had never carried out a plan, to which should be added the qualification 'successfully' (84.600), draws attention to the success of her unselfconscious acts, and the failure of her egotistical plans. The *a priori* opposition to plans should be compared with the *a priori* condemnation of role-playing in *Anna Karenina* (see below, pp. 79 ff.); no reasons are given for denying that in certain contexts planning may be the most rational and sustaining procedure.

Indulgence in plans and possibilities diminishes the capacity for action, and often leads to the neglect of present tasks, even when those tasks are necessary steps to the fulfilment of the desired plan; Fred and Will illustrate this point in different ways (cf: 22.162; 23.172). Failure to carry out the initial steps may then lead to surrender to the imagined world, where action is not only easy but comes without effort or obstacle. Possibilities become more real than actuality, and dwelling upon them becomes a surrogate for action; at this stage men become passive victims of their distorted mental vision and thus of the world around them, of which they remain ignorant. 'We are on a perilous margin when we begin to look passively at our future selves, and see our own figures led with dull consent into insipid misdoing and shabby achievement' (80.574). Although this passage in fact refers to a particular case of resignation in the face of apparently insuperable obstacles, it equally describes in a general way the mesmeric effects of imagination. For Dorothea the 'real future' had to replace the imaginary, and the real yoke of marriage, the ideal (20.144; 48.353). Other factors may combine to condition surrogates for action, of course. Casaubon's desire for public esteem, together with his half-conscious fear that he might fail to elicit or deserve it, drove him to avoid any revealing tests. In addition, his own self-proclamation, aside from its excesses, committed him to specific actions he had no guarantee of achieving, and itself discouraged him from the attempt.

We are told that the world 'is full of hopeful analogies and handsome dubious eggs called possibilities' (10.61); Will's hopefulness about the future (e.g. 'prospects' 37.269), akin to Fred's optimistic expectations about Featherstone's will, is a sign of mental immaturity. 'What can the fitness of things mean, if not the fitness to a man's expectations?' (14.100); but there is no 'fitness' in things, and all the major characters have to learn that nature is simply neutral with respect to them. It should be noted that a man is passive in relation to those images which are the brood of his desires, and frequently the charm and plausibility of a man's images reside in their vagueness; this feature only increases the danger of self-deception. Will had 'dreamy visions of possibilities' in connection with Dorothea (47.343); expectant beneficiaries of Featherstone's will were liberal in their speculations (32.224; 35.242). Speculation ran freely at the auction at which Will bought the painting for Mrs. Bulstrode, over Lydgate's medical powers and over Bulstrode's behaviour towards Raffles: 'everybody liked better to conjecture how the thing was than simply to know it; for conjecture became more confident than knowledge, and had a more liberal allowance for the incompatible' (71.529). It is rewarding, however, to postulate a deeper reason. Knowledge is a boundary to speculation, just as the facts delimit possibilities (45.323); independent of the domain of the self, the facts challenge its power. Although real power resides in knowledge, a mentally immature person feels greater power over what he merely imagines, since he has yet to define the boundaries of the self; but, of course, this power is as phantom as the world in which it is exercised.

Occasionally the term 'possibility' is contrasted with 'probability'. Mary Garth was accustomed to think rigorously of probabilities (57.422) and eventually Dorothea looked with a healthy sense of probabilities at Casaubon's labours (48.351). Probabilities are calculable in the light of available knowledge, as even Casaubon admitted to himself in the matter of his health (42.309)—it is significant that in this context he used precisely the scientific method he eschewed in his academic work, and turned to Lydgate for confirmation by the same method. Casaubon's egoism drove him to calculate; but fear might well have had the opposite effect, as it did on Mrs. Bulstrode, who avoided estimating the probabilities of her husband's situation (68.503). One final observation. We have already noted the use of imagination for the purposes of establishing connections between phenomena, in particular causal connections. We should remember that in advance of any acts we may be contemplating, the consequences of them are merely possibilities in the sense just discussed.

PROVIDENCE AND POWER

We have considered the view that to imagine possibilities is to exercise one's power, and also that the continued exercise of that power is usually implied in the possibilities imagined. At this stage egoism may operate once more. For even partial awareness that one is imagining only possibilities is accompanied by the desire that some special agency might intervene in the natural course of events in order to realize those possibilities; the characteristic sign of this desire in *Middlemarch* is the occurrence of the terms 'chance', 'luck', and 'Providence'. When a character alludes to these concepts it can be taken to indicate either his assumption that special dispensation has been granted him, or his desire that it should be granted; in the latter cases it implies his awareness that only an extraordinary turn of events can avert the disaster that threatens him. Characters who hope to be released from the causal web in which they find themselves enmeshed, are often partially aware that such a hope is forlorn.

We are told, in connection with Will Ladislaw, that 'exiles notoriously feed much on hopes' (82.586). The metaphorical force of this remark may be discerned by inverting it: those who feed on hope are exiles—from the actual world. Fred's release from financial difficulties was to come 'purely by the favour of providence', just as his ability to repay Garth rested on 'the mysteries of luck' (36.250; 23.168). Certainly he shared a family trait in this respect; both his father (13.95; 25.193) and his sister Rosamond, as we shall see, frequently trusted in Providence. Fred believed that the intervention of chance on his behalf would relieve him of the necessity of doing anything himself—a commonplace desire (cf. Will, 60.441; Brooke, 49.356; Finale, 611) which is much emphasized also in *Anna Karenina*. And when some action seemed unavoidable, he always tried to persuade someone else to perform in his stead (12.90; 24.177; 28.187; 40.296; 52.376); as Mary Garth remarked, there was a gap between what he said he could do and what he did (52.379), a gap which is manifest, of course, in the lives of Casaubon and Lydgate, but also in varying degrees in those of all the main characters. No doubt Fred's notion of happiness was the same as his sister's, 'a paradise where everything is given to you and nothing claimed' (36.257). Like her brother Rosamond indulged in impracticable wishes instead of practical effort (64.480); she trusted to chance that Lydgate would not learn of her approach to the auctioneer not to sell their house, until too late; and she trusted 'her own petty magic' to calm Will after Dorothea had found them together, confident 'of making the thing that is not as though it were' (78.569). Unexpected pleasures in her eyes, were due to Providence; she had 'a Providence of her own who had kindly made her more charming than other girls' (27.195) and which arranged the entry of Lydgate into her life. It should be observed, however, that when she succeeded in any of her schemes, albeit after a war of attrition, she did not lay the credit to Providence, but to the general recognition of her own judgement.

Lydgate explicitly associated trust in chance, particularly in the form of gambling (in either a literal or metaphorical sense), with lack of money; even money gained in a profession, he believed, would come only by chance (63.472), a proposition he later falsified during his successful London career. Gambling was like a disease, and could not bring the sort of power for which he longed (66.490); but it 'implied no asking and brought no responsibility' and he turned to it. His 'immense need to win' drove him to the same company in the Green Dragon which helped Fred's decline. Lydgate is brought down to the level of her brother, and by implication of herself, by his own wife; he deceived himself into believing that 'an assurance of luck to the needful amount' (67.496) would deprive gambling of its more immediately dangerous consequences. Circumstances never, of themselves, bring about any fundamental change in men's character in *Middlemarch*; at most they bring to light, and challenge, previously hidden traits. It would seem, therefore, that 'learning from experience', whatever explanation is given of the notion, must be taken to refer to some development of powers or capacities—which may or may not be common to all men. Thus, Lydgate's longing for luck in financial difficulties was no new development in his character. Earlier, he had refused to face the problem of Farebrother's candidacy for the hospital chaplaincy, since he hoped that 'chance' would 'exclude the necessity for voting' (18.134). And a related occasion: he had not intended to marry, but now that Rosamond had appeared, 'other schemes . . . would simply adjust themselves anew' (36.254). Lydgate's surrender to chance and to the dominance of his desires over his better knowledge emphasizes the gap between his professional life as a rigorous scientist, and his life as a social being; it was not only Casaubon who arranged his knowledge in pigeon-holes (cf. 2.14).

Bulstrode had always assigned a prominent place to Providence in his scheme of things; it needs to be noted only that his fervent prayers are often the invocation of chance to divert the causal sequence of things to his own advantage—'he tried to believe in the potency of . . . prayerful resolution' (69.511). He made only provisional arrangements to leave Middlemarch when Raffles first appeared; like Fred and Lydgate, he felt that Providence might intervene, and 'that something would happen to hinder the worst' (68.505). It seemed to him 'a sort of earnest that Providence intended his rescue from worse consequences' (69.511), when only Garth appeared to have met Raffles; all the obvious antecedents to that meeting were ignored. Providence would deliver him from the haunting ghost of his past, and secure the secrecy of Lydgate's medical advice on the treatment of Raffles (71.526, 532).

Ascription of events to Providence, and appeals for its intercession are all signs of self-concern, and often also of a bid for power. But there are other ways in which the characters in *Middlemarch* seek power, all of them revealing the egoism of those concerned. Casaubon and Lydgate both wanted submissive wives (7.46; 11.70; 36.261) who would 'recognize' the pre-eminence of their husbands (29.206; 27.197; 58.425)—and Providence had supplied Casaubon with the wife 'he needed' (29.206). Both men discovered that absolute control over the life of another, making it merely an appendage of their own, was not possible (see my later discussion of such 'possession' in Proust's novel). Having failed to control the judgement of professional scholars by will alone, because he had not submitted any relevant achievements, Casaubon sought to control his wife's judgement; it was precisely because he was 'jealous of her opinion' that he feared Will's influence upon Dorothea (42.307). He was afraid of the 'future possibilities' to which her altered judgement might lead her, because he had already begun to suspect that 'he was not unmixedly adorable'; and adoration, however inappropriate, was more soothing to the ego. Not all egoists are secretive; but those who are, fear openness because it threatens their self-deception that the world is at their command. This is one reason why Casaubon and Bulstrode fear the influence of Ladislaw's ready tongue (e.g. 42.306).

Casaubon and Lydgate both longed for the power that scholarship can bring, although in the one case it was theoretical scholarship, and in the other essentially practical (e.g. 66.490). Casaubon never risked the test, and felt helpless against Dorothea's ardent nature which always yearned for practical action. Lydgate was thwarted by his more powerfully egotistical wife. He gradually distinguished between the imagined adoration he desired and the prestige Rosamond sought, and came to recognize that he was not master over her at all (58.425; 64.483). Bulstrode and Featherstone both sought to gain power over others by means of manipulating money; and perhaps because money appeals more directly to men's basic desires and needs than affairs of the mind, they were more successful than Casaubon and Lydgate. The strength of Bulstrode's cupidity had been 'a power enabling him to master all the knowledge necessary to gratify it' (53.381)—in contrast to Casaubon. It was one of his principles to gain as much power as possible, that he might use it for the glory of God (16.115). He wanted to rule dictatorially, and his habit of supremacy was disrupted by Ladislaw's unwillingness to accept his expression of penitence (13.97; 45.331; 61.456). It is worth remarking that Raffles exercised power over Bulstrode (53.388) because he played the same game, only more ruthlessly, and that the banker finally despaired only when he lost all grasp over the sick man's mind (69.511).

We may infer that some search for power is deemed a natural human tendency; it is taken as part of the attempt to achieve self-identity. Farebrother remarked that 'the stronger thing is not to give up power, but to use it well' (52.375), and the epigraph to Chapter 64, apparently written by the author herself, is important:

> . . . power is relative; you cannot fright
> The coming pest with border fortresses,
> Or catch your carp with subtle argument.
> All force is twain in one: cause is not cause
> Unless effect be there; and action's self
> Must needs contain a passive. So command
> Exists but with obedience.

Again: 'power finds its place in lack of power' (epigraph, Ch. 34). Victims must share responsibility for their submission. Each individual, also, is responsible for the outcome of the battle between reason, will and desire; will, by itself, is powerless against desire (69.510; 70.519), and the desires of each man compete against the desires of all. Featherstone's attempt to control the future by the provisions of his will, and Casaubon's attempt to retain power over Dorothea after his death (48.350; 50.362), contrast with Dorothea's own 'delightful plan' to extend the domain of the self, by making 'a little colony' where she would be everyone's friend (55.401). Earlier, she had spoken of 'a little kingdom' where she would 'give laws' (37.269), and fulfil her 'need to rule beneficently' (37.265).

CONSCIOUSNESS AND CONSCIENCE

It is characteristic of all of us, in so far as we are egoists, to locate the cause of our dissatisfaction in the behaviour of someone else who we take to be selfishly seeking his own ends. Casaubon initially suspected that a deficiency in Dorothea explained his modified delight following their engagement (7.47), and was shocked to discover that a close union was 'more of a subjection than he had been able to imagine' (20.150). Similarly, Rosamond's 'discontent in her marriage was due to the conditions of marriage itself, to its demands for self-suppression and tolerance, and not to the nature of her husband' (75.552). Lydgate, too, thought of himself as the sufferer, and of others as the agents who had thwarted his purposes (73.540). 'One likes to be done well by, in every tense, past, present and future' (35.247). And Dorothea raged at Will after she found him with Rosamond (80.576).

Egoists are mistaken about both the nature and extent of their selves in relation to the world around them. Indeed, the main characters may be seen as illustrating not only various types and degrees of egoism, but by the same token various degrees of empiricism, and the differing effects of the incursion of the actual world into their imagined world. In general, the greater the egoism, and hence the self-deception, the greater the humiliation of its discovery; Casaubon and Bulstrode suffer more than Lydgate and Dorothea. The one exception is Rosamond, whose intellectual deficiencies seem to protect her from full realization of their consequences. Characterization of egoism is likely also to be characterization of the intimately related problems of self-knowledge and self-identity. There are numerous references in *Middlemarch* to a character's private vision, inmost soul, inward life or consciousness, and some of the implications that can be drawn from these references need to be spelled out. Briefly, each of us has to learn that our inner self is known to others only indirectly, through various manifestations, each of which is open to diverse interpretations; secondly, we have to learn that others have their own inner selves known to us only through their manifestations; thirdly, we have to learn that a moral life consists in some sort of rapport between our own inner selves and those of other people, in the context of a morally neutral physical world in which we all live. Alongside these views, a reader should remember objections that Wittgenstein made, some of which I have already mentioned. Inner states cannot provide a criterion of identity which would make it intelligible to ascribe such states to others; for one has to learn the conventions that establish samenesses, and no convention about a man's inaccessibly private states could be taught. And even to pick out inner feelings presupposes the use of concepts. Further, learning a concept requires the possibility of public correction, and correction is impossible if it is impossible to discover whether mistakes have been made. We should remember that on the traditional view of knowledge presupposed in *Middlemarch* the ultimately secure foundation of knowledge is provided by a man's inner feelings—about which he cannot be mistaken. But on Wittgenstein's argument, such a man could never acquire concepts to pick out his feelings, and they could not constitute an incorrigible base for knowledge.

Although Fred was too self-concerned to understand others (12.89; 23.172) he had an 'inner self' before which he could be ashamed (as when he sought, too hastily, to leave Featherstone, having gained a loan), and which Farebrother recommended him to consult about his duties (14.101; 52.376). Casaubon, likewise, was too languidly self-conscious to give to, or take from, others; and he became morbidly suspicious as a consequence (29.206; 42.306; 44.322). Least of all was he likely to detect those subtle signs of inner turbulence, recognizable only to those who know us well, or to those between whom exists the happy freedom which comes from mutual understanding (30.213; 78.570; 62.462; cf. 27.196). The egoism which drives a man to seek pre-eminence, may condemn him to lonely isolation, immured from the world which alone can confer that pre-eminence. Casaubon, Lydgate, Bulstrode, Dorothea, and Rosamond all experienced loneliness and isolation because of failure in mutual understanding.

Since antiquity the notion of conscience has been associated with that of consciousness, and this connection is retained in *Middlemarch* enabling us to infer from the novel several orthodox views. These are probably the commonplaces critics have in mind when they describe the novel as 'philosophical'. Just as the agent alone knows what his conscience tells him, so he alone knows the reports of his consciousness or awareness; reflection upon these reports is an essential step in the formation of moral decisions. We should not suppose that the reports a man gives himself are peculi-

arly true: 'speech is representative: who can represent himself just
as he is, even in his own reflections?' (70.521). What one is
conscious of is a function of the combined operations of sense-
experience, imagination, and reason; and the passions can dominate all these, and dull or distort one's awareness. Nevertheless,
leaving aside the accuracy of his reports, it is a man's moral duty
to determine precisely what he is thinking at any one moment;
and we should suspend judgement of other men until we have
some inkling of their own account. One reason is that, on the view
presupposed in the novel, each man's knowledge is essentially
constructed out of his first-person accounts. 'What is the report of
his own consciousness about his doings or capacity', what hind-
rances and hopes condition his labours (10.62)? 'Who can know
how much of his inward life is made up of thoughts he believes
other men to have about him, until that fabric of opinion is
threatened with ruin' (68.504)? As Bulstrode discovered, 'the pain,
as well as the public estimate of disgrace, depends on the amount
of previous profession' (53.386; 85.602). The moral aim is 'the
reaching forward of the whole consciousness towards the fullest
truth, the least partial good', to try to make life less difficult for
each other (72.537; 39.287); and to this end, it 'signifies nothing
what other men think' (20.151; 56.412). And the only sure means
is by personal feeling, for truths known through the hard process
of feeling are unassailable by argument (45.334; 56.408; 69.510).
Conscience would thus seem to be the repository of moral knowledge, acquired through personal experience, in some sense, and
not by means of argument (cf. 44.322). Only the totally avaricious
man, the man who believes exclusively in his own greed, we are
told, lacks a conscience as an inner criterion of moral action
(61.453). Even at moments of intrigue, characters are shown to
experience the nagging pricks of conscience. Bulstrode's 'moral
sensibility' was early on padded by 'inward argument' (61.451);
and later, when the 'resurgent threatening past' had awakened his
conscience, or activated suppressed memories, he had to soothe it
consciously (70.521; 71.532; 73.541; 75.554). To say that 'an uneasy conscience heareth innuendoes' (31.220) is not only to say

that an uneasy conscience is still an active conscience; it is also to draw attention to the intimate link between conscience, consciousness, and imagination. It hears innuendoes because it perceives data in the light of preconceived interpretations. It is notable that appeals to conscience are not said to be appeals to intuition, in any sense; on the contrary, both the recognition of, and reliance upon, the judgements of conscience, rest on experience. Dorothea had to learn about the self-subduing acts of fellowship from her experiences (82.588—cf. her teasing remark to Celia that 'you would have to feel with me, else you would never know' 84.602), and it may be presumed that Garth's 'clear feeling' within him had similarly been learned by experience to be reliable (56.412). In spite of this important qualification there is a tendency to take conscience as the ultimately reliable criterion of moral knowledge. But whenever this is done, as it is in *Anna Karenina* (see p. 107), it is hard to retain any role for interpretative imagination, or for thought in general; and it is also hard to see how conscience is going to be affected by the continual stream of experiences everyone, quite reasonably, is alleged to have. There is a danger of conscience becoming immune from thought and experience. We should notice that in both *Middlemarch* and *Anna Karenina*, conscience is assumed to be, in some sense, the same in everyone, and to issue the same verdicts in like circumstances.

On the view we are discussing, the acquisition of fellow-feeling, at least in one respect, is difficult. It requires 'a perpetual claim on the immediate fresh application of thought, and on the consideration of another's need and trial' (66.489); one single good resolve is quite insufficient, and would suffice only if everybody were co-operating towards its enactment (18.139). Furthermore, neither ignoring motives, as recommended by Casaubon, nor exclusive attention to intentions, as recommended by Bulstrode (2.16; 70.516) ensures moral action. Both motives and intentions are at the mercy of desires, and a man's deliberated actions should be determined by weighing their probable consequences to others (37.267; 24.183). Religion, and any morality dependent upon it, can change only when the emotions which fill it are changed, for emotions, it will be remembered, are the factors which dominate our thought and action; emotions are themselves affected by circumstances, but in the end our good depends on the quality and breadth of our emotion (61.454; 62.459; 47.344). At this point the relations between thought and emotion are obscure, because, earlier, emotions were said to falsify rational thought. If the dominating emotion is one of fear, exemplified, say, in concern for rewards (Bulstrode, 70.516), then our lives will be tainted. The nature of fear is not explored, nor is it explained why fear may not sometimes be a justifiable emotion; but the view is probably that as a motive, fear is generally to be condemned—or avoided. Bulstrode's fear of consequences was so great that he believed he could mollify them by doing something spontaneously (61.454); he failed to see that spontaneous action was impossible when under the dominance of fear. Fear, indeed, is intimately related to egoism in *Middlemarch*, since it is often founded upon non-rational guesses about the world, unsupported by factual evidence or probable hypotheses. Even the egoist's excessive concern for favourable public estimates of himself is partly motivated by fear; it is notable, for instance, that Bulstrode always surrendered a bid for power in the face of adverse judgements which might affect him— thus, at different times, he gave in to Vincy, Lydgate, Raffles, and Will Ladislaw. Whatever inner processes actually or hopefully informed his life, Bulstrode was forced to recognize that 'acts present themselves to onlookers' in 'rigid outline' (61.452)—a view hard to reconcile with the central roles assigned to imagination; as Lydgate discovered, 'circumstances would always be stronger than his assertion' (73.541) because there are no essential constraints upon interpretation. The very fact that imagination must operate within and upon perception guarantees that, for any act, 'it is always possible for those who like it to interpret [it] into a crime: there is no proof in favour of the man outside his own consciousness and assertion' (72.538). Perhaps this passage indicates a yearning for an inner criterion of certainty in morality.

Usually, we are more concerned with self-justification than with self-knowledge (34.241; 17.128), but we should try to disregard this concern for others' opinions of us (68.504). Although nothing, in fact, forces us to identify our acts by strict classification, we may achieve self-knowledge only by recognizing the degree of egoism in our imagination (65.488; 42.307; 58.425). When, as frequently happens, reason is subject to desire, it may argue against the surer judgement of conscience, and become 'unreason' (47.345; 61.453); Bulstrode habitually 'washed and diluted' his acts 'with inward argument and motive' (85.602). We must therefore return to the unanalysed, and possibly unanalysable, starting-point of all knowledge, namely feeling. What we often call 'knowledge', of course, has been derived from the authority or opinion of others, and sometimes this has to suffice; but in morality it does not. To 'feel the truth' of a commonplace, such as 'we must all die', is very different from the 'acquired knowledge' of 'merely knowing' that it is true (42.311; 80.517); such personal realization is a necessary step not only towards self-knowledge, but also towards understanding of others. No one knows with certainty what is in another man's mind, and in the absence of a logical guarantee that he understands that man, he lacks the fullest reassurance that his own experience of the external world is what he believes it to be. But this scepticism is irrelevant and would preclude all action (23.176; 70.516); it is also likely to bolster our egoism at the most unsuspected places. Scepticism, then, which has been accepted throughout as an inalienable part of an empiricist account of knowledge, in the end has to be discarded, or at least ignored, if moral concepts are to be immune from its threats. Although we are told in the novel that inner conviction is no guarantee of truth, there is a tendency to treat conscience as such a guarantee in the moral realm, analogous to, or perhaps even an instance of, the incorrigible inner feelings that are supposed to be the ultimate foundations of knowledge. The fundamental working assumption for an empiricist who wishes to act morally, in the account I have inferred from *Middlemarch*, is that all men have sufficiently similar sense-experiences in similar situations to establish communication and understanding; and that this belief, while it may puncture the egoism which seeks to assert the uniqueness of ourselves, is the sole foundation of sympathy with others. Although men frequently mistake their own symptoms, their own self-estimate is important (75.552; 10.62; cf. Finale, where both Lydgate and Dorothea judge themselves to have been partial failures), at least as a starting-point towards self-awareness. The egoist is subject to self-deception because he does not spell out the data he has available; he fails to recognize that for every difference which sets him apart from others, there is a similarity which makes the comparison intelligible; he fails to grasp that knowledge of himself and of others go hand in hand.

CONCLUSION

The predominance of imagination-vocabulary in *Middlemarch* is undeniable: there are numerous references, as we have seen, not only to 'images' and 'imagining', but to 'conjectures', 'creative inclination', 'foreseeing', 'preconceiving', 'constructing', 'fashioning', and 'fancying'. I have argued that we may infer from the novel a view according to which we may distinguish three related roles of imagination.

As a presupposition of perception, imagination would provide concepts for the minimally coherent ordering of our transient sensory-experiences. We become able to think of our experience as continuous, and as connected in some way with other phenomena, themselves continuous as well as independent of us.

Constructive imagination, or fancy, is able to conjecture, plan, hypothesize, and interpret; it is able to build composite images and pictures whose only connection with the actual world is through their diverse constituents. While it is free to transcend a man's past and present experience, and enables him to establish causal connections and interpretations of indirect evidence, it is also subject to his brute psychological nature, in particular his desires. We saw various ways in which imagination is used for the purposes of interpretation. We discovered that all the major characters, at some time, mistake the mere possibles of imagination for the actual world. In his imagined world every man can be master; we noted that many characters sought to extend their domain by seeking power in their dealings with other men. Sometimes such power could be maintained only by pretending that the facts were other than they were, or by hoping for the intercession of special causes operating solely on behalf of the agent. Nevertheless, the search for power should also be understood as part of a search for self-identity. In this connection we noted the close relation between 'consciousness' and 'conscience'. In spite of their self-concern, egoists do not achieve full consciousness of themselves, their surroundings, or the relations obtaining between these two sets of data. If they did, they would recognize within themselves a criterion of right action: the judgements of conscience. Indeed, we may assume that when an egoist recognizes his conscience sufficiently to suppress it, as happened with Bulstrode, at those moments he begins to achieve full self-consciousness.

The third role of imagination is in the sympathetic understanding of other men; such understanding cannot be reached by those exclusively concerned with themselves, but it rests upon the use of imagination to interpret the outward signs of men's inner lives. Lydgate and Casaubon differed entirely on the uses to which they put their constructive imagination in their professional work; but they both failed to see that such imagination is also essential in their social lives. The mental world of the imagination is quite separate from the actual world in which we live; to connect the two demands a disciplined exercise of will-power. It is only by his imagination that a man can understand the actual world; but it is also by the imagination that he can deny himself knowledge of himself, his world, and other men.

If past beliefs and present desires govern our interpretations of our sense-experience, can we be sure that any given description is correct? Casaubon's misinterpretation of Dorothea's behaviour after their marriage was based, in part, on his earlier misinterpretations; the chances of reaching the truth seem to diminish with each step. We saw, however, that such absolute scepticism is regarded as 'irrelevant'. We all know perfectly well, in a rough and ready manner, what descriptions are acceptable accounts of 'the facts'; and our recognition of the revisability of our accounts itself rests on assumptions about the relative stability of 'the facts' we believe ourselves to be talking about.

Hume argued that any knowledge we may have of 'the facts' is itself based upon assumptions about causal connections. If we say, therefore, that from *Middlemarch* we can infer the view that a large part of morality depends on a grasp of the causal law, that is, on a realization of the complex web of causal relationships to which our individual lives are bound, we are saying, in effect, that morality depends largely upon recognition of 'the facts'. Such realization and recognition depends, of course, on the use of interpretative imagination, not on *a priori* assumptions according to which all things are probable (cf. 51.372).

In conjunction with the different roles of imagination we noted two types of egoism. The sense in which we are all egoists is that in which our experiences are private; we all have this 'equivalent centre of self' (21.156). Necessarily what I perceive is governed by my viewpoint, interests, knowledge and psychological make-up; necessarily only I have access to my imagination, the realm in which I exercise absolute control. But this epistemological egoism, which is as unavoidable as the imagination presupposed by perception, tends to go hand in hand with ethical egoism, the view that only I matter. Ethical egoism can be defeated only by further use of the human capacity which helped to sustain it: imagination. Having used our imagination in perception, in the interpretation of our sense-experience, and in the construction of hypotheses about the connections between phenomena, we must use it again to assume that we all have analogous experiences. Self-knowledge entails a grasp of the similarities and differences between us and other men; with self-knowledge goes self-identity. Many of the characters in *Middlemarch* may be understood to be searching for self-identity; a prominent way in which this is done is by getting other people to take notice of one. Casaubon, Lydgate, Fred, Bulstrode, Rosamond, and Dorothea all strove for recognition, in various ways, by people other than themselves; and Will Ladislaw was greatly concerned that Dorothea should notice him (22.161;

37.270; 43.317; 62.464). Although, at times, we all assume that others judge us according to our own self-estimate, and see things from our own viewpoint, we nevertheless need reassurance on the point; to gain such assurance, we must make known 'our world' and thus give something of ourselves—we can escape, in this way, some of 'the miserable isolation' of egoism (64.473). To say, therefore, that the self is the principal obstacle to knowledge (42.307)[1] is to draw attention to the two types of egoism and the dangerous freedom of imagination. For empirical knowledge can begin to be secure only when we grasp the perils inherent in the very mechanisms by which, alone, it may be achieved. It should be unnecessary to repeat that what makes a judgement empirical must not be misconstrued as an overriding objection to its reliability. Yet such misconstruction is partly responsible for attempts to find a basis for empirical knowledge possessing the same credentials as *a priori* knowledge. The view that inaccessibly private feelings constitute an incorrigible ground for empirical knowledge, fails to recognize how concepts are taught and learned, and how they function.

II

GEORGE ELIOT AND PHILOSOPHY

I shall now consider briefly philosophical remarks in some of George Eliot's other writings, but with no intention, in so doing, of legitimizing my interpretation of *Middlemarch*; and in outlining some of the sources of her views, I shall stress the importance of G. H. Lewes.

In a letter of 1849 (*GEL*, I, 277)[2] George Eliot declared that she did not go to the authors she most respected as to a textbook or moral code. A major problem is to determine precisely what con-

---

[1] Cf. *Middlemarch*, 42.307: 'Will not a tiny speck very close to our vision blot out the glory of the world, and leave only a margin by which we see the blot?' and George Eliot's review of Tennyson's *Maud, Westminster Review*, LXIV, October 1855, p. 597: 'that optical law by which an insignificant object, if near, excludes very great and glorious things that lie in the distance, has its moral parallel in the judgment of the public'.

[2] All references to letters are to the standard edition of G. S. Haight, *The George Eliot Letters* (7 vols., New Haven, 1954–5).

stitutes an influence. Not all influence is either positive or direct, and agreement with what one reads does not establish its influence; a book may articulate one's own previously unexpressed, and hence unclarified, views, or it may express what one has either expressed already oneself or could have expressed without assistance. Natural egoism frequently favours the latter view. To avoid begging the question about influences, and also a minimally rewarding search, I shall give a partial list of views that appear in George Eliot's own writings and in the writings of the authors she acknowledged; in some cases it is impossible to distinguish between sources of her views, and texts which merely confirmed her already established views.

The list of philosophers whom George Eliot herself mentioned as influences is short: Thomas à Kempis for his stress on resignation; Rousseau, Comte, and Mill, especially for his *System of Logic* (1843). Incidental references occur to Cudworth, Hume, Voltaire, and Kant, among others. Between 1844 and 1846 she translated David Friedrich Strauss's *Das Leben Jesu*, and she translated Spinoza's *Tractatus Theologico-Politicus* in 1849, his *Ethic* in 1854, and Feuerbach's *Essence of Christianity* is 1853.

As early as 1859, upon the publication of *Adam Bede*, a distinguished French critic, Emile Montégut, wondered how much Spinoza had influenced the novelist's thought; unfortunately, when his articles were eventually published in *Revue des Deux Mondes* in 1883, he did not develop the speculation. As far as I know, however, he was the first critic to engage in a philosophical consideration of George Eliot's novels. It seems more than likely that George Eliot first became interested in Spinoza through her friend Charles Bray, with whom she had many discussions, and with whose book *The Philosophy of Necessity* (1841) she must have had acquaintance. I believe that she came to Spinoza with prefocused interests and interpretations, through the work of Bray— to whose own book I shall return in a moment. As a professional philosopher (perhaps because of that fact) I can find little in Spinoza that would have been of service to George Eliot; further, discussions with G. H. Lewes would have shown her the incompatibility of the philosopher's main views with her own dominant beliefs. In particular, the metaphysical foundations, the logical structure of the argument, the technical meaning of such central terms as 'actio' and 'passio', are alien to George Eliot and nothing of them appears in her work. In Rousseau she could have found reference to the imperceptible influence of outward factors on our inward being, such that we may come to act in ways against our nature and knowledge; also the views that men act or are motivated by passions not intellect (equally she could have read this in Aristotle and Hume and countless others), that virtuous actions can be made habitual, that wisdom is found in all conditions of life. Love of the country, and country people is also proclaimed; but most notable was Rousseau's view that 'a succession of small duties always faithfully done demands no less than do heroic actions' (*Les Confessions*, Bk. III). She could also have found pronouncements on the interconnection of the sciences, and on the nagging realization that one's thoughtless actions might have had evil consequences—memories of such actions can perpetually haunt. In Comte, George Eliot could have found the view that description alone is what is needed, or indeed possible, in empirical investigation; no underlying causes can be known, and metaphysics is to be consigned to the flames (again). In Bray she could have read that both the material and moral worlds are subject to the same laws, laws of necessity; and she could have found similar views in Spinoza and Mill; further, Spinoza, Bray, and Mill all argue that such necessity allows freedom of will—whether they argue this successfully is a quite different question. In Feuerbach she read that man is the criterion of truth, and that religion is reducible to anthropology and psychology; certainly views she could have read elsewhere, notably in Hume.

A further word on Bray is now in place. *The Philosophy of Necessity* is an enthusiastically eclectic work, derived principally from Jonathan Edwards's *Freedom of the Will* (Boston, 1754), but also containing copious quotations from Hume, Brown's criticisms of Hume, Mackintosh, Bentham, and many others. In 1835 Bray had accepted phrenology as of fundamental philosophical and scientific relevance, and the phrenological views of George Combe and Sidney Smith are also prominent in his book. One reason for denying the major influence of Spinoza on George Eliot is that Bray expresses views that George Eliot herself espoused over the next thirty years and couched in almost identical words. For example:

all the knowledge that we acquire of an external world is of its action through the medium of the senses upon only a few of the mental faculties. . . . Nothing is therefore known to us as it is (p. 98). . . . Reason is dependent for its exercise upon experience, and experience is nothing more than the knowledge of the invariable order of nature, of the relations of cause and effect (p. 172). . . . Man is not only responsible for that portion of his happiness which depends upon his own body and mind, but for that which he derives from the great body of Society, of which he is a member (p. 179). . . . Abstractedly, all actions are alike . . . *in themselves*, they are all equally deserving of praise or blame . . . because they are all the produce of causes, arising out of natural constitution and circumstances over which the individual has no control (p. 253). . . . Pleasures and pains are the sole springs of action . . . and a man necessarily seeks his own happiness (p. 261); the feelings that prompt us to action are mere blind impulses (p. 281). . . . What is man, viewed philosophically by the aid of the doctrine of Necessity? A mere link in the chain of causation, connected with innumerable links before his existence, and with the future chain ad infinitum, the consequences of his existence being endless. . . . A mere atom in the mass of sensitive creation (p. 271).

Later, Bray asserts that 'an internal monitor has been superadded called Conscience, which if *attended* to, and not *perverted*, will dictate, on all occasions, what is right and what is wrong' (p. 277). What is required for moral action is 'moderation and consistency in our desires and expectations'; 'the main thing to be taught is the habitual predominance of the moral feelings' (pp. 287, 292). Notice the attempt to avoid determinism by 'superadding' conscience. How it is supposed to function, however, is unclear.

Let us contrast with these views George Eliot's own pronouncements on moral issues. At the outset of her literary career in 1851, she wrote in the *Westminster Review*, that the key to life 'is the recognition of the presence of undeviating law in the material and moral world. . . . Human duty is comprised in the earnest study of this law and patient obedience to its teaching' (*Essays*, pp. 28, 31).[1] Four years later, in 1855, she asserted that nothing extrinsic could constitute a truly moral motive to action, and she frequently repeated thereafter that fear of consequences as a motive to action was really only a form of egoism (cf. *Essays*, p. 374): 'the immediate impulse of love or justice . . . alone makes an action truly moral' (*Essays*, p. 135). Only the 'direct prompting of the sympathetic feelings' can ensure benevolence; in their absence a deed may become one 'of deference, or obedience, or self-interest, or vanity' (*Essays*, p. 187). Here we note an important change between 1851 and 1855; formerly she advocated an essentially passive morality of submission; but soon she came to condemn any notion of obedience, especially to extrinsic laws or dogmas. And in 1857 (*Essays*, p. 379) she asserted that in proportion as morality is emotional it will exhibit itself in direct sympathetic feeling and action; only where emotion is weak may rule or theory strengthen a motive to action. In all other cases it is internal feeling that matters. In 1855, she tried to expand upon her views of morality: 'morality . . . is dependent on the regulation of feeling by intellect. All human beings who can be said to be in any degree moral have their impulses guided, not indeed always by their own intellect, but by the intellect of human beings who have gone before them, and created traditions and associations which have taken the rank of laws' (*Essays*, p. 166). Ten years later, in 1865, she expressed a similar view: 'Our sentiments may be called organized traditions; and a large part of our actions gather all their justification, all their attraction and aroma, from the memory of the life lived, of the actions done, before we were born' (*Essays*, p. 409). On the one hand, we are told that what makes an action moral is that it must be done from direct motives, that is, immediate impulses; on the other, we are told that such impulses take their form from our

[1] Reference to the essays is to the edition by Thomas Pinney, *Essays of George Eliot*, London, 1963.

prehistory, as it were, or from our memory of it, and that many of our actions gather all their justification from what others have done before we were born. So what makes an action moral is one thing, and what justifies it is another; further, what justifies it is nothing we ourselves do or can possibly influence, since it is passed. The latter view, of course, cannot avoid a perpetual regress: if what I do now gains its justification from what my great-grandparents did a hundred years ago, then, equally, what they did then, gains *its* justification from what others did before them; and so on. George Eliot has confused causal explanation of an action with its moral justification.

So far we have noted four of George Eliot's philosophical views: those concerning the undeviating law in both the moral and material worlds; those concerning direct feeling of sympathy as the only moral motive; those concerning the influence of past traditions upon one's impulses; and those concerning the justification of our actions by reference to past actions, not ours. When we turn to her pronouncements upon art, we find that her theoretical statements are less than consistent. Briefly, her views may be summarized as follows:

1.   'It is a quite sufficient task to exhibit men and things as they are' and this is what great artists do (1855, *Essays*, p. 146; 1856, *Essays*, p. 310).

2.   'Each man sees things not as they are, but as they appear through his peculiar mental media' (*Westminster Review*, LXVI, July 1856, p. 272); the reason is that 'the most active perception gives us rather a reflex of what we think and feel, than the real sum of objects before us' (1855, *Essays*, p. 89).

3.   'No one can maintain that *all* fact is a fit subject for art' (1855, *Essays*, p. 146). The first two views are not obviously compatible; the second and third views taken together imply that art is selective.

4.   The morality of art lies in its effects, namely, those of arousing sympathy in the audience (1856, *Essays*, p. 270); on the other hand, the morality of action lies in the motives, namely, those of sympathy (1857, *Essays*, p. 374). 'In proportion as morality is

emotional (i.e. has affinity with Art) it will exhibit itself in direct sympathetic feeling and action' (ibid., p. 379). It follows, of course, that the morality of art is separable from the morality of the artist; for the product of his actions, that is, his art, may not have been informed by moral motives, while yet having moral effects of arousing sympathy. Writing on Ruskin, George Eliot asserted that 'in making clear to ourselves what is best and noblest in art, we are making clear to ourselves what is best and noblest in morals' (*Westminster Review*, LXV, April 1856, p. 626); but this does not accord with her standard view that what is best in art is its effect, and what is best in morality is its motive—the occurrence of the term 'sympathy' in both accounts does not establish the required relation. (In *Middlemarch* (see above, p. 44) we were told that consideration of probable consequences was necessary to morality and that motives and intentions alone were insufficient.) In the same article she wrote: 'the truth of infinite value that he teaches is *realism*—the doctrine that all truth and beauty are to be attained by a humble and faithful study of nature' (ibid., p. 626). Nine years later (1865, *Essays*, p. 413) she still seemed to suppose the possibility of a passive theory of perception: 'The great conception of universal regular sequence, without partiality and without caprice . . . could only grow out of that patient watching of external fact, and that silencing of preconceived notions, which are urged upon the mind by the problems of physical science.' But no amount of watching, however patient, will establish a *universal* sequence.

I have already adverted to the tension between passive and active theories of perception, in connection with the pier-glass example in *Middlemarch*. A passage in 'Leaves from a note-book' apparently written after *Middlemarch* seems to recognize, for the first time, the tension: 'it is difficult to strike the balance between the educational needs of passivity or receptivity, and independent selection. We should learn nothing without the tendency to implicit acceptance; but there must clearly be a limit to such mental submission, else we should come to a stand-still' (*Essays*, p. 443). In her famous first review of 1851, however, George Eliot had quoted long passages

from Mackay's *The Progress of the Intellect* which emphasized much
the same problem, and stressed the role of 'faith' in knowledge;
the quotation clearly shows that the notion is intimately related
to the notion of imagination (with its various roles) I have alleged
underlies the narrative in *Middlemarch*. This is Mackay:

immediate as well as the more remote inferences from phenomena, are
the blended fruit of faith and knowledge; and . . . though faith, properly speaking, is not knowledge, but the admission of certain inferences
beyond knowledge, yet it is almost impossible, in tracing back the
operations of the mind, to find any, even the most elementary inference,
which is not in some degree a compound of both, and which may not
ultimately be resolved into a consistent belief in the results of experience. . . . True faith is a belief in things probable; it is the assigning to
certain inferences a hypothetical objectivity, and upon the conscious
acknowledgment of this hypothetical character alone depends its
advantage over fanaticism. . . . Reason alone can in each case determine
where credulity begins, and fix the limit beyond which the mind should
cease to assign even a qualified objectivity to its own imaginations.
In its advanced stages faith is a legitimate result of the calculation of
probabilities; it may transcend experience, but can never absolutely
contradict it. Faith and knowledge tend mutually to the confirmation
and enlargement of each other; faith by verification being often
transformed into knowledge, and every increase of knowledge supplying a wider and firmer basis of belief. Faith, as an inference from knowledge, should be consistently inferred from the whole of knowledge;
since, when estranged and violated, it loses its vitality, and the estrange-
ment is as effectual when it is hastily and unfairly inferred as where it is
wholly gratuitous. The same experience which is the source of knowledge being, therefore, the only legitimate foundation of faith, a
sound faith cannot be derived from the anomalous and exceptional. It
is the avidity for the marvellous, and the morbid eagerness for a cheap
and easy solution of the mysteries of existence—a solution to be implied
in the conception of an arbitrary and unintelligible rule, which has ever
retarded philosophy and stultified religion. Faith naturally arises out of
the regular and undeviating. (Vol. i. p. 35, quoted in *Essays*, pp. 33 ff.)

In *Impressions of Theophrastus Such* (1879) George Eliot, in addition to exploring the theme of egoism throughout the essays,

turned once more to the roles of imagination. She seemed to have reverted to the notion of passive perception. 'The power of precise statement and description is rated lower' than that of 'high imagination' which induces people to confuse '*it seemed so*' and '*I should like it to be so*'. Many people's 'supposed imaginativeness is simply a very usual lack of discriminating perception'; in contrast, 'a fine imagination . . . is always based on a keen vision, a keen consciousness of what *is*, and carries the store of definite knowledge as material for the construction of its inward visions.' 'Industrious submissive observation' must provide the foundation;

powerful imagination is not false outward vision, but intense inward representation, and a creative energy constantly fed by susceptibility to the veriest minutiae of experience, which it reproduces and constructs in fresh and fresh wholes; not the habitual confusion of provable fact with the fictions of fancy and transient inclination, but a breadth of ideal association which informs every material object, every incidental fact, with far-reaching memories and stored residues of passion, bringing into new light the less obvious relations of human existence.

It is important not to be 'so absorbed in ideal vision as to lose consciousness of surrounding objects'. All these extracts are from Chapter 13 'How we come to give ourselves false testimonials, and believe in them.' In the same chapter occurs a passage on the 'facility of men in believing that they are still what they once meant to be':

When we come to examine in detail what is the sane mind in the sane body, the final test of completeness seems to be a security of distinction between what we have professed and what we have done—what we have aimed at and what we have achieved—what we have invented and what we have witnessed or had evidenced to us—what we think and feel in the present and what we thought and felt in the past.

At the beginning of the essay occur further remarks for consideration alongside my interpretation of *Middlemarch*. In new situations 'comparison would teach us in the first place by likeness, and our clue to further knowledge would be resemblance to what we already knew'; it is in this connection that we must recognize that 'the only method of knowing mankind' is 'to judge of others by one's self'—but the dangers of both this method and its opposite should also be recognized. The full force of these baldly stated views is perhaps conveyed with greater impact in *Middlemarch*, where they are not stated as such, but rather enacted; such was one of George Eliot's artistic intentions. Frequently she contrasted 'presenting' or 'painting' with mere 'describing' (e.g. *Westminster Review*, LXVI, July 1856, p. 260), and she criticized Kingsley because he 'can never trust to the impression that scene itself will make on you' (1855, *Essays*, p. 126). The distinction, which she borrowed from Lessing, plays a special role in George Eliot's thought. When accurate, descriptions were usually thought to be so because the speaker had disengaged his interests. George Eliot, on the other hand, believed that effective communication rested precisely upon an artist's emotional involvement; 'presentation', therefore, such as that achieved by Goethe when 'he quietly follows the stream of fact and of life' (1855, *Essays*, p. 146), was to be the old notion of description, but with the addition of the very involvement that used to be excluded.

We have seen that from her early reading of Bray, George Eliot was impressed by the causal relations between phenomena; and in her review of Mackay her reference to 'faith', clearly based on Mill's discussions of induction, paves the way to a grasp of the roles of imagination in perception. Nevertheless, it is only after her union with G. H. Lewes, in 1854, that she began to write, explicitly: 'I only try to exhibit some things as they have been or are, seen through such a medium as my own nature gives me.' (*GEL*, II, 362).[1] And Blackwood, reporting her views, explicitly uses the notion of imagination as gap-filling, which we saw in

---

[1] Cf. *Adam Bede*, Ch. 7: 'my strongest effort is to avoid any such arbitrary picture, and to give a faithful account of men and things as they have mirrored themselves in my mind. The mirror is doubtless defective, the reflection faint or confused; but I feel as much bound to tell you as precisely as I can what that reflection is, as if I were in the witness-box narrating my experience on oath.... Examine your words well, and you will find that even when you have no motive to be false, it is a very hard thing to say the exact truth, even about your own feelings—much harder than to say something fine about them which is *not* the exact truth.'

Middlemarch: 'any real observation of life and character must be limited, and the imagination must fill in and give life to the picture' (*GEL*, III, 427). Although George Eliot had read the philosophers who espoused these views before she met Lewes, the credit must go to him for her realization of their importance; before her union with him, she had not acknowledged the force of those ideas; afterwards, she often did so, although, as we have seen, she also tried to retain a notion of passive perception. It is not surprising that Lewes convinced George Eliot of the importance of those views; for years he had himself stressed them in his philosophical writings. It is to Lewes, therefore, that we must now turn.

In his article on recent work in aesthetics in the *British and Foreign Review*, vol. 13, 1842, Lewes concentrated mainly on Hegel's *Lectures*; he made a number of references to the articles by 'a philosophic critic' (in fact, J. S. Mill) in the *Monthly Repository*, vol. 7, 1833 and the *Westminster Review*, vol. xxix, April 1838, offering the cogent criticism that the author 'has looked at the creative *mind* of the artist, not at the *work of art*' (*BFR*, 1842, p. 15) —this criticism, which he applied also to Hegel, is one of the earliest formulations known to me of a salient objection to the whole expression theory of art and it is repeated by Dorothea to Will Ladislaw in *Middlemarch* (22.166). Lewes agreed with Hegel that any moral teaching in art must be indirect, through inspiration rather than doctrine. He also endorsed one tenet of Hegel's theory of language; namely, that names have the same value in the mind as visual images or representations, that words seldom, and need never, raise images in our minds; rather, words are the representatives in our minds of the things they stand for (*BFR*, p. 6)—a view which is prominent in Locke. Such a view could underlie the following remark in *Middlemarch*: 'Private prayer is inaudible speech, and speech is representative: who can represent himself just as he is, even in his own reflections?' (70.521). Lewes also argued that an artist should not dogmatically teach any moral truth, but should convey it 'indirectly' (*BFR*, 1842, p. 21); he agreed with Hegel that any philosophy in art must be only 'implicit' (ibid., p. 23) and quotes with approval a passage by R. H. Horne: 'the true mission of art is to enlarge the bounds of human sympathy' (ibid.).

In the *Westminster Review*, vol. xxxix, 1843, Lewes introduced the English-speaking public to the works of Spinoza. He pointed out that a prerequisite to understanding Spinoza is understanding Descartes; and that an entry into Spinoza's thought is best made via his abridgment of Descartes's *Meditations*—this must be a slip on Lewes's part; presumably he had in mind Spinoza's *Principia Philosophiae Cartesianae*, which at most could be considered an abridgement of Descartes's *Principles of Philosophy*, not the *Meditations*. At the same time he urged the reader to remember the fundamental differences in the method of Descartes and Bacon; in the light of this comparison he rejected Spinoza's view that 'the mind is a mirror reflecting things as they are' (*WR*, p. 398); he drew the distinction between consciousness of one's own states, and consciousness of the 'not-self', and quoted Bacon with approval: 'The human understanding is like an *unequal* mirror to rays of things, which mixing its own nature with the nature of things, distorts and perverts them' (*Novum Organum*, Aphorism 41). 'There can be no doubt that—*as regards myself*—consciousness is the clear and articulate voice of truth; but it by no means follows, therefore, that—*as regards not-self*—consciousness is a perfect mirror reflecting what is, as it is' (*WR*, 1843, p. 399). After providing a translation of the opening sections of Spinoza's *Ethic* and an account of what he 'implicitly teaches', Lewes expressed his own views. 'The mind can never know the *essences* of things, but only their appearances—which is as much as saying that the mind can know nothing but its own ideas'; we are not conscious of anything 'external to our own consciousness'. Hume is credited with 'the immortal discovery' ('though Spinoza had, in his way, also foreseen it') that 'a perception is a state of the percipient, and that mind is the collective unity of these various states'; it is the mind which 'gives forms to things unknown'; 'the mind is not a passive mirror reflecting the nature of things, but the partial creator of its forms' (*WR*, pp. 399–401). There are several interesting historical features of Lewes's article. He detected connections between Bacon and Hume; he interpreted Hume in a more Kantian light than had been done before (or much since); and he provided the transition between Hume and the combined doctrines of Comte and Mill which he later espoused. It is a coincidence that Lewes's article on Spinoza immediately preceded, in the same issue of the *Westminster Review*, Alexander Bain's famous review of J. S. Mill's *System of Logic*, perhaps the most influential British nine-teenth-century philosophical treatise. And in that review Bain summarized Mill's view that hypotheses are deductions from laws not proved but conjectured or imagined to exist; and further that 'the actions of men, like all natural events, [are] subject to invari-able laws'. These views reappear in Lewes and George Eliot.

In the same year, 1843, Lewes wrote an article on contemporary French philosophy for the *British and Foreign Review*, vol. 15, chiefly notable for its précis and championship of the work of Auguste Comte. The following passage is of particular interest for our purposes:

If, in contemplating phenomena, we do not immediately connect them with some principle, it would not only be impossible for us to combine our isolated observations, and consequently to draw any benefit from them, but we should also be unable even to retain them, and most fre-quently the important facts would remain unperceived. We are there-fore forced to theorize. A theory is necessary to observation. (*BFR*, 15, 1843, p. 397)

Once more Bacon is credited with having foreseen this method; but the following account by Lewes would probably not charac-terize Bacon's method: 'the characteristic of science if prevision: if from your knowledge you can foresee and predict certain re-sults, which occur as you predicted, then indeed your knowledge must be true' (ibid., p. 400). Lewes sketched Comte's three stages of knowledge: the fictitious stage, in which men seek to know the essences of things; the metaphysical or abstract stage in which abstract forces are supposed to inhere in various substances; the positive or scientific stage in which the mind, convinced of the futility of all enquiry into causes and essences, applies itself to the

observation and classification of the laws which regulate effects—
the highest stage of knowledge would be the discovery of one
single law under which all others could be subsumed. Galileo,
Descartes, and Bacon all glimpsed this truth. Comte believes that
all branches of knowledge pass through these stages.

It will be evident that certain of the remarks we have quoted
from Lewes's articles of the same period exhibit tensions, if not
contradictions: Bacon, Hume, Kant, and Comte are not obviously
in accord unless certain amendments are made to their theories. If
Lewes wished to avoid his own strictures on eclecticism (*BFR*,
vol. 15, 1843, p. 375) we would at most be permitted to say that
he was suggesting historically antecedent pointers to his own
adopted positions. A passage in a review of Hamilton's edition of
Reid, in the *British Quarterly Review*, vol. 5, 1847, is important:
'The irresistible desire for a "system", so far from being the
characteristic of a philosophical mind, is, in the present state of our
knowledge, the certain indication of an *ill-trained* intellect' (p. 464).
Should we apply this stern judgement to Lydgate as well as to
Casaubon?

The opening pages of Lewes's *Comte's Philosophy of the Sciences*
(London, 1853), a collection of previously published articles, contains a passage which, as Lewes was well aware, comes straight out
of Hume (and ultimately from Aristotle—Lewes was sensitive to
analogies between Hume and Aristotle, cf. his *Aristotle* (London,
1864), p. 241): 'There never will be a Philosophy capable of satis-
fying the demands of Humanity, until the truth be recognized
that man is moved by his emotions, not by his ideas: using his
Intellect only as an eye to *see the way*. . . . Intellect is the servant,
not the lord of the Heart' (p. 5).

Lewes turned his attention to 'The Principles of success in
Literature', a series of articles in the *Fortnightly Review*, vol. 1, 1865;
apart from a quotation from George Eliot's review of Young's
work (*Westminster Review*, vol. LXVII, 1857—we have already
quoted from this review), it is chiefly interesting for remarks upon
the role of imagination in both art and science: 'Everyone who has
seriously investigated a novel question, who has really interrogated

Nature with a view to a distinct answer, will bear me out in saying that it requires intense and sustained effort of imagination. The relations of sequence among the phenomena must be seen; they are hidden; they can only be seen mentally . . . experiments by which the problem may be solved have to be imagined' (p. 573). Although Lewes defined imagination as 'simply the power of forming images' (p. 576, repeated p. 577), he ascribed a central role to it which seems not to be adequately covered by the definition. 'The chief intellectual operations—Perception, Inference, Reasoning, and Imagination—may be viewed as so many forms of mental vision'; 'the eye sees a certain coloured surface; the mind sees at the same instant many other coexistent but unapparent facts—it reinstates in their due order those unapparent facts. Were it not for this mental vision supplying the deficiencies of ocular vision, the coloured surface would be an enigma' (pp. 188, 189). 'In general men are passive under Sense and the routine of habitual inferences . . . they can see little more than what they have been taught to see'; 'the superiority of one mind over another depends on the rapidity with which experiences are thus organized' (pp. 191, 192). Later, he writes: 'From known facts the philosopher infers the facts that are unapparent. He does so by an act of imagination (hypothesis) which has to be subjected to verification. . . . It is because we see little that we have to imagine much'; 'the imagination is most tasked when it has to paint pictures which shall withstand the silent criticism of general experience, and to frame hypotheses which shall withstand the confrontation with facts' (pp. 574–5, 579). Lewes emphasized that 'no man imagines what he has not seen or known', but that its specific character, differentiating it from memory, is 'its tendency to selection, abstraction, and recombination' (pp. 578, 586).

Early in the series of articles, Lewes had remarked that 'much of our thinking is carried on by signs instead of images' (p. 190), thus emphasizing a criticism he had made of Hobbes years before (*A Biog. Hist. of Philos.*, vol. 2, new edition, N.Y., 1857, p. 504); in his later articles, however, he seemed concerned to stress that 'vigorous and effective minds habitually deal with concrete images' (p.

190). In the history Lewes frequently stressed that 'the mind is an *active* co-operator in all sensation' (e.g. p. 452); naturally, Kant is credited with the full development of the doctrine: the 'two-fold co-operation of object and subject is *indispensable* to all knowledge' (p. 644). One other observation is of interest. 'All things necessarily stand related to all other things', and with the advice to a reader to turn to Mill's discussion, Lewes seems to mean that all things are related causally (p. 586), in spite of his insistence that we happen only to use the notion of cause for successive phenomena; and yet, he also distinguished between a cause and 'the whole group of conditions which preceded' any event (p. 587). It is not at all clear how we would establish the causal relations between all things. Nevertheless, precisely this view is taken by George Eliot herself.

From these quotations it will be evident that Lewes himself occasionally subscribed to the view that one receives impressions passively; the very term 'im-pression' carries the implication unless one explicitly denies it. George Eliot herself asserted that 'to receive deep impressions is the foundation of all true mental power' (*GEL*, V, 155), and the Humean doctrine behind this view, that all one's ideas are ultimately based upon sensory impressions, also informs her belief that no one 'could be prepared for true fellowship without having had his share of sorrow as well as of joy' (*GEL*, V, 213). This latter belief is also in accord with Feuerbach's dictum that 'love does not exist without sympathy, sympathy does not exist without suffering in common' (*The Essence of Christianity* ed. 1854, p. 53). In a famous letter of 1875 to Mrs. Ponsonby (quoted in Cross's *Life*), during which George Eliot repudiates 'necessitarianism', she wrote: 'the most thorough experientialists admit intuition—i.e. direct impressions of sensibility underlying all proof—as necessary starting points for thought' (*GEL*, VI, 167). When Lewes himself asserted that 'all cognition is primarily emotional' (*GEL*, VI, 125) he was merely reasserting a view expressed before he met George Eliot, in his early Comte articles.

George Eliot was anxious to relate emotions to particular thoughts and situations, not to abstractions: 'emotion links itself with particulars, and only in a faint and secondary manner with abstractions' (1857, *Essays*, p. 371); 'appeals founded on generalizations and statistics require a sympathy ready-made, a moral sentiment already in activity' (1865, *Essays*, p. 270; cf. the reference in *Middlemarch*, 46.337: 'A few rows of figures are enough to deduce misery from'). It is a contingent fact, she believed, that men grasp the force of a view only by means of particular examples; hence Lecky is praised for 'being strongly impressed with the great part played by the emotions in the formation of opinion' (1865, *Essays*, p. 412). Deductive reasoning is only opposed when it is used to deny empirical evidence, when an *a priori* conclusion is made 'the standard by which he accepts or rejects evidence' (1856, *Essays*, p. 256); this is why 'there is nothing like acute deductive reasoning for keeping a man in the dark' (1856, *Essays*, p. 405). 'Deduction, as Mill shows, is not properly opposed to induction but to experiment, and is a means of registering and using the results of induction, indispensable to any great progress in science' (1855, *Essays*, p. 152).

The only effect George Eliot desired from her work was that readers should be better able to enact tolerant judgement, pity, and sympathy (*GEL*, II, 299; III, 111); as an 'aesthetic' teacher, rather than a 'doctrinal teacher' she hoped to rouse 'the nobler emotions' (*GEL*, VII, 44). Her ideal in her novels was to make 'matter and form an inseparable truthfulness' (*GEL*, V, 374). None of these views gainsay my discussion of the philosophical views inferrable from *Middlemarch* and her other writings. But a summary of my discussion is now in place.

From *Middlemarch* we inferred the view that man is naturally egoistic and seeks, above all, to satisfy his desires, for his desires govern both his perception and his action. The only way to defeat moral selfishness is by means of the imagination, the very capacity that may itself have been a victim of a man's desires. Experience is the basis of our knowledge and the only test of our hypotheses; but imagination is needed to recognize the implications of our experience, for example, that our acts have consequences beyond our awareness, and that we are subject to the causal action of countless outside factors as well as of our own past. Imagination, in brief, is the means by which we get beyond the immediately present sense-experience; it enables us to gain knowledge of others, and to feel sympathy for them. Nevertheless, our own descriptions of our experience reflect our interests and knowledge; our mental vision is necessarily focused in one way rather than another, and it is a duty to discern how that focus differs from the focus of other people.

I have frequently drawn attention to an apparent tension in George Eliot's writings between a passive and an active theory of perception. It seems that Lewes never fully persuaded George Eliot of the role of the perceiver in constructing his own perceptions; for he held that we cannot just receive data neutrally, as it were, from the external world, because our recognition of the data as being of a particular kind necessitates the use of concepts. He subscribed, then, to a Kantian notion of imagination irradiating perception. Nevertheless, even on such a view, the foundation of our knowledge is our experience, however it is classified; we have only the experiences we have. This tautology, derived from Hume, seems to me to have persuaded George Eliot to settle for an essentially passive theory of perception. Initially, we just have impressions of a certain sort, with respect to which we are passive; but to interpret them, we must use our imagination, and at this stage we become active participants in the construction of our knowledge. For practical purposes, therefore, George Eliot was willing to ignore the role of imagination as a presupposition of perception; it was not obviously a claim open to empirical verification, and if it were in fact universally true, no avoiding action could be taken. Having set it aside, however, the moral injunction becomes much plainer: we must ask ourselves precisely what is the nature of our experiences (no matter how they came about, or whether they have already been 'processed' in some unavoidable way). Indeed, George Eliot seems to subscribe to most of Hume's causal doctrine:[1] upon receiving impressions of a certain sort, a

[1] For a brief account of Hume's views see my 'Another Look at Hume's Views of Aesthetic and Moral Judgments', *The Philosophical Quarterly*, 20, January 1970.

causal chain is started as a result of which a man just feels in a particular way towards the external phenomena; in so far as this sentiment depends on a man's internal constitution there is nothing we can do about it; the only task for reason and intellect is to ensure to the best of our abilities that we have perceived the phenomena correctly. And we can only establish *that* by comparing our descriptions with those of other people who, for the sake of the argument, are already assumed to have had analogous experiences.

All philosophers make assumptions in the course of their arguments; anyone who stresses the roles of imagination is likely to be particularly aware of the ubiquity of assumptions. Oddly enough, George Eliot did not seem to have that awareness; probably because, since her aim was to prescribe a certain moral position, its logical foundations were of minor concern to her, and, furthermore, the vocabulary would be a natural part of her intellectual inheritance. Thus, if artists are to arouse sympathy by presenting things as they are, the view that all perception is distorted by idiosyncrasies must be underplayed; again, although experience is the foundation of views about causal sequences, the universality of causal relations is a postulate—albeit one that is useful for certain moral doctrines concerned with responsibility and sympathy. In parenthesis, it should be noted that an occasional effect of gloom which attends George Eliot's moral precepts, is attributable to this purely logical postulate about causes; we shall find that in Proust's novel a similar, purely logical point about the nature of knowledge, is presented as a melancholy and regrettable fact about human failings.

A distinction is sometimes made between a moralist, who prescribes moral policies by means, say, of rhetoric, examples, and other persuasive devices, and a moral philosopher, who is concerned with the nature and validity of the concepts and arguments used in the presentation of moral policies. We know of George Eliot's intentions to arouse the reader's sympathies, and also her intention to fuse form and content; if we take notice of her intentions, and consider them relevant to our judgement of her work, then we are forced to consider what ideas she expressed. And we are also forced to do this if we wish to consider her as a moralist. Obviously, according to the definition just given, George Eliot is not a moral philosopher. But for a reader there is a task akin to that of a moral philosopher; because an attempt to discern the meaning of the ideas she herself expressed, or of those that may be inferred from her writings, is likely to go hand in hand with an attempt to discern their interrelations and their cogency. Furthermore, a clear grasp of the ideas that inform her work cannot diminish a reader's appreciation of her achievement as a novelist.

CHAPTER 2

Action and Passion in Anna Karenina

Anna Karenina is a novel from which serious moral views can be derived, but it is neither a theological nor a philosophical tract. Nevertheless, I shall try to *state* explicitly, from a philosophical standpoint, what I take Tolstoy only to have *shown* or implied within his novel, without implying in any way that he ought to have stated it himself.

The question 'How to live?' is compounded of two other intimately related questions: a practical question, 'What is to be done?' the answer to which issues in public action; and a prior question, 'What is the meaning or significance of the situation?' answers to which issue in, at most, further internal decisions. I shall show how these two questions recur throughout the novel, and what prevents the main characters from answering them. To make a character explicitly ask 'What is to be done?' emphasizes the moments of decision which explain subsequent actions, and the points at which change might have been consciously initiated. On a deeper level, however, the question can be taken to relate to the problem of what it is to be a human agent, and not a passive victim of circumstances. It is for this reason that I introduce a pair of technical terms, *actio* and *passio*, to denote a distinction implicit in the text. *Actio* refers only to what a man is both conscious and in control of, whether in his inner life or outward behaviour; a man is in one sense responsible for what he does only in so far as he acts, is active, or is an agent. Emotional states and thoughts which possess or take control of him, together with habits and what he does unwittingly, fall under the heading *passio*. Essential to *passio* is the fact that the sufferer, sometimes through wilful ignorance, is out of control in the relevant area. A man may be a victim not only of his inner life but also of what he has brought about, albeit not intentionally or wilfully. Lacking such control a man is denied self-fulfilment; for underlying the *actio/passio* distinction in *Anna Karenina*, is the view that a fundamental duty is to discern and seek to realize one's essential nature or real self; whatever masks knowledge of this potential or inhibits its actualization is to be condemned. Some of the difficulties in these notions will emerge later on, but the over-all view presupposed in the novel may be characterized as follows. In order to discover some of the factors which deny a man agency, it is important to decide how his external behaviour reflects his inner life of thought and feeling; and a consideration of both natural and conventional expression, which this involves, is itself open to assessment in the light of the *actio/passio* distinction. For the most part the significance of a man's acts must be inferred, like his intentions, from the descriptions given of those acts; there are many ways of describing most events and not all descriptions of what a man has brought about could refer to the fulfilment of what he wanted, intended or tried to do. Even when a man's actions are the expressions of his internal decisions and emotions, it may be impossible to determine what his internal states were if we consider what he does as an isolated and discrete performance (cf. previous chapter, pp. 11, 41). Further, the significance of what he does, and its connections with other doings, will emerge only from consideration of their context; it cannot be discerned as an immediately perceptible property of his performance, because it entails reference beyond the present. These points will become clear with the examples in the following discussion. I begin, however, with a very brief consideration of some stylistic and structural features of the novel; others will emerge in the detailed exposition, but it will be convenient to bear some of these factors in mind, particularly as Tolstoy was rightly proud of the architecture of his work, and also of having hidden the seams which bound it together.

From *Anna Karenina* we can infer the view that for understanding each other, and their common lot, the similarities between men are as important as the differences. We cannot always tell by observation how much of a man's behaviour is spontaneous and how much is conventional. To the extent that it is conventional, the external similarity of his behaviour to that of other men may mask differences in the internal states behind it; on the other hand, when men respond to situations spontaneously, we are shown that men tend to act in the same way. Mutual illumination of characters in the novel is achieved by comparison between them; but such comparison is also used for the contrasting purposes of securing their individuality and binding them together with each other. The nature of each character and of their responses are largely defined, as it were, as the intersection of multiple comparisons with other people. Many of these cross-references are obvious, such as the parallel dreams of Anna and Vronsky, the family resemblances between Stiva and Anna (they are equally incapable of hiding their marital discord from their children; they each seek to live in the present, etc.), Dolly and Kitty, Nikolai and Levin, the equal ambitiousness of Karenin and Vronsky and the fact that both are passed over in promotion, the search for a pattern in life by Kitty, in her 'unnatural' period, and by Levin, and their equal hot temper. Both Kitty and her mother receive proposals of marriage by means of chalked messages, which provides an analogy between the worldly-wise Prince and the young Levin. Vronsky's attitude to marriage, shown at the end of Part I, is contrasted with Levin's, characterized earlier in the same part; both desired definiteness (III, 26, 20);[1] Vronsky could not remember his father, nor Levin his mother (I, 16, 6), and both Levin's parents had died when he was young, as had Karenin's, who also could not remember his father (V, 21). Before asking Anna to marry him Karenin had weighed all the arguments for and against (V, 21), and Koznyshev behaved in the same way towards Varenka (VI, 5) reaching the opposite conclusion. Like Oblonsky, Koznyshev went to the country for rest, but unlike him, regarded the social influences of the town as corrupting (III, 1). Oblonsky, like Karenin, could not

---

[1] All my references to, and translations from, *Anna Karenina* are taken from volumes 8 and 9 of the twelve-volume edition of Tolstoy's works: *Sobranie Sochineniy*, Moscow, 1958. Roman numerals refer to the Part, and arabic numerals to the chapter within the Part.

cope with tears (I, 4; II, 13), but not because he had suppressed deep emotions and feared them, as Seriozha also came to do (VII, 19), but because his shallow emotions were aroused too easily, even by drink, as Dolly observed (VI, 31). It seemed to the men that childbirth brought Vronsky closer to Anna and Levin closer to Kitty (IV, 18; VII, 13). Sometimes the illuminating comparisons are far apart: Oblonsky told Anna that she married in ignorance of love, and Anna told Vronsky that Karenin married in ignorance of love (IV, 21; II, 9); Dolly talked to Anna of what most hurt her, as Anna spoke to her, at the end (I, 19; VII, 28); Karenin's self-pity (V, 22), like his denial of Anna's existence for him (III, 13), resembles Anna's self-pity and her denial of his existence for her (VII, 12; II, 22). Levin believed that Koznyshev's good works arose from a lack of something, and revealed a negative trait; similarly Oblonsky suggested that Levin had been acting only with a negative idea of justice (III, 1; VI, 11). Parallels nearer together also abound: Kitty declared that she was not to blame for Levin's distress at the consequences of Vronsky's arrival, and Anna made the same declaration, for the same reason, but about Kitty (I, 15, 28); as Anna loved Vronsky too much, so did Kitty love Levin (V, 8, 16); Anna's first thoughts were of Seriozha both when she was met by Karenin and when she met Vronsky (I, 31; IV, 23); neither Karenin nor Anna could look for solace to religion (III, 13, 15), and both had to suffer in solitude (V, 21, 29); as Karenin wished primarily to punish Anna, so she wished to punish Vronsky (III, 13; VII, 26), and Levin wanted Kitty to suffer for having made him suffer (II, 16). These natural reactions of seeking vengeance are to be read in the light of the epigraph to the novel, from *Romans* 12:19, 'Vengeance is mine; I will repay, saith the Lord.' Karenin and Anna were equally insistent that the other should not be happy (III, 13, 16). Three less prominent examples must suffice to show the ubiquity of such comparisons: the life of the hero in the English novel Anna reads on the train returning to Petersburg (I, 29) is precisely the sort of life she and Vronsky come to lead; as Vronsky was attracted by Golenishchev's breeding, so was Levin by Veslovsky's (V, 7; VI, 8), and each of these minor characters admired the principal's wife; just as Kitty never reflected on Mme Stahl's body under the quilt, so Levin failed to consider the dying Nikolai's, whereas Kitty had now learnt to do so (II, 34; V, 18). It should not be thought from these few out of the numerous such comparisons that they are all of the same type, that their effects are identical, or that they perform the same functions; but the careful analysis necessary to establish differences between them is not here relevant.

Two linguistic observations, however, are in place at the outset. First, the infrequency of cognitive verbs should be noted. Characters are rarely said to 'know' or even 'think' something; on the contrary, they are more frequently said to *not* know or realize or consider or understand. What they are said to do, invariably, is to 'feel' (*chuvstvovat'*) that something is the case, or occasionally 'see'. Levin is not alone in explicitly contrasting what he thinks with what he feels (I, 11). One point here is that, in certain contexts, a man may legitimately claim certainty and incorrigibility for reports of what he senses internally, because only he can know; but he can make no unchallengeable reports of what it is that he perceives, for here the reference is external and open to public scrutiny. The verb 'to feel' may be used in both reports, but this does not secure the unassailability of our perceptual judgements. A consequence of conflating the two types of report is the assumption that in all cases the cause of one's sensations is identical with the object of one's perceptions. These points will be clarified by the examples in the discussion. The second linguistic observation is that emotions are said to communicate themselves (*soobshchat'*) to other people; those infected thus become victims of internal states not their own, and the emotion communicated to them is thus, for them, *passio*.

I turn now to the first of my two main questions and to the obstacles which make it difficult for characters to answer it.

WHAT IS TO BE DONE?

All the main characters explicitly ask this question, and most, finding no acceptable answer in their particular context, consequently do nothing; they allow themselves to be passive precisely when action is called for. After his affair with the governess has been discovered Oblonsky asks this question (I, 4, 10, 11), and both Dolly and Anna ask each other in the same context (I, 19). At the prospect of being confronted by both Levin and Vronsky, Kitty asks it (I, 15). After observing Anna's animated conversation with Vronsky, Karenin asks himself the question, and again when Dolly tries to dissuade him from divorce (II, 8; IV, 12). Levin asks it after reflecting upon the peasants, and the moment before Kitty passes in the carriage,[1] and he asks it again when his brother Nikolai is dying (III, 12, 31). The moment before he shoots himself, Vronsky asks it (IV, 18), and in her final demented soliloquy, Anna asks it (VII, 27). The significance of the question, and its recurrence, should not be overlooked. By asking the question a character takes the first steps towards action in the fullest sense; by failing to answer it, or to carry through his answer, or by turning away from his answer, he succumbs to *passio* which he has himself brought about. *Actio* is essential not only for self-respect but ultimately for sanity, as we shall see; doing comes to be identified with living. Anna explicitly associates these two notions (VII, 12) and exemplifies the reference to sanity. The closing sentence of Part IV, echoed in the closing sentence of Part VII after Anna's death, had already marked the connection, however; the one thread that guided Levin through his depression was his work—*delo*, related to *delat'*, to do.

Having refused to consider seriously the question he had asked himself, Oblonsky is prepared to accept his valet's view that things will 'right themselves' (I, 4; IV, 7). At the beginning of her affair with Vronsky, Anna persuades herself that since nothing has happened no action is required by her (I, 32); in part this view is fostered by her familiar environment, where not only many things go on as before, which was also precisely Vronsky's reaction (I, 34), but 'everything did itself' anyway (III, 17). This social conditioning, together with his physical fear of a duel, also

---

[1] The scene in which Kitty passes in the carriage should be compared with that scene in *Middlemarch* (62.465) in which Dorothea passes Will Ladislaw.

explained Karenin's inactivity (III, 13). Vronsky told Kitty that he never made up his mind without consulting his mother (I, 12), and in spite of his characterization as an energetic man we shall discover that he was not, strictly, a man of action; on a number of occasions he submits 'against his will' (*nevol'no*) to Anna (III, 22; IV, 1, 2; V, 8), and like her and her brother and her husband he hopes that the situation will change of its own accord, and that 'something other than what was due from him' would clarify their difficulties (IV, 1). Karenin persuaded himself, when Anna recovered after her confinement, that 'nothing need be changed' and thus no action by him was needed (IV, 19). When they begin to grasp the complexity of the situation in which they are called upon to answer the question 'What to do?' and to act, these same characters ascribe to the situation an elemental force, which opposes them and both causes and justifies their failure to act. Karenin, Vronsky, and Anna look upon society as such a constraining force, and Levin views the peasants in a similar light (e.g. IV, 22; II, 13); at times, these views lead to fatalism, as when Anna asks Dolly whether things could have been otherwise (VI, 23). There is a sense, however, in which the characters know that they are no less responsible for what they have allowed to come about, by not acting, than they are for what they actively do; the frequent requests for forgiveness and the insistence that they are not to blame, for example by Oblonsky and Kitty (I, 1, 9, 15) and by Anna (I, 28), are evidence for this half-realization. There is a number of different factors which causally explain inaction, and to these we must turn.

Anna's habit, mentioned nearly a dozen times, of half-shutting her eyes[1] was taken by Dolly as an indication of her wilfully averting attention from the facts of the situation and from her vital impulses (it should be noted that Dolly judged Anna's life with Karenin as artificial as she later judged Anna's life with Vronsky (I, 19; VI, 19)); and that expression of self-denial, leading as it did to self-deception, was matched in Karenin by the cracking of his

---

[1] This is, of course, a natural symptom of short-sightedness. There has been much discussion of the personality traits of myopics.

knuckles. Both traits show how the characters are reacting to a situation, and indicate tension between their inner states and their outward behaviour (For Anna's gesture, see: I, 23; IV, 3; VI, 19, 21, 23; VII, 10, 28; for Karenin's see: II, 8, 9, 27; III, 14; IV, 19; V, 22). Karenin's refusal to engage in life led to ignorance of it and of what to do when called upon to act (IV, 20); 'every time he had come up against life itself he had stepped aside' (II, 8), and his object, 'of settling matters with the least disturbance' (III, 13— hence Oblonsky's assurance, 'I'll settle it all for you so that you will not notice' VII, 18) led him to avoid personal confrontation or, if unavoidable, to secure the presence of a third person (II, 26: Vronsky and Anna each return with a third person when the other has decided upon a frank discussion, V, 31, 32). Karenin preferred to communicate with people by letter. He wrote to Anna—in French, to avoid, surprisingly, the coldness of the Russian 'you'; the same reason for which Vronsky spoke to her in French (II, 22) —and to his lawyer. It comforted him to have 'translated this matter of life into a matter of paper' (IV, 8) and he wrote again to Anna, thinking he could 'say it better in a letter', as he admitted to Oblonsky (IV, 22). The habit infected the Countess Lydia Ivanovna after she had taken him up, for she wrote two or three notes a day to him: 'it had an elegance and secrecy about it that was lacking in their personal dealings' (V, 23). Although it was indeed literally necessary, the underlying irony should not be missed in the observation that Anna decided to write to Karenin in order to enter into dealings with him (V, 29). Whereas Karenin's absence or denial of emotion blinded him to a reality in which emotions were a dominant factor, Vronsky's excess of emotion, in the form of passions, was equally blinding, as we shall see. But before elaborating upon this point and upon other difficulties in the way of answering the question 'What is to be done?' it will be convenient to indicate in advance what the proper solution is supposed to be.

To know what to do a man has only to look within, to his conscience. All the major characters are shown as hearing the voice or experiencing the pricks of conscience, whether or not they recognize them for what they are, or heed them. Karenin, Anna, Vronsky, and Levin are all said to know things 'in the depths of' their hearts: Karenin that he was a wronged husband and that he wanted Anna to suffer for having destroyed his peace of mind (II, 26; III, 14); Levin that he ought not to have visited Anna with Oblonsky, and that Koznyshev lacked 'vital impulses' (VII, 11; III, 1); Anna that her position was false, and later, after receiving Karenin's first letter, that everything would go on in the old way (III, 15, 22). Vronsky 'in his heart' felt that those who offered advice on the effects of his affair were right (II, 21), although he successfully drove away this strange feeling; Oblonsky, on the other hand, failed to heed because he failed to recognize the warning given by the voice of conscience when he called, the first time, to intercede with Karenin on Anna's behalf (IV, 22). And his sister Anna failed to heed the warning of an inner voice about Vronsky's slavish adoration at the ball (I, 29). These cases can be taken to show two activities of conscience: judgements about right and wrong, and judgements simply about what is the case. It is important to stress the implication that conscience is concerned with non-moral knowledge, because the view is canvassed and accepted, at least by Levin, that we all really know the true nature of the situations in which we find ourselves, and thus also know what we should do. (We saw in the last chapter that a similar view was canvassed in *Middlemarch*.) An infallible judge in his heart decided which of two possible courses of action was the better, and this judge operated 'when he did not think, but just lived' (VIII, 10); knowledge of right and wrong, he asserts, must be 'given' since he could not have acquired it from anywhere (VIII, 12). In the same passage, in which he repudiates the role of reason, and to which we shall return, Levin concludes that his new-found knowledge is no real discovery: 'I have only come to know what I know.' Later we shall question the consistency of these statements with what is stated or can be inferred from elsewhere in the novel. It suffices to remark here that much remains unclear about the efficacy of conscience and its judgements. For example, even if conscience gives unmistakable guidance at the outset of a chain of actions, does it continue to guide after a wrong step has been taken? Does it operate anew at each fresh decision point, or is its power diminished with each false step? What guidance was Anna's conscience towards extrication from her predicament, after she had ignored its early warnings? Although these questions could be appropriately pressed only if a thesis were being argued, they pinpoint obscurities in the views that can be inferred from the novel; and such obscurities may affect one's overall assessment of the novel.

A man whose actions are in accord with the judgements of his conscience may be said to act 'naturally', that is, according to what it is in his nature to be. In returning now to a detailed discussion of the difficulties in the way of answering the question 'What is to be done?' we shall see both why and how it is that most men's performances fail to come up to this definition of action.

ROLE-PLAYING

Levin, Koznyshev, Karenin, Anna, and Vronsky are explicitly described as adopting and playing roles, at one time or another; the significance and implications of this need to be spelt out. Six times Vronsky is described as consciously adopting (*izbirat'*) a role; for example, that of seducer, magnanimous lover sacrificing his career, painter, and wealthy landowner (II, 4; III, 21; V, 9; VI, 25). He was humiliated by Karenin's forgiveness of Anna at her bedside, and felt that he had exchanged roles with the husband; from which it must be inferred that he had earlier seen himself in the role of a simple but grand and in no way deceitful lover (IV, 18). This is explained in part by reflection on the nature of Vronsky's code of principles (III, 20). Although the rules which comprised the code defined without doubt what should and what should not be done, the code as a whole covered only a very small number of circumstances; they did not cover his relations with Anna, for example, nor with anyone who was either ignorant of, or who ignored, the provisions of the code. Hence Vronsky's bewilderment with Karenin when no challenge to a duel is forthcoming. Vronsky was less concerned with the rationality and moral worth of his principles of conduct than with their 'simplicity' and 'clarity'; and these properties also beguiled Levin, Anna, and, to a certain extent, Karenin. But neither the contingencies nor the complexities of life can be contained within rules of conduct that are both simple and rigid, as is implied throughout the novel (although denied by Levin at its conclusion). Playing a role and the adoption of simple and rigid rules of conduct are contrasted, in *Anna Karenina*, with unselfconscious involvement in life, which was why Mihailov was repelled and insulted by Vronsky's artistic efforts (V, 13). Vronsky did not derive inspiration for his painting directly from life, but indirectly from other painters' interpretations of life; in this way he found inspiration easy (V, 8), but it was not a true engagement in the creative, artistic experience, which was why he could give it up so painlessly. It should be noted, in this connection, that Levin's book had been an escape from life (V, 15); was the children's book Anna was writing a similar consolatory escape (VII, 9)? Does her writing escape being the adoption of a role in being an attempt to mitigate unfulfilled motherly instincts? To answer this question we must consider what roles are implied to be; but we should note, in passing, that even when Vronsky surrenders to his passions (IV, 2), what he does is in accord with the role he has determined previously to play (I, 34; II, 4).

Roles, it is implied, occur within, and are defined by, a social context. It is clear that their adoption presupposes possible recognition by other people. One does not adopt a role if no one is going to know. Anna remarked to Dolly that Vronsky needed an audience (VI, 19), and in describing the improvements he had made to the estate, Vronsky is said to have felt the need to boast before someone new (VI, 20). Karenin was pleased with the saintly role he was performing in the eyes of the Countess Lydia Ivanovna (V, 25). Just as the context circumscribes the role, so the role circumscribes the behaviour of him who adopts it; within the domain of each role, it is implied, neither natural nor spontaneous behaviour is possible. The cases from which we can infer all this also imply a distinction between 'spontaneous' behaviour which is impulsive, unselfconscious and usually unreflective; and 'natural' behaviour which refers to the enactment of a man's real nature when he follows his conscience, but does not have the usual reference to what is judged individually characteristic or socially customary. Condemnation of role-playing seems to rest on the assumptions that since any man is to be defined in terms of his internal essence, roles, regarded as existing only in external social contexts, inhibit the realization of that essence. But the view that self-knowledge largely depends on following one's conscience is not obviously connected with, and leaves unjustified, the further implicit view that habitual, conventional, passionate, and even role-playing activities must be excluded from the real nature of all men. And it is unclear why a man may not intentionally adopt a role for certain ends without being dominated by it, forgoing close personal relationships, or inhibiting self-fulfilment; at this stage it is unclear how it would be possible to *act* without reference to rules or roles.

We can infer the view that once the outlet for the external expression of a man's natural and spontaneous feelings is closed, their internal occurrence comes to be ignored, and in the end may cease; in such cases, it may be assumed that the spontaneous feelings were natural to the character in question, and would not have constituted *passio* if expressed. The dominance of habit has to be actively opposed in all quarters, for there are no conditions of life to which a man cannot get accustomed (VII, 13). The legacy of persistent role-playing is apparent when Koznyshev considers whether to propose to Mlle Varenka. Koznyshev was only minimally concerned that failure to remain true to the memory of Marie would 'detract from the poetic role he played in the eyes of others' (VI, 4); it was lack of practice in expressing his natural feelings, brought about by constant role-playing, that led him not to say 'what ought to have been said' (VI, 5), and habitual reliance upon exclusively rational appraisal that enabled him to convince himself that he was right. The artificiality of Kitty's behaviour when she adopted the role of ministering angel under Mme Stahl's influence, is contrasted with the natural spontaneity of her behaviour when Nikolai was dying. Levin was appalled by Dolly's invitation to visit her during Kitty's stay, because it would have involved, he felt, the adoption of the role in which he appeared before Kitty to forgive her (III, 24). Three points emerge from this example. First, the factor of how other people view what one is doing: not only may they be wrong in their interpretation, but a man can be a disinterested observer of his own past actions in the same way as others view his present actions. By this means a man may come to see his past actions as having resulted from the adoption of a role. Secondly, although Levin had different but strong motives and inclinations to go, the possibility that others would fail to recognize them and would think up other motives, offering an account in terms of role-playing, was a sufficient deterrent to his going. He was wrong, of course, in assuming that others would have so carefully reflected upon his motives, and also in meanly ascribing to others mean descriptions of himself. Kitty reprimanded him for ascribing mean motives to her and others (V, 16) but she also came to realize that it was all part of his self-denigration, which she believed to be not entirely genuine (VI, 3). The third point is that someone may have a need which is partly alleviated by the adoption of a role; it is implied, indeed, that the explicit adoption of a role by a character is always an indication of the presence of a need, although the precise nature of that need cannot always be inferred from the role adopted. It is this third point which explains why Anna, who is in fact a mother, is also said to have assumed 'the greatly exaggerated role of the mother living for her son' (III, 15). Anna resented the fact that people said her husband was a man of integrity, so moral and religious; they did not know that he had crushed everything living out of her, so that she had been forced to divert, as it were, the love proper to him on to her son (III, 16). 'On her first born . . . had been placed all the force of the love that had not secured satisfaction' (V, 31); the distortion consequent upon this unnatural attitude had serious effects upon her relations with Vronsky. Karenin, too, was concerned with what people would say; and he was pleased to think that the decision he had reached, and which would be conveyed to

Anna in the first letter, happened to correspond with the require-
ments of religion: 'no one in the circumstances would be able to
say that he had not acted in conformity with the principles of'
religion (III, 13). The point is, however, that although his decision
was in conformity with, it most certainly had not been reached for
the sake of, religion; but people whose knowledge of him was
restricted to observation of his outward behaviour, need never
know this inner fact which explained it. He failed to see that one
who acts for the sake of religion may thereby be less true to his
inner-self than one who, fulfilling that self, merely acts in conformity with religion.

Social roles may be contrasted with social functions or offices,
and the duties attendant upon these tasks may themselves be contrasted with natural duties, such as those of motherhood or being
a family member. Koznyshev, for example, refers to the duties
attendant upon the social tasks of juryman or telegraph clerk (IV,
10). Natural duties such as motherhood may well clash with
desires and with the possibility of performing roles. Dolly came
to accept the peasant woman's remark that with children 'You
can't work or anything. They only bind one' (VI, 16); such duties,
linked with a person's nature, appear, misleadingly, to limit
personal freedom because they are constraints upon desires. We
find that unhampered indulgence in his desires is associated with
avoidance or denial of a character's natural duties. It is implied that
the adoption of a social role is a self-conscious act for which the
agent is responsible, and is to be contrasted with what he would
naturally do, other constraints notwithstanding. It is further
implied that where the demands of roles are allowed by an agent
to subdue duties attached to his nature, he is alone responsible for
having brought about his own state of *passio*.

Although the adoption of social roles or the playing of parts,
and even conventional social behaviour in general, are said to be
false or artificial (I, 19; II, 8—at one point it is said that to act
comme il faut is not to act or to respond to life at all (V, 7)), there is
no suggestion that man is not, or ought not to be, a social being.
The view of man as a social being is quite compatible with the

notion that a man is to be defined in terms of his essence or inner nature; the tension between the realization of this nature and the constraints imposed by the social life men must live, mirrors the tension between a man's inner states and their outward expression, to which we shall refer later. In spite of this, it is also implied that those whose lives consist exclusively in the narrowly rule-bound performance of social roles will have no reserves of knowledge, experience, or energy, to cope with the crises of life. First, because the clear but simple rules necessary for the performance of roles cannot provide for the contingencies of life; secondly, because the continued exercise of rule-bound responses atrophies the natural capacities for those spontaneous responses which may carry one through a crisis. Karenin, whose life had been geared to professional ambition, felt totally isolated in his misery (V, 21); partly because he failed to find 'the ordinance to which the newly-arisen situation was subject' (II, 8), partly because he persisted in his old habit of striving 'to withhold every manifestation of life in himself' (III, 13). As a result, he was unable to establish any natural human relationship, as shown in the episode with the Countess Lydia. It is his emotional need which explains Karenin's participation in the seance which, intellectually, he knows to be a hoax (VII, 21)—his flirtation with religion should be compared and contrasted with those of Kitty and Levin, respectively. Such needs are often co-extensive with a marked tension between unwilling knowledge and willing belief; for example, at the moment before Anna confessed that she was Vronsky's mistress, when returning from the races, it is said of Karenin that what he knew was so terrible that he was prepared to believe anything—anything, that is, that could serve as a soothing denial of what he knew (II, 29). Anna is terrified of being left alone without Vronsky (VI, 23) and yet because of misunderstandings and obstacles partly of her own making she has to suffer in solitude (V, 29). Karenin, Anna, and Vronsky are social beings, whose world is defined by their society and the various roles that may be adopted and enacted within it. However isolated he felt, Vronsky, after Anna's death, goes off to the front with other people. In vivid contrast, Levin, whose first remark to Vronsky had been that 'one is never bored by oneself' (I, 14), required solitude for reflection and equilibrium. He was always uneasy in, and sought to escape from, society (VI, 30) and Kitty, herself a product of such society but also the repository, latterly, of motherly common sense, felt that he thought too much because he was always alone (VIII, 7). Levin's gathering of his spiritual resources is contrasted with Vronsky's regular 'days of reckoning' which were concerned with matters far from spiritual (III, 19), although his code of principles was indeed the point of reference on such occasions. But if Levin found dissatisfaction with his reflections and with himself when alone, and alleviated it by acting, Vronsky and Anna could not survive alone, and sought to avoid being alone by the trivial and unfulfilling expenditure of time in the company of others. The only close personal, adult relations that Anna and Vronsky established were with each other, in spite of the fact that they needed a constant background of people; Vronsky's definition of a close acquaintance is one who asks no personal questions. Levin, on the other hand, expected open discussion of personal matters, however disconcerting this was to social beings such as Oblonsky (I, 11).

In so far as the notion of playing a role is taken to imply a contrast between what is merely social and what is natural for an individual, the intentional adoption of a role is sometimes seen as the expression of a desire to be other than one naturally is; and sometimes a character only discovers his nature by realizing that he had been playing a role. Only after her father had recognized and commented upon Mme Stahl and Kitty's behaviour, did Kitty realize that she had 'deceived herself in imagining that she could be what she wanted to be' (II, 35). Perhaps it was in Levin's nature frequently to dream of a new life; yet others sometimes believed him to be only playing a role and to have deceived himself about his motives or his actions, particularly in connection with the peasants (cf. VI, 11). Occasionally he recognizes this possibility; 'he felt himself and did not want to be anyone else' (I, 26). A fundamental problem, as Levin explicity realized in this same passage, is whether a man is a perpetual victim of outside factors, such as his past and his environment, or whether he can make what he will of himself.

Those characters who undergo change, at least in the sense of coming to be their true selves, do so primarily as a result of close human relationships, for which the spontaneous expression of natural responses is assumed to be necessary. Oblonsky and Karenin, who do not appear to change as a result of their marriages precisely because they do not involve themselves, by giving themselves, in deep or sustained human relationship, can be taken to show, in different ways, how such relationships challenge both the egoism and the freedom of those concerned. At this point the present notion of role-playing relates to the notion of both self-identity, in the sense of discovery and realization of the self, and of freedom. It is implied that while the exclusive adoption of roles precludes involvement (the view I challenged), precisely because roles are seen as self-interested, it allows for indulgence in egoistic fancies; and also that the sort of freedom necessary for self-identity is confused, at least by Vronsky and Oblonsky and to a certain extent by Levin, with the freedom to pursue self-gratifying social roles. In such cases the characters concerned suffer *passio*, and fail to act. When Anna realized that she would never experience the freedoms of love and 'could not be stronger than herself' (III, 16) she was referring, in part, to the power of her social habits and needs which were incompatible both with her passionate desires and with the development of her true nature. But there is also much in the novel to suggest that no one knows freedom in love, a view which perhaps influenced Proust.[1] First, because love so often becomes a passion that subdues and subjects the individual will; secondly, because love requires some sort of self-denial in

[1] In *Contre Sainte-Beuve* Proust asked why Kitty was said to have a 'sly' look whenever she spoke of religion (V, 19). Surely the look expressed her attitude to Levin's professed agnosticism, which she thought both funny and in a sense not genuine (cf. VIII, 7). This partly explains her following remark, 'everything is possible', the implicit rider being 'for one with faith'. There is, however, added point to her remark, because it echoes Vronsky's early assurance to Anna, 'there is a way out of every situation' (II, 22), and Oblonsky's identical assurance both to Anna and then to Karenin (IV, 21, 22).

order to establish a bond with its object. Dining with three
bachelors just before his wedding, Levin is teased about the im-
pending loss of freedom, and reflects that the perfect happiness of
losing his identity in Kitty's would indeed be a loss of freedom (V,
2). Vronsky told Anna of their indivisibility (II, 7) and Levin had
felt the same about himself and Kitty (IV, 15; V, 4); and after
their first quarrel he discovered that he was not simply close to her,
'he did not know where she ended and he began' (V, 14). Nevertheless, both then and later when Oblonsky caused Levin to
reflect that he was tied too much to Kitty's apron strings (VI, 11),
he began to feel that he should assert his manly independence. In
Levin's eyes this probably referred to masculine activities such as
shooting, although there may have been elements of what was
undoubtedly central in Oblonsky's eyes, namely, those activities
associated with the social role of an independently minded husband. In any case Oblonsky gives the wrong reason for attempting
to preserve some sort of independence; it is not, as he thought, for
self-respect (the term which had earlier been a matter of dispute
between Levin and Koznyshev—III, 3), which might be attainable
without such independence, but for self-identity which might not
be thus attainable. Vronsky resented the threat to his freedom that
Anna's demands increasingly made on him. Initially he was concerned only that the possibility of freedom, should he want it, had
not been undermined (VI, 25); but he became like a man who
thinks he is compelled to stay with his legs doubled up and who
consequently gets cramp (V, 28); he felt not only the need to
assert his independence, therefore, he came to see this assertion as
a right (VI, 31, 32). Oblonsky retained his freedom, and bachelor
tastes (III, 7), by not accepting the natural duties that go with
having a family; whereas Dolly was prevented by just these duties
to her children from having the freedom she craved. Both the
presence and thought of Seriozha were felt by Anna, at various
times, as a constraint upon her freedom and a curb upon carefree
indulgence in her passions; this feeling of constraint, which suppressed the natural motherly duties she felt, combined with her
genuine love for him in exacerbating her divided loyalties. It

should be noted, however, that Anna consistently carried a mis-leading, and long out of date, picture of Seriozha in her mind (I, 32; V, 29); the point is that Anna had attained maximum posses-sion over someone who, at the age of four, had already achieved sufficient independence for self-identity. The egoism of passion, which demands exclusive attention and satisfaction, can be taken to relate to the possessiveness of close relationships. Kitty's mother was loath to give her youngest daughter any freedom before marriage (I, 12); Karenin was loath to give Anna the free-dom that divorce would provide (IV, 22). When characters expli-citly reflect upon threats to their freedom, what they refer to is the loss of some egoistic indulgence; the social round, for example, or the structure of society, is not always described as a restriction upon freedom. Vronsky, who regrets that society will not accept Anna, still readily repairs to it in order to escape her demands and to show his independence; indeed, he contrasts 'complete freedom' unfavourably with the 'social round' (V, 8).

I have argued that we can infer the view from *Anna Karenina*, whether or not it is Tolstoy's own view, that to adopt a social role is to adopt a rule-bound mode of conduct which fails to cater for the unpredictabilities of life, and conflicts with natural duties and spontaneous impulses. Further, the view holds, the adoption of roles precludes intimate personal relations, and provides no re-serves for riding out storms; on these occasions, social beings whose lives have consisted in role-playing become totally isolated in their misery. Some people, it is implied, adopt roles to fulfil needs, but others adopt them in order to be other than what they are; in either case, the self-knowledge derivable only from self-confrontation is denied them. Sustained human relationships challenge the egoistic sense of freedom and independence; but the urge to assert one's independence may have arisen as much from concern for self-identity, as from concern for what society expects of a certain social role. A man, therefore, who asks 'What is to be done?' but expects an answer in terms of rules or roles is doomed to failure, and is unlikely to hear or heed the voice of conscience which alone can give him the correct answer.

With such an emphasis upon the intuitive judgements of conscience, it is important to clarify the functions and value of rational thought, and this we shall do in due course. It might be thought that conscience would be influenced, at least, by memories. A preliminary word is in order here, however. The old landowner whom Levin met at Sviazhsky's, whose ideas had 'grown out of the conditions of his life', was 'perfectly correct in the judgements he had been worried into by life' (III, 27, 28). On the other hand, Koznyshev's philanthropy had been reasoned out and had not been motivated by 'an impulse of the heart'; in Levin's view, his brother lacked 'the vital force' which drives a man to select and stick to one path in life (III, 1). When Kitty came to repudiate her behaviour at the German spa, she described it as 'all thought up' and 'not from the heart'; she declares that she 'cannot live except from the heart', whereas Varenka 'lives according to principle' (II, 35). In this limited respect Varenka resembles both Koznyshev, which throws further light on his failure to propose to her, and also Karenin, whereas Kitty resembles Levin and Anna.

We can infer the view that our thoughts are controlled by at least three separate factors: by our desires, our interests, and our reasoning. All serve to blind us to the truth and all may lead to self-deception. Reason and reasoning mislead because our ways of thinking may be subservient to our interests, but also because the general categories and concepts of reason obliterate the uniqueness of particular circumstances. If a man obeys the judgements of his conscience he will not be led astray, since they tell him not only what is right and wrong, and what to do, but also which of his spontaneous passions to curb; further, of course, only by following his conscience may a man discover his true nature. Anna discovered that 'in dreams, when she had no control over her thoughts, her position appeared to her in all its hideous nakedness' (II, 11). The key to right action, according to the view I have inferred, is thus not controlled thought and spontaneous passion, but rather spontaneous thought, in accord with conscience, and controlled passion, where the latter expression refers to the realization of those passions alone which conscience sanctions. Levin's conclusion, at the end of the novel, that 'the path of thought is strange and not natural to man', coupled with his rejection of the powers of reason in the search for knowledge of how to live and what to do, fails to convince because it entails the denial, and not merely the proper use, of what has been shown to be a natural capacity (VIII, 13, 12). But we are shown no cases where spontaneous thought alone, without any emotional elements, either guides a man aright or leads to action. On the contrary, an emotional response is implied to be a living response, for man is both a thinking and a feeling being; the heart and not the intellect provides the motive power to action, as Aristotle observed, although thought, in the sense of the judgements of conscience, prescribes the action to be taken.[1] There is a number of other interesting obstacles to answering the question 'What is to be done?' connected with reasoning, and these we shall examine shortly. First, however, it is important to consider what happens when characters confuse passion with action; for living is equated with acting, and failure to act or incapacity for acting may lead to insanity, as in the case of Anna, and spiritual death.

ACTION AND PASSION

These terms may be illustrated by reflection upon the characterization of Anna and Vronsky. The animal magnetism that existed between them is shown in their earliest meetings, at the station and on the train (I, 18, 30). Anna's effect on those around her is defined in terms of attractiveness, seductive fascination, bewitching charm. Seven times in one sentence, and then again, Anna is described at Kitty's ball as 'charming' (I, 23); by extension of the metaphor, both she and Vronsky are described as 'bewitching' (I, 12; VI, 25; VII, 11); she is said to be fascinating or attractive (VI, 7; VII, 9), and also well aware of the power of her attractiveness (VI, 17, 25, 32). We should also note that Kitty recognizes this sort of power in herself (I, 22; II, 30) and also, with alarm, in Levin (VII, 1). The reason for Anna's effect on others is her vitality. When he first

---

[1] Cf. George Eliot, *Adam Bede*, Ch. 17. 'It isn't notions sets people doing the right thing—it's feelings.'

saw her at the station, Vronsky noticed that it was 'as if an excess of something overflowed her being' (I, 18); and thereafter Anna is shown as driven by a desire 'to live' (I, 29). Much later, Anna declared to Dolly that her main desire was to live (VI, 18), and Dolly reflected that such a desire was perfectly natural since God put it into the soul of each of us (VI, 16). Anna's surplus of energy partly explains the failure of her imagination to reflect reality. Seriozha and Vronsky were incomparably greater in her imagination than they were in reality (IV, 2; I, 32) because her energy, denied outward expression, had been diverted inwards and had augmented to excess the natural power of the imagination. Further, when her natural vivacity did escape its artificial bonds, imposed by her life with Karenin, it was bound to appear in manifestations regarded as excessive by others. Dolly was wrong to suppose that Anna's flirting with Veslovsky revealed 'a new trait of coquetry' (VI, 22), since Anna is explicitly described on her first entry as throwing 'the ball of coquetry' at Vronsky (I, 18).

In addition to her charm, however, we are also shown at the outset what can only be called the seeds of Anna's mental imbalance; an imbalance brought about in part by the denial of her vitality and natural energy, and in part by the violent collision between duty and desire. Her nightmare on the train back to Petersburg, which foretold her own death, was prefaced by the words: 'What am I doing here? Am I myself or someone else?' (I, 29). Before long, the conflict in her heart between love for Seriozha and love for Vronsky, together with the consequential clash of duty and desire, led her to feel that 'everything in her mind was beginning to be double' (III, 15, 16: I take *dukh* here to cover both 'mind' and 'heart'). At times, she hardly knew what she feared and what she desired (III, 15). Her own fear of these states of mind communicated itself to Vronsky, who clearly disbelieved his own explanation of them as effects of pregnancy (IV, 3); and neither he nor she is comforted by labelling the cause of the jealous behaviour that resulted from her mental stress, 'the demon' inside her (IV, 3). Indeed, this move merely encourages Anna to talk of 'another woman' inside her, and of whom she is afraid

(IV, 17); the consequence is that she is less inclined to search out the true causes of her troubled state, and more inclined to surrender as a victim of it. Her jealousy becomes more obsessive and gains greater control over her mind; her seemingly inevitable decline is accompanied by tortured thoughts of her shame, by assertions that she is not to blame (e.g. VI, 23, an echo of an earlier disclaimer, also to Dolly, in I, 28), and by fears that she will not be forgiven (III, 15).

During all this time 'her chief preoccupation was herself'; both how she could please Vronsky enough to maintain possession of him, and how she could save herself (VI, 25; V, 8); and the former was deemed to be the solution of the latter. It was not wholly because of her understanding of Vronsky that she saw the only solution both for herself and Vronsky, as the provision of physical pleasure: 'She took both of his hands in hers, and drew them to her waist, not taking her eyes off him' (VI, 32); 'He took Anna's hand and looked enquiringly into her eyes. Understanding that look differently, she smiled at him' (VI, 24).[1] Physical contact with those she loved had always been important to Anna, as was emphasized in the physical pleasure she derived from Seriozha's caresses (I, 32; V, 27, 29), and in the continual reference to the physical emblem which represents her, as it were, throughout the novel: her beautiful hands. These references, fifteen in all, serve to focus attention on a particular feature of the situation, as when Dolly's children play with Anna's ring, or when Anna opens her small red bag, so like Varenka's (II, 34), and which reappears at her death, delaying her first jump (I, 29; VII, 31). But there is a deeper significance which we shall discuss shortly.

If Anna's most poignant moment is parting from Seriozha when carrying, unopened and forgotten, his birthday presents (V, 30), perhaps her most degrading is when she wondered: 'Is there any new feeling I can think up [*pridumayu*] between Vronsky and me?' (VII, 30). Having reached the stage of living only for her feelings, the only things she felt she knew with certainty were her

---

[1] Cf. the scene in *Middlemarch* (64.474) in which Lydgate tries to induce Rosamond's comprehension of their difficulties by means of physical contact.

appetites (VII, 29); she had arrived at the state in which Vronsky found it formerly easiest to indulge, but from which, and as a result of giving himself to her, he was beginning to emerge. He always required novelty, and balked at repetition; he had, for example, 'admired her so often' (VI, 32; V, 33). It was a savage irony that in the nightmare that presaged her suicide, Anna had found the feeling of falling pleasant or joyful, presumably for its aspect of release or freedom (I, 29); it would thus be a new feeling to indulge in. The virtues of Anna's inner nature lay in her vitality; but, having failed to find outlets for it, having failed to heed the judgements of her conscience about herself and her situation, she became a victim of her internal states and the external circumstances which had been allowed to crush her. Man has to act in the external, social world; and he can do this, it is implied, only by discovering and enacting his true inner nature; failure here renders him a victim both of the external world and of inner states not truly part of his essence. Anna's suicide, although an attempt at action, was an escape from it. The literal and inevitable answer to Anna's final utterance, 'What am I doing?' must be: nothing.

In contrast to Anna's small, white hands, Vronsky is represented, emblematically, by his strong, white, even teeth; hands which are associated with touch, are contrasted with teeth which are associated with what may be devoured (I, 34; II, 4, 21; IV, 3; V, 7, 31; VI, 17). Described by Anna as an intelligent dog, and as a setter (I, 23; VII, 30), Vronsky resembled the animals among which he felt at home, and which he could master; his smile is reminiscent of a horse, and Anna sees herself as no longer having the same 'flavour' for him (VII, 30). However much his 'inner life' was absorbed in his passions, its outward course ran along the inevitable lines prescribed by his interests and the code of rules we have already mentioned (II, 18); furthermore, his two passions of the moment, Anna and horses, did not interfere with each other (ibid); he had other passions, of course, of which one was ambition, which did clash with his love for a time (III, 20). Even so, he always needed an occupation (II, 18; VI, 21) of some kind, both to stave off boredom which, for him, arose as much from the repetition of a familiar activity as from the total freedom to do anything at all, and to refresh himself for further indulgence in his passions. These occupations, and they include all the roles he adopted during his life with Anna, were not in the strictest sense actions; they were simply indulgences of another sort, in which he could let himself be carried away—distractions (II, 18); Dolly used the same word to characterize Oblonsky's capacity for letting himself be completely carried away by his feelings (I, 19). But over and above the features already mentioned, two terms serve to define Vronsky: 'pleasure' and 'desire'. The first term, 'pleasure' (*udovol'stvie*), is introduced in the first extended account we are given of him, after he had captivated Kitty (I, 16): 'He could not believe that what gave such great and enjoyable pleasure to himself, and above all to her, could be wrong'. The importance of the term has been emphasized, shortly before, in the conversation between Oblonsky and Levin on the two kinds of love Plato defines in the *Symposium*; Oblonsky remarks that there can be no conflict between proper Platonic love and non-Platonic love, because of the latter all that may be said, crudely, is: 'Thanks ever so much for the pleasure' (I, 11). After Vronsky had escorted the foreign prince to Petersburg, Anna asked him: 'Don't all of you like those animal pleasures?' (IV, 3). The second term, 'desire' (*zhelanie*), is equally important. It is shown that he belonged to a class in which 'the real people' surrendered unblushingly to every passion (I, 34); and how the desire for adultery absorbed him for a year, 'taking the place of all his former desires', until it was achieved (II, 2); and how he experienced the 'desire to find any diversion from the monotony of his life' (V, 7). The full force of the term comes out, however, only when Anna and Vronsky are in Italy; her new-found happiness has just been described, and he has taken up painting (V, 8):

Vronsky, meanwhile, in spite of the complete realization [*osushchest-vlenie*] of what he had so long desired, was not entirely happy. He soon felt that the realization of his desires brought him no more than a grain of sand out of the mountain of happiness he had expected. Their realization showed him the eternal error men make in imagining that happiness is the realization of desires. For a time . . . he had felt all the charm of freedom in general, which he had not known before, and of freedom for love, and he was content; but not for long. He soon felt that in his heart there rose up a desire for desires: *ennui*. Independently of his will, he began to clutch at every passing caprice, taking it for a desire and a purpose. . . . As a hungry animal seizes upon everything it can clutch at in the hope that it may be food, so Vronsky. . . . He took up painting, putting into it all the unused stock of desires that required satisfaction.

Vronsky is thus a man of passion in both the everyday and technical senses: a man whose aim is indulgence and self-gratification, and a man who is both a victim of his desires and strives to act only according to social roles. In the passage quoted above we find him searching for objects to fit his antecedent, unfocused desires; and the attempt both to anchor and then to justify what was virtually a pathological state, was precisely mirrored in Anna when she became a victim of her own jealous states: 'She was jealous not of any particular woman but of his love. Not having as yet an object for her jealousy, she was on the look-out for one' (VII, 23). In this connection it should be noted that the 'activities' in which Vronsky engages, or to which he surrenders himself, are primarily physical; it is doubly significant that the verb most generally used to describe the mode of his decisions is 'to feel' (*pochustvovat'*), which combines tactile associations with those of a mental attitude less than fully intellectual. He neither reflected upon the past nor thought carefully about the future, which may explain why he is almost unique in not feeling jealousy and is also the ironic explanation of why he was incapable of self-deception and self-torment (V, 14). Further, although all the main characters contemplate, with varying degrees of seriousness, the possibility of death as the best way out of their troubles, it could be said that Vronsky alone does not think about it; he merely attempts suicide, and with that random yet stereotyped gesture comes as near death as does Anna in her fever. Vronsky certainly centred his love on Anna; he would rather cut off his hand than have her humiliated (III, 20). But his understanding of her was too limited, so that he neither showed her this loyalty nor sought to attack the root cause of her smothering demands. Paradoxically, it was Anna who should have been a woman of action, because she was driven by living impulses; yet she succumbs to *passio*; on the other hand, Vronsky, whom all would have described as a man of action, never was really such. By the adoption of social roles and the indulgence in his animal desires, Vronsky showed two wrong answers to the question: 'What is to be done?'

OTHER OBSTACLES TO ANSWERING THE QUESTION

On the view that I have inferred from the text, the inadequacy of one's reason to answer the question 'What is to be done?' is related to the general inadequacy of language to convey the uniqueness and complexity of the situations in which action is required. We are shown cases in which individual emotions and associations are too powerful to be represented by general concepts; for Levin the words 'mother' and 'love', and for Anna the words 'love' and 'son' were too sacred for everyday utterance (VI, 2; V, 2; II, 7, 23). Two other types of case are also shown: those in which someone says something other than he intended, which usually occurs when his emotions have achieved temporary dominance over the weaker voice of conscience, or over antecedent thought; and those in which what is being experienced seems to be inexpressible in words at all.

Take, first, some of the cases where a character does not say what he had intended. When Anna asked Vronsky to go to Moscow to beg Kitty's forgiveness, 'he saw that she was saying what she forced herself to say, not what she wanted to say. . . . She strained with all her strength of mind to say what ought to be said. But instead of that her eyes rested on him, full of love, and made no answer' (II, 7). In this instance conscience initially triumphed over and then succumbed to emotion or desire; a case of *passio*. The same evening Karenin waited to confront Anna with his views on her behaviour. As usual he prepared a speech, 'as if it were a ministerial report, under four headings.'[1] But when

---

[1] Cf. the scene in *Middlemarch* (67.500) when Bulstrode seeks to win over Will Ladislaw; Bulstrode 'thoroughly prepared his ministerial explanation'.

he came to deliver it he 'did not notice that he was saying something quite different from what he had prepared', and was getting
involuntarily excited about something he had already decided
concerned her conscience alone (II, 9). What he said, in fact,
centred on himself and his feelings to which no references were
made in his prepared speech. Even when he had regained his composure after the emotional episode of his proposal to Kitty, Levin
did not say at all what he wanted to say, when he called to discuss
wedding arrangements (IV, 16). Koznyshev, before proposing to
Varenka, 'repeated to himself the words in which he wanted to
express his offer, but instead of those words some unexpected
consideration occurred to him and he suddenly asked' the difference between two kinds of mushroom (VI, 5). In all these cases of
emotional stress we are shown how a man's utterances may
achieve both form and impetus independently of his will or intentions. The unusual loquacity of both Anna and Karenin at the
races is explicitly said to be the expression of their inner distress
and uneasiness (II, 27, 28).

The much larger range of cases in which the complexity of the
situation itself, or of the individual's feelings about it, persuade a
character of the inadequacy of words, also reveals more clearly
than any other means one of the problems of the inner–outer
dichotomy; that is, the gap and the tension between a man's inner
life of feelings, thoughts, and emotions, and his public life in which
these are made manifest to others. There was discussion of this
issue in the last chapter, and it will appear again when I consider
Proust's novel. After she had committed adultery, Anna 'found
no words to express the complexity of her feelings', just as 'she
could not put into words her sense of shame' (II, 11); Nikolai, in
his death agony, 'had no words to express this desire for deliverance' (V, 20). At least three differences in the cases may be noted.
Sometimes, a character who wished something to be mysterious
and therefore valuable, persuaded himself that it was inexpressible;
Kitty believed that Mme Stahl's religion was one that could be
loved, but she 'did not find this out from words' (II, 33). This misinterpretation of the signs is something I shall return to shortly.

Sometimes, a character refused to express what was expressible because he unconsciously knew that a cherished illusion would be destroyed; Kitty was dismayed to hear her father describe Mme Stahl as a pietist, and thus 'to find that what she prized so highly had a name' (II, 34). Levin believed that the most valuable feelings and deepest truths, in so far as they were related, were ill served by verbal articulation; he 'did not like talking about the beauty of nature. Words for him took away from the beauty of what he saw' (III, 2). Thirdly, there are cases of close human relationships where factors other than mere words are more powerful means of communication. When Levin visited Nikolai, 'these two men were so akin and so near to each other, that the slightest gesture, tone of voice, told both more than could be said in words' (III, 31). Note should also be taken, in passing, of cases where a question is known by the questioner to be superfluous, because he already knows the answer, but which nevertheless must be asked, sometimes for reasons relating to the questioner's own states, sometimes for reasons relating to the hearer, as when Anna asked Vronsky why he was on the same train to Petersburg (I, 19); and also of cases where both speaker and hearer understand that an utterance is to be taken in a sense opposite to its literal meaning, again because other than linguistic purposes are being served, as when Vronsky refused to understand, while clearly understanding, Anna's fearful prognostications after her nightmare (IV, 3).

Language is not the only means of communication; gesture and facial expression are perhaps more basic, direct, and spontaneous ways of manifesting one's inner states. By far the most significant point to be made here is in connection with hands. In Part I alone there are thirty references to hands, and in the novel as a whole over 250 references; a total which is more than twice the number of references to eyes. Like eyes, hands may be used for the natural expression of inner states, but unlike eyes they may also be used for the conventional expression of inner states not actually present; physically, hands are the basic mode of touch, and are thus to be associated with the non-cognitive verb which, as we have seen, characteristically describe individuals' first responses, 'to feel'.

Aside from the conventions of greetings, hands are also used as signs of affection and emotional bond; it was because they were in public, after Vronsky's accident at the racecourse, that Karenin offered his arm three times to Anna (II, 29). But stress on the conventional may lead not only to diminution of communication of the inner states with which they were originally associated, but also to the agent's diminished awareness of what his inner states are. Indeed, the conventional gesture can become a substitute for the emotion it originally expressed. Oblonsky's gratitude for the revival of the old custom of hand-kissing (IV, 21) should be seen both as a desire for titillation and as a desire to avoid emotions of a deeper or more disturbing kind. Objecting to a man's long finger-nails, Levin remarked that in the country the one object was to have hands that could be used (I, 10), and it should be observed that the peasants are never described as engaging in any of the elaborate gestures of the main characters. If hands are thus seen as a bridge between inward states and their natural or conventional expression, and also by means of touch as a direct mode of communication with others, the full significance of the physical emblem which represents Anna is apparent.

If the presence of emotions can be an obstacle to the accurate perception of the situation in which one finds oneself, it is also an obstacle to correct interpretations of others' gestures and looks. Unlike the Prince, Kitty's mother, because she was already emotionally biased towards Vronsky, failed to infer from Vronsky's and Levin's behaviour their intentions with regard to Kitty (I, 12). A dozen times or more, misunderstanding arises when one character, prevented by egoism or emotional predisposition, fails to put himself in another's position. The dramatic point of the half-dozen occasions when a character succeeds in doing this, and for the first time in his life, is that the triumph of natural responses over self-interest is only momentary, and fails to check his self-destruction. Karenin (II, 8; IV, 19), Anna (IV, 4), and Vronsky (III, 22) provide the most notable examples. Consider, first, some of the cases of straightforward misunderstanding. Gazing into Varenka's eyes Kitty wondered what gave her such tranquillity, what it was that she knew: 'But Varenka did not even understand what that look of Kitty's asked' (II, 32). Here, Kitty is balked at the outset because she is asking for an explanation of what she had already wrongly described. This incident may be compared with the account of the priest's blessing at the wedding. Levin 'looked round, and their eyes met. And by the expression in hers he concluded that she understood just as he did. But that was not true: she had hardly understood a word of the service and was not even listening to the words of the ceremony' (V, 4). Earlier, after his acceptance by Kitty, Levin had gone to a discussion meeting with Koznyshev. Levin saw from the secretary's face 'what a nice, kind, splendid fellow he was. That was apparent from the way he got mixed up and confused in reading the minutes. . . . What was so remarkable to Levin was that he seemed to be able to see through them all at present, and from little previously unnoticeable signs recognized the soul of each, and saw clearly that they were all good' (IV, 14). Throughout this and the surrounding episodes Levin deduced from the pleasure attendant upon his heightened state of perception the significance of what he perceived. Levin's euphoria is balanced by Karenin's hyper-sensitivity, equally egoistic and distorting of vision: 'He felt that he could not endure the general strain of contempt and bitterness which he distinctly read on the face of . . . everyone without exception he had met during the last two days' (V, 21). Anna, whose excess of passion and demented jealousy is partly paralleled in Levin (see his behaviour when he suspects Kitty of encouraging Veslovsky—VI, 7) quite failed to understand Vronsky's reaction to her news that she had told Karenin everything. 'She was not listening to his words, she was reading his thoughts from the expression on his face. She could not know that that expression arose from the first thought that occurred to him—that a duel was now inevitable' (III, 22). With masochistic deliberation Anna misread Vronsky's physiognomic expressions; at the very end of Part VI, when she insists upon accompanying him to Moscow, she believes his look to be that of a vindictive man lashed to fury—it is Anna's description, not the narrator's—'she saw that look and surely [*verno ugadala*]

guessed its meaning' (VI, 32). Later still, when the thorny question
of children had again provoked argument, she once more mistook
his look of pain, failing to check her interpretation for consistency
with what he said: '"Here it is—now he has ceased pretending and
I can see all his cold hate for me" she thought, not listening to his
words but watching with terror the cold, cruel judge who looked
at her mockingly out of his eyes' (VII, 25). It should be noted that
before his wedding Levin was panic-struck by the belief that he
did not really know Kitty's thoughts, wishes, and feelings; Anna
had claimed similar ignorance of Vronsky's internal states (V, 2;
IV, 3). Later Levin acknowledged that no one either knew or was
obliged to know his feelings (VII, 14); and Anna, during her final
soliloquy, wondered whether, in any case, it was possible ever to
tell another person what one was feeling (VII, 29). These sceptical
doubts should be compared with Levin's reactions when Oblonsky
arrived to stay accompanied by Veslovsky; suddenly feeling out
of temper with everything, Levin is able to think up perverse and
unflattering interpretations for the most casual and conventional
greetings offered by his friends and relatives to the new arrivals
(VI, 6). The main point here is not that Levin's perception and
interpretation are distorted by his mood, nor that he takes conventional gestures far too seriously, holding the egoistic and in-
considerate view that one ought only to express exactly what one
feels and thinks. It is, rather, that unless 'true' expression is to be
arbitrarily restricted to 'natural' and spontaneous reactions such as
writhing or crying with pain, all outward expression of inward
states must be grounded on convention in order to be intelligible
to others; but this same fact also secures the possibility of mis-
interpreting outward expression. As we saw when discussing
Middlemarch (see above, pp. 41, 50), this possibility is not a reason
for scepticism, but it is a reason for avoiding over-confident and
hasty inferences, such as we saw Anna indulge in above; the solution is to search for other clues in a person's behaviour which may
serve as checks upon one's inferences; these other clues, of course,
may themselves be derived by means of the same sort of fallible
inference that is in question, but consistency and coherence among

one's inferences, together with the assumption that some must be reliable in order for knowledge claims to be made at all, are the only criteria that may be demanded. Nevertheless, as the example of Anna clearly shows, a person who is suffering from a pathological state or other major distortion of vision, may yet make a set of inferences from someone's behaviour to their inner beliefs and feelings, which, although consistent and coherent as a set, is entirely wrong.

THE SECOND QUESTION: 'WHAT IS THE MEANING OR
SIGNIFICANCE OF THE SITUATION?'

In almost all of the interpretations that may be put on it, this question is prior to the question about what should be done; one cannot decide what to do unless one has already decided what is the nature of the situation; otherwise one's performance is not a 'doing', not *actio*. I shall translate the term *smysl* as 'meaning' and the term *znachenie* as 'significance', in order to emphasize that utterances, gestures, looks (cf. VI, 32), situations, questions (cf. I, 7) are significant to people only under specifiable conditions, in particular contexts—a point to which I shall return, in a slightly different way, in the final chapter. Failure to grasp any significance in a situation or in people's responses, may be caused by ignorance, lack of thought, dominance of one's passions, egoism, refusal or inability to put oneself in another's place, or combinations of all these. For example, Levin was disturbed by the apparent independence of Sviazhsky's clear and logical beliefs and convictions, and his decisive actions which seemed to proceed in a direction opposite to those convictions (III, 26).

A man may ask a question, however, which although it occurs within, and may have arisen because of, a particular situation, is much more general in scope, and refers not only beyond the present context but even to the sum of all possible contexts: 'What is the meaning of life?' (*smysl zhizni* is the invariable expression in the text). The precise meaning of the question, and the sort of answer the questioner would deem appropriate, are still determined by the particular context of its occurrence. When

Vronsky felt that the meaning of life for him lay in seeing Anna, he is referring to the goal (*tsel'*), mentioned in a preceding sentence, which may unify all his actions (I, 31); possession of Anna will be the heading under which most of his actions are to be subsumed. We should note that the overriding dominance of one such object for all one's activities is itself likely to turn *actio* into *passio*, especially where possession of the goal is something for which one is prepared to become a victim. When Levin saw Kitty pass him on the road in the carriage, he reached a similar conclusion, or better, since this implies rational procedures rather than passive realization, a similar view occurred to him; life with her could be the goal of his subsequent actions, and when achieved the focus for them (III, 12). 'Focus of activities' is the explanation of Anna's reference to Vronsky as 'the meaning of life for her' (III, 15), as it is also, implicitly, in the following chapter, when she reflects that during her life with Karenin she had continually tried 'to find a justification of her life' (III, 16).

Although a character may know that something provides a focus for his activities, or some of them, and for that reason alone comes to value the focus, he may know no other reason why such a focus is valuable. Just as Levin lost his former intellectual interests when his life initially centred on Kitty, so Vronsky, when Anna became the focus of his life, found to his surprise that ambition, society and the court, which had earlier comprised the meaning of his life, now had no meaning for him (IV, 11, 18). One danger in cases where the focus of one's life is identical with the object of one's desires, as with Anna and Vronsky, is that the activity of thought becomes subordinate to the overwhelming passion for gratification of the desire. The implication of this observation is that instead of a character searching for, and subsequently finding, an answer to the question 'What is the meaning of my life?' by means of reflective thought and rational appraisal, the supposed answer comes about independently of the character's own efforts; and such passive realization diminishes the element of *actio* in performances based upon it.

Related to the senses of significance, meaning, goal, and justification, often covered by the one word 'meaning', are two other expressions, 'pattern' (II, 30) and 'outlook on life' (III, 26). The implication is that whoever discerns a pattern in, or imposes one on, the phenomena, may be able to determine a focus for his activities; and if one has so far failed to find or impose such a pattern, it will be helpful to discover how others view the situation. Kitty, for example, believed that Varenka had already found a pattern in life for which she was herself seeking; and Levin believed that Sviazhsky's composure and decisiveness must have come about as a direct effect of his outlook on life, or, in other words, of the particular set of descriptions under which he viewed the world (II, 30; III, 26). In both these cases the external behaviour of another person is taken as a guide to their internal composure, and this itself is explained as having its cause in a particular way of looking at things. Shortly before her suicide Anna reviewed her relationship with Vronsky and decided that, at the bottom of his heart, he would be glad if she left him: 'This was not conjecture— she saw it distinctly in the piercing light which revealed to her now the meaning of life and human relations' (VII, 30)—this is an assertion in Anna's voice, not in that of the narrator. In the quotation the expression 'meaning of life' can be taken to refer both to 'goal' and to 'pattern'. In referring back to her lament that 'there is nothing to be proud of', it refers to 'goal'; but it also means 'pattern' when referring further back to her assertion that what Vronsky looked for in her was 'not love so much as satisfaction of his vanity'. The pattern she believed herself to have found provided no more justification (*opravdanie*) for her life with Vronsky than it had for her life with Karenin; we, as readers, are shown that her impulsive hypothesis, arrived at in a condition of *passio*, provides no justification of her behaviour based upon it and contributes to that behaviour being itself *passio*.

When Levin reflected on the meaning (*smysl*) of death, following Nikolai's (V, 20), he was concerned not only with what purposes were achieved by death, but also with a question how any pattern may intelligibly incorporate the notion of death other than as a merely terminal point. Frequently in the concluding chapters Levin is said to puzzle over 'what he was living for' (*dlya chevo*), and a goal and pattern revealed themselves to him only when he stopped reflective thought: 'when he stopped worrying himself about it, it was as if he knew both who he was and what he was living for, because he acted and lived resolutely and definitely' (VIII, 10). It should be noted, first, that although this view was sufficient for the peace of mind of the individual concerned, it was only *as if* he knew the answer to his problem; secondly, the alleviation of his worries came about, not as a result of his remedial efforts to remove them, but when he turned aside from them. These points are of the greatest importance for an assessment of the concluding part of the novel, and they must be spelt out. In the quotation above, Levin recognizes that he has stopped worrying about his problem. And yet he also offers the fact of his resolute action as a reason for the view that he must have solved his problem. But nothing has been shown to support the missing premise needed to make this reasoning cogent, namely, that behaviour described as resolute cannot take place without antecedent mental conclusions. This would be to assume a too simple correlation between internal states and the behaviour deemed to be their external expression. Levin, we know, was prone to this sort of mistake; when Nikolai was dying Levin had been impressed by the nursing of Agatha Mihalovna and Kitty: 'The proof that they certainly knew the nature of death lay in the fact that, without doubting for a second, they knew how it was necessary to act with the dying, and were not afraid of them' (V, 19). Levin appears to have been beguiled by the necessity of decisive action when dealing with the sick, into assuming that the sureness he observed could be attributable only to a particular inner state, namely, one of certainty with respect to some metaphysical problems. In fact, however, he had already experienced occasions when the demand for physical action precluded the possibility of reflective thought, and whatever phenomenal properties belonged to that action could not have been ascribed to antecedent rational decisions or conclusions; the most prominent such occasion was when he went mowing with the peasants (III,

4), to whom he also ascribed wisdom about his intellectual problems. Although the most effective scything movements were unconscious, and were specifically described as being interrupted by conscious thought, Levin when mowing had this in common with Kitty when nursing: they were too busy to think of themselves. Three conclusions might be drawn from this observation. Questions about the meaning of life are ultimately self-referential since they come back to its meaning for oneself; excessive attention to such self-referential issues might detract from the effectiveness of one's actions on behalf of others and support for this view might be derived from the fact that many activities which require one's exclusive energies leave no time to think of oneself. Thirdly, and this applies with particular force to the quotation about Kitty and Agatha above, for dealing with the dying it may be quite unnecessary to have reached conclusions on the metaphysical nature of death. But this does not mean that we have found central cases where the question 'What is to be done?' is not preceded by the essentially prior question 'What is the meaning?' On the contrary, we merely have cases where it is important not to confuse the different senses of the prior question. Kitty knew what to do when nursing Nikolai precisely because she had weighed up the significance of the situation, what it amounted to; we are told that she tried 'to find out all the details of his condition' (V, 18). Levin is wrong to assume that this task cannot be accomplished without or is identical with establishing the meaning of a situation in its teleological and metaphysical senses; we may say that he confuses establishing the nature of a situation (*znachenie*) with establishing the nature or analysis of the concepts in terms of which one describes the situation (*smysl*). One man may know that another is dying without ever having reflected upon the concept of death. It is the necessity for action, often immediate, that determines the range of candidate answers to the question 'What is the meaning, significance of this situation?' Although particular situations also provide the occasion for more general conceptual and philosophical reflection, failure to engage in or conclude such reflection does not preclude action in the light of one's assessment of the situation.

And a possible conclusion now emerges: answers to questions concerning 'the meaning of life' (*smysl*) are not reached prior to action; on the contrary, they are reached only as a result of action, by reflection upon that action. If and when answers are found, then they may well affect subsequent actions, but those actions, like all others, must still be preceded by answers to the quite different question: 'What is the significance of this situation in so far as we have to act?'

At the end of the novel Levin felt that he had intuitive knowledge that he should live for God, in spite of the fact that his reason had provided no help in establishing the meaning of his life or impulses (VIII, 12); the justification of his subsequent repudiation of all reason is not entirely clear, however (VIII, 19). Anna, Vronsky, and Karenin, having asked the question 'What is to be done?' do not fully exercise their reason upon trying to answer it, by first establishing the nature of the situation in which they have to act; and they rapidly succumb to *passio*. Had Levin been content to accept his view that when he stopped worrying he managed to act decisively, then there would be doubt whether what he did on those occasions amounted to *actio* at all. And yet the judgements of conscience, if obeyed, retain precisely this element of passivity, which would seem to limit the agent's contribution to any proceedings. What notions of freedom are compatible with a morality defined in terms of acting out one's internal essence and obeying inner instructions? Furthermore, Levin's inner voice had earlier told him that it was wrong to take part in something he did not understand (V, 1), which seems to call for the use of reason, at least for assessing the nature of the situation. Levin's general prescription 'Live for God' cannot be more than a principle under which specific actions may be subsumed. To advocate its use instead of reflection upon the particular case which confronts each individual would entail forfeiture of the notion of human agency. Finally, no matter how a man comes by knowledge, if he knows what to do in a given situation, then it must be possible in principle for him to give an account of what he is doing; when this condition is unfulfilled he cannot himself know what he is doing, he would not technically be acting, and his performance would be *passio*. Levin tends to confuse *how* he knows, which he believes to be mysterious, with *what* he knows, which at least in connection with action, cannot and must not be. It is this confusion which partly explains his eagerness to find life both more consistent and simpler than it really is (I, 11; III, 12); like Vronsky and Karenin, Levin had difficulty in facing the fact that life is illogical and disordered (II, 8), or, perhaps, has no order other than we impose, and that to cope with the indescribable complexity of every living thing (Mihailov's phrase—V, 11) no simple solution could possibly suffice for *actio*. To impose or to advocate simple solutions at the outset would be to assume that we know what, by definition, we cannot yet know, namely, the internal essence of each one of us, to the discovery and realization of which our energies ought to be devoted; for we are shown that self-knowledge and morality are in this way interdependent.

CONCLUSION

I have intentionally omitted discussion of many prominent features of the novel. I have been concerned only to suggest aspects that would justify a description of the novel as 'philsophical'. We have inferred a view from these aspects about what it is for a man possessing intellect and emotion to *act*, and what may prevent him from acting. But no thesis is argued for in *Anna Karenina*; nor does what I have stated amount to 'the point' of the novel. A summary of my account, nevertheless, may mislead not only in those directions, but also appear to simplify and trivialize what is self-evidently detailed and complex. It might be more accurate to characterize the novel as presenting a reader with a large number of cases and considerations, both practical and theoretical, which may incline him one way and another when he seeks to answer some fundamental problems. Many, but not all, of the considerations with which we are presented support a conclusion that may be stated briefly, although it is not, as such, stated within the novel at all. A focus for such a statement is provided by Koznyshev's observation that philosophy is the search for the necessary link between personal and common interests (III, 3),[1] although the brevity, and attendant incompleteness, of this generalization disguises both the complexity of the issues and the forms such a search may legitimately take in practice. A man lives by acting, and he acts by being himself; but he cannot be himself until he has discovered what manner of man he is; and he cannot make that discovery by pursuing self-interested activities; for although it is a discovery he seeks to make, it cannot be found by searching; rather, it is a discovery which comes upon a man only when he is in a condition to receive it. Perhaps an active man would be one who achieved a perfect blending of mind and body, reason and the passions, such that neither dominated the other and the voice of conscience could thus be clearly heard. But this is speculation, for we are shown no such man, although it seems correct to infer from the cases we are shown, that just as no man achieves complete self-realization, so no man is perfectly active. If the presentation of *passio* in *Anna Karenina* is felt to be more persuasive than that of *actio*, one reason immediately suggests itself: the theory of knowledge underlying the account is deemed to have no conclusive answer to scepticism. Such a view, which, as we saw in the last chapter, threatened to undermine the positive account of morality in *Middlemarch*, misconceives the nature of empiricism in particular, and of concepts in general.

A second point should be made in conclusion. Alongside the sympathetic understanding aroused for them, a reader is left in no doubt about how he is supposed to judge Anna, Vronsky, Karenin, and Oblonsky. For example, Anna's natural vitality had been curbed by the artificial existence she had led with Karenin; when, given momentarily favourable conditions, those impulses over-

[1] In Cross's *Life of George Eliot* (Cabinet Edition, vol. 3, pp. 34–40) occur extracts from George Eliot's *Notes on the Spanish Gypsy and Tragedy in General* (1868); in a passage very close to Koznyshev's distinction between the individual and the general, she wrote that to be really tragic a work 'must represent irreparable collision between the individual and the general (in differing degrees of generality). It is the individual with whom we sympathize, and the general of which we recognize the irresistible power' (p. 36).

flowed, they subdued and made their victim both their possessor and those to whom she was tied by various bonds. They launched their victim on a path which led to self-destruction. Anna's suicide, even if adequately prepared for in terms of her emotional excess and incipient mental imbalance, was an escape from, or a refusal to grapple with, the problems of life; it was a solution to nothing. Levin, on the other hand, continued to deploy his energies, because he had found a simple guiding principle, failure to find which had been one of Anna's reasons for suicide. But Anna's failure, together with her suicide, and Levin's success, are equally false conclusions in the light of everything else we have been shown in the novel; they are conclusions apparently imposed by the author upon the implicit argument, and against its principal burden. For example, the energies of both the peasants and those with family duties, such as Kitty and Dolly, are shown as being geared to, and expended in, their daily tasks. Levin concludes from this, not only that they must be happier than he, but that he should suppress and deny his natural capacities for reflection in order to engage in unthinking labour. But we have been shown in the cases of Anna's suppression of her vital impulses and Karenin's of his emotions, that any such suppression is wrong and has evil consequences. Levin would be ensuring that he did not attain self-knowledge; to assume that the problems with which he had been grappling would disappear if he turned his attention away from them, would be the first step towards a wilfully adopted self-deception. This last example serves to illustrate, although on a different level since it concerns the author's handling of his own material,[1] what we have been shown throughout, namely, the various obstacles to action and the various senses in which action and passion cannot coincide.

[1] A reader might wonder how to take Anna's delirious, 'dying' wish to secure Karenin's forgiveness (IV, 17). Both Karenin and Vronsky deemed her response to her husband to have been one of ecstatic tenderness, and there is a further statement, apparently in the author's voice, that her repentance was sincere (IV, 17, 18, 19). It would seem, therefore, that Karenin's genuine forgiveness, secured under these peculiar conditions, is brutally rewarded, in the light of Anna's subsequent departure with Vronsky.

Even if my statement of what can be inferred from the novel is accepted, it will be evident that I do not believe to be cogent all the philosophical views I have outlined. But it would be a task for another occasion to show in detail the respects in which I believe those views to be muddled or mistaken.

CHAPTER 3

The Self and Others in The Brothers Karamazov

ONE disadvantage of the largely descriptive methods that I shall adopt in this and the next chapter, circumscribed as they are by my particular interests, is that I may succeed only in distorting each novel by laboriously re-telling it in my own terms. I must reaffirm that I am not aiming to explain or analyse the impact a particular novel may have on variously constituted readers. But because of their impact it must be admitted that some readers may find it harder to ignore the ideas expressed in Dostoevsky's novel, than it is to ignore the ideas in the other novels I am discussing. For the moral policies are not only baldly stated in *The Brothers Karamazov*, but their statement assumes importance in the plot and structure of the novel. In addition, they provide criteria by which the actions portrayed may be judged. To this extent, therefore, they are easier to discuss, because they are easier to identify; on the other hand, obscurities in the explicit moral posture tend to appear more prominent than they might otherwise do, and a reader may be more confused and puzzled about its precise meaning and ramifications.

Unlike *Middlemarch*, there is in *The Brothers Karamazov* little indication of the theory of knowledge underlying the moral views stated, but the stress on the nature and effects of pride broadens the characterization of egoism encountered in George Eliot's novel. Emphasis upon the dangers of passivity, and upon the need for living responses, which we discussed in connection with *Anna Karenina*, becomes in Dostoevsky's novel a bold assertion, tied to explicit theological beliefs, of self-effacement and commitment to others. Finally, the portrayal of the psychology of love and hate, together with the effects of dreams and the pleasures of masochism, point forward to Proust's novel, although without the epistemological foundations provided in that novel.

The structure of *The Brothers Karamazov*, on one level, is very simple. We are first presented with a characterization of different sorts of malaise, all fundamentally deriving from the same causes: the absence of faith in God, and the assertion of self. We are then given an explicit statement of moral and theological views which throw light on the types of malaise, and also point the way to effective regeneration. Finally, we are shown various stages in the regeneration of some of the central characters. The fundamental moral and religious views expressed in the novel cover nearly everything that happens in the novel, and this is appropriate, it might be thought, since there can be nothing to which God's laws do not apply.

The central characters may be taken as constituting a chain or scale of being, where 'being' is defined in terms of moral consciousness, and that, in turn, is defined in terms of faith in God, belief in immortality, and service to others. At the top of this scale is Zossima, followed by his disciple Alyosha; they are followed by those characters who achieve some measure of regeneration, Dmitri, Grushenka, Ivan, and possibly, Katerina; Fyodor and Smerdyakov occupy the lowest positions. Progress up the chain or scale depends upon recognition by an individual that he has a soul as well as a body and a mind, and that the soul must be made the centre of his being; the body is the source of experience, and also a prime driving force, while the mind is a mere tool, possessing no motive power of its own. The relative non-being represented by the lower members on the scale is associated not only with moral blindness, but also with falsehood, cruelty, self-interest, and failure to communicate with or to understand others. The moral policies and modes of living that are to be combated by the explicit moral doctrine of the novel, are themselves both stated and shown in action in the lives of the principal characters. After describing the positive doctrine, I shall spell out what may be called the negative or false doctrine which forms the target. Dmitri and Ivan form the focus for the false doctrine, showing its embodiment and effects on persons. But there is also a more abstract attack upon types of reasoning; here, the law and science, represented by psychology, are pilloried. Both are essentially reductionist in form, and encumbered with their own rules of procedure—which they wield with morally dangerous aesthetic indulgence—they fail to recognize all the factors of which man is made; on the practical level, they fail, for example, to take account of such phenomena as self-punishment, and on the theoretical level, they fail to see that man has a soul over and above his mind and body. Legal reasoning exemplifies the activity of the mind in one of its purer forms, while psychology, unlike the sciences which restrict their attention to the functions of the body, seeks to account for the processes of the mind. Both the law and psychology, however, fail to grasp that a man's whole being not only may be, but ought to be, subservient to his soul.

THE POSITIVE DOCTRINE

I shall begin by outlining the positive doctrine. This will enable us to see later how everything else in the novel falls within its scope. The moral tone of the work is introduced by the narrator's evaluation of the principal characters. We are told, for example, that Alyosha was entirely convinced of the existence of God and of immortality, and that he sought truth, immediate action, and service to others (I, 5).[1] We are also told that by choosing an elder one renounced one's will in the hope of self-conquest, and in the hope that after a life of obedience one attained perfect freedom from the self. The narrator adds, rather complacently, that the institution of elders is a two-edged weapon, in that it can lead to Satanic pride and thus bondage—and since these traits are revealed in the Legend of the Inquisitor, a reader may take the possibility as partly explaining Ivan's curiosity in visiting the monastery.

After preliminary descriptions we are shown the elder Zossima

---

[1] All my references to, and translations from, *The Brothers Karamazov* are taken from volumes 9 and 10 of the standard edition of Dostoevsky's works, ed. Grossman, Dolinin *et al.*: *Sobranie Sochineniy*, Moscow, 1958. Roman numerals refer to the Book, and arabic numerals refer to the chapter within the Book.

in action, as it were; first, advising Fyodor, then, as the chapter titles tell us, advising peasant women with faith and also a woman with no faith in the future life (Madame Hohlakova), and finally Ivan. The elder's particular approach and understanding of each appears unusual and bears out that reputation for keen intuition, of which we have already heard; only later is it explained in terms of his experiences and beliefs. Fyodor's claim to feel lower than the people he meets (II, 2) may be contrasted with Zossima's later admonition to his disciples to accept that one is lower than one's fellows. Zossima tells Fyodor that he who lies to himself comes to lose respect for himself and for others, and having no respect (*uvazhat'*) ceases to love others and gives way to vice (II, 2). Madame Hohlakova, like Miüsov, and later Ivan (II, 4; II, 8; V, 4), claims to love the people, but in none of these cases is it the sort of love Zossima enjoins. What is needed is 'active love', and with the 'self-forgetfulness' thereby achieved, no doubts can hinder belief in future life (II, 4). In contrast to Alyosha, Ivan, and Madame Hohlakova are beset by doubts largely because they are concerned with themselves, and also because they implicitly require reasons to back up their 'love'. Later in the novel we find Rakitin asking why he should love either Alyosha or Grushenka, since one loves people for some reason (VII, 3), and Grushenka replies that one should love people without a reason. Rakitin's question is echoed by the defence counsel's claim that sons should stand before their fathers and ask 'Why must I love you?' (XII, 13). In the present context, however, whereas Fyodor was urged not to feel such shame, Madame Hohlakova is urged not to be so fastidious; the reason is the same in each case, since both states reveal pride and concern for self, illustrated again in Zossima's parable of the man who only loved humanity in general (II, 4)—a parable precisely foreshadowing Ivan's own confession to Alyosha (V, 4).

The fullest and most sustained statement of the positive moral doctrine of the novel occurs in Book VI, devoted to the life and sayings of Zossima. Echoing the words of his elder brother, Zossima several times urges his fellow monks to accept personal responsibility for all things and for all men (VI, 1, 2; cf. IV, 1). In his final talk to them, and in the biographical notes recorded by Alyosha, Zossima's bow to Dmitri is finally explained in terms of the close parallels between their youthful army experiences (VI, 2; III, 4), and his fears for a man whom he himself once resembled. Readers become aware, moreover, of the dramatic irony in Zossima's fears, for there are marked similarities between the murder committed with 'extraordinary audacity' by Zossima's Visitor— with his confession to Zossima and subsequently to everyone else, and the presumed guilt of the boastful drunken peasant—and the audacious murder by Smerdyakov, with the confession to his own pseudo-elder, Ivan (but to no one else), and the presumed guilt of the drunken, boastful Dmitri. Further, Zossima's regeneration begins after hitting Afanasy, and Dmitri's begins when he climbs off the wall after hitting Grigory, although it does not get under way until his dream of the babe.

Zossima's own ethical pronouncements are prefaced by those of his Visitor Mihail, who held that to transform the world it was necessary to turn men into another path psychologically, since no scientific teaching would teach men to have equal consideration for all. Mihail believed that heaven lies hidden within each man. Men had ceased to understand, however, that true security is to be found in social solidarity and not in isolated individual effort; searching for the greatest fulness of life for oneself only results in isolation, solitude (VI, 2). In spite of these views, however, Mihail postponed public confession of his murder because of fear of the consequences, (cf. the chapter on *Middlemarch*, above, p. 45), particularly the consequences of such a memory in the hearts of his children. Zossima insisted that such egoism can be checked only by serving the higher truth, and quotes from the Gospel of St. John 12, v. 24 a passage which also serves as the epigraph to the novel: 'except a corn of wheat fall into the ground and die, it abideth alone: but if it die, it bringeth forth much fruit.'

Zossima himself held that the spiritual and higher part of man's being is rejected by the methods of science, which restricts itself to objects of sense, and as a result foolish desires and habits are fostered. In a passage strongly reminiscent of remarks upon

Vronsky in *Anna Karenina*, Zossima asserts that it is a distortion of human nature to see freedom as the satisfaction and multiplication of desires; for by thinking up desires for himself a man sets himself in bondage, withdraws his concern for the rest of humanity, and becomes isolated from it (VI, 3). Fyodor may be taken as an example of such self-isolating indulgence. The only way to cut off one's superfluous wants is through obedience, prayer, and fasting. But in contrast to the peasants, who retain their faith in God, the upper classes seek to follow the methods of science, and want to base justice on the dictates of reason alone (Ivan wanted empirical evidence of justice (V, 4) as Alyosha did when Zossima died (VII, 2)); what follows is only more bloodshed, since the notion of crime becomes meaningless without belief in God (VI, 3). It should be noted that the peasants are not painted in a Levin-like glow; Grigory and Marfa are steadfast but also obstinate, and the jury brings in a verdict which seems to reflect incomprehension and prejudice, rather than immovable faith and intuition.

Zossima asserts that although much is hidden from men on earth, they have been given a mystic sense of a living bond with the higher heavenly world; this is what philosophers mean when they say that reality on earth cannot be apprehended. Indeed, by loving everything one will come to perceive the divine mystery in things. Loving humility (*smirenie lyubovnoe*) is the strongest of all things, and the only means of salvation is to make oneself responsible for everything; this is aided by the fact that 'all is like an ocean, everything flows and touches: a touch in one place resounds at the other end of the earth' (VI, 3). Nevertheless such love is hard to acquire, and it is easy to succumb to Satanic pride, imagining that one is doing something fine—a condition, the reader is entitled to assume, experienced by the Inquisitor. In what serves to answer Ivan's earlier horror of the doctrine that children inherit the sins of their fathers, Zossima asserts that children especially should be loved, because they are sinless like the angels (VI, 3). One truly lives only through feeling contact with other mysterious worlds, and if the feeling grows weak one becomes indifferent to life, and may grow to hate it. Smerdyakov illustrates the tenet that 'hell is the suffering of being unable to love' (VI, 3); for he who curses God and life, curses himself.

Zossima urges that no man can judge another; if 'after your kiss, he goes away unmoved' it shows that his time has not yet come. But it will come, even if only in another place. Christ's response to the Inquisitor conforms with this tenet. There is a difficulty, however, with such a view. If, whatever happens, a man's time to be cleansed will come in due course, the act of loving and not judging would seem to benefit primarily the bene-factor, not the beneficiary; and the pride of Satan would be even harder to avoid. The benefactor cannot defend his loving another on the ground that it may prove the finally effective trigger for the other man's self-judgement, since that would itself imply that the man had been judged to need self-judgement.

The scope and consequences of these views are best grasped not in the abstract statements we have just summarized, but in the particular cases in the novel to which they may be applied. What I have called the negative doctrine of the novel consists, first, in failure to observe the positive doctrine; in this direction, there-fore, we may expect to find the effects of pride and self-concern, and the effects of failing to believe in God, selflessly love others, or refrain from judgement. Secondly, however, the negative doctrine is itself formulated, and we shall need to consider its tenets.

UNDERSTANDING OTHERS

The narrator in *A la recherche du temps perdu* (III, 378), as I mention again in the next chapter, remarked that Dostoevsky presented his characters and their actions not in a logical sequence, beginning with their cause, but in the reverse order, beginning with the effect that strikes us. Thus many events are left unexplained at the time of their first description, and remain mysterious or puzzling both to other characters in the novel, and to the reader. Smerdya-kov's strange behaviour before Ivan left for Moscow is explained only much later (V, 6; XI, 7). Only after the second visit to Smerdyakov does Ivan fully realize and also explain to himself why he had described his listening to his father's stirrings down-stairs as 'infamous' (V, 7; XI, 6, 7). The anxiety Dmitri felt while drinking with Pyotr Ilyitch before driving to Mokroe, is first explained by his anxiety over the condition of Grigory, and later by his consciousness of having finally stolen Katerina's money (VIII, 5, 6, 7; IX, 7).

Two purely literary features of the novel may be noted at this stage. The number of references to eyes far exceeds the combined total of references to all other bodily characteristics. One reason is that through his eyes a man is most likely to reveal his inner self; the self that will enable us to understand his outward behaviour (cf. the previous chapter, on *Anna Karenina*, p. 98). Constantly characters gaze intently and searchingly into each other's eyes (e.g. III, 5; V, 3; XI, 5; XII, 5; Epilogue), and there are frequent refer-ences, especially from Book XI onwards, to flashing, burning, gleaming eyes. There are contrasts, of course. If Ivan readily detected the look of expectation in Alyosha's eyes, Smerdyakov's inner self was not obviously revealed in his outer expression (V, 3; III, 6). Katerina was quite mistaken in detecting simple-hearted-ness in Grushenka's eyes (III, 10). In addition to enquiring eyes and to eyes which betray inner states, there are what may be called spectator-eyes. In the case of the boys who stare at Kolya's per-formance by Ilusha's bedside (X, 5) their eyes mostly betray in-comprehension. But there are other cases where spectators take on the role of *voyeurs*. When Ferapont burst into Zossima's cell, the inquisitive eyes of the monk from Obdorsk could be seen under his arm (VII, 1); when Dmitri was arrested in the tavern the face of Trifon Borisytch inexplicably appeared in and disappeared from the doorway (IX, 6); the inquisitive public stared at Grushenka and at the famous counsel during the trial (XII, 4, 10).

A man's eyes often reveal his mode of consciousness. That mode is also indicated by how events strike him. In the course of the novel the adjectives and adverbs 'sudden' and 'unexpected' (*vdrug, vnezapnyy, neojidannyy*) occur over six hundred times; the related terms 'surprising', 'peculiar', and 'odd' also occur frequently. Three broad classes of phenomena in the novel are qualified by these terms. First, actions, particularly utterances and gestures, are said by observers to be sudden. These actions may not be unexpected by the agent or even by the reader. The second class of sudden events consists of internal states and feelings, some of which are publicly expressed. Thus when a man smiles suddenly, the smile may be unexpected by observers, and the state which explains it unexpected to the agent. Unexpressed private states, when sudden, are known only to the agent and to the reader in so far as he has access to the agent's mode of consciousness. The third class of sudden events consists of physiognomic changes observable by other characters, such as blushes and frowns; some of these will be the involuntary expression of internal states.

A general point emerges from these two literary observations. Behaviour is often inexplicable without either assumptions about, or knowledge of, the inner man it betrays and expresses. If behaviour is inappropriately described a misleading base is provided for all subsequent inferences (cf. the previous chapter, pp. 71, 79 ff, 82, 99–102; and the next chapter, p. 165). This is one reason why Fetyukovitch warns the prosecutor that psychology is a knife that cuts both ways (XII, 10). A comic example is provided by the three interpretations of the way in which Dmitri walked into court (XII, 3). A second feature which hinders understanding is the fact that events often have multiple causes. After recounting the Legend of the Inquisitor Ivan returned to his father's house, but found to his surprise that he felt profoundly depressed (V, 6). Several factors contributed to his depression: loathing for his father's house, parting from Alyosha, vexation at his failure to express himself more adequately to Alyosha, apprehension at the unknown future ahead of him on his journey, an unfocused irritation with Smerdyakov; and, a reader may be tempted to add, a half-realized feeling of guilt. Again, several causes explained the flippant and malicious behaviour around the coffin of Zossima (VII, 1), including jealousy of the elder and hostility towards the institution of elders. Reverting to the trial, the third doctor asserts that Dmitri's excited state before his arrest might have been due to several causes such as jealousy, anger, and drunkenness, all perfectly obvious. But the prosecutor does not accept this notion, and his approach needs brief consideration.

The prosecutor believes that a man's actions are ultimately explicable by reference to his prior thoughts which constitute his motives, aims, and reasons (he draws no distinctions between these concepts). But this belief entails a simplification of phenomena which we shall recognize, in a different form, in Ivan. For the investigator and the prosecutor both fail to see that not everything a man does represents the execution of intention. Thus, while Dmitri can explain his hatred of his father only by reference to his undisguised feelings, he can quote no purpose at all (*tsel*) behind his picking up the pestle on the way to his father's house (IX, 3, 5). On the other hand he falsely declares that he does not know why he jumped off the fence after hitting Grigory; presumably he did not cite his pity for his servant because he feared that he would be disbelieved, and also because he was bewildered about the type of answer the prosecutor would accept (IX, 5). Sometimes, of course, an agent is fully conscious of his purposes. Dmitri reluctantly confesses that his purpose (*tsel*) in hiding half Katerina's 3,000 roubles constitutes the disgrace of it (IX, 7); on the other hand, when asked to explain what need he had to boast of having spent three thousand roubles, Dmitri first suggests such multiple causes as bravado, shame at his extravagance, the effort to forget the money he had sewn up; but finally he himself asks why men sometimes tell lies. Part of the explanation in the present case, recognized by the reader but not by the investigator, resides in the notion of self-punishment, to which we shall turn shortly. It is sufficient to note here that the prosecutor, like the investigator, persistently postulates underlying motives and causes. He argues that the underlying cause (*prichina*) of Dmitri's continual anger was jealousy (XII, 7); and he argues that Smerdyakov cannot have committed the murder (XII, 8) since no motive (*motiv*) can be supposed in his case. It must be remembered, of course, that the prosecutor's task is to secure conviction, and to this end he assumes the prisoner's guilt until innocence is proved; thus his task is merely to postulate hypotheses with which the available evidence is consistent. The reader is well aware, however, that the prosecutor is not only highly selective in what he accepts as evidence—for example, he accepts Katerina's but not Ivan's frenetic outburst—but that he is blatantly inconsistent, and also falls into Smerdyakov's traps. His general claim that Dmitri lived always in the present (XII, 9) does not cohere with his persistence in postulating Karamazov's motives.

The defence counsel has no difficulty in showing the inadequacy of the prosecutor's hypotheses, which he believes reveal an abuse of psychology (XII, 10) and an inadequate application of 'accepted judicial methods' (XII, 2). Observers at the trial, however, felt that in his own use of these procedures he was, as it were, playing a game. His arguments that there was no money to be stolen, and that there was no murder in a true sense, carry to extremes what is an essentially aesthetic approach to the situation, and as such, as we shall see later, is morally reprehensible. The early part of his argument consists, it is true, in showing that there are other hypotheses than those of the prosecutor with which the evidence is conformable, especially if a wider spectrum of evidence is considered. But although the reader knows that many of the defence hypotheses are correct, it is not obvious that counsel himself thinks so—in this way the dramatic irony of his incidental truths is increased. Nevertheless, Fetyukovitch provides us with three important observations. First, he points out how the mind can be biased by the use of such terms as 'parricide' and 'murder'. It may also be influenced by the mere weight of apparent evidence, even if every item taken separately is shown to be suspect. The reader is also shown a case where simple reiteration of a hypothesis is taken as corroborative evidence, as when Pyotr Ilyitch's surmise about Dmitri came as a direct confirmation of a theory held by all as to the identity of the criminal (IX, 2). This incident also exemplifies the second point, namely, Fetyukovitch's warning against assuming that everything is as we make up our minds to believe it (XII, 12). He urges that by the use of imagination we can invent new persons, and accuses the prosecution of having invented a new Dmitri, an invention derived from an illicit inference—the inference that because

Dmitri admittedly was in the garden, he must therefore have committed the murder (XII, 12). On the comic level we remember Madame Hohlakova, who claimed that whatever she imagined came to pass (IX, 1), a claim little distinguishable in her case from the claim that she imagined whatever came to pass. Imagination may influence the mind not only in a constructive way, however, but also in a blinding way. Dmitri regarded Grushenka's Pole as non-existent because his desires blinded his imagination. The third of Fetyukovitch's points is his argument that in the sphere of actual life, men ought to act only on convictions justified by reason and experience, tested by analysis. Action must be rational, not dreamlike and mystical—like the religious associations of certain words and ideas. Recognizing this tenet one could not fail to see that Fyodor was in no proper sense a father to his children, and hence that his murder by any of his children could not be parricide (XII, 13). Now these last views are in fundamental opposition to the tenets of Zossima, and represent in their most persuasive form the conclusions of the free-thinking characters in the book—Ivan (before his regeneration), Smerdyakov, Rakitin, Kolya, and that abstract bogey behind much of the theoretical discussion, atheistic European (French) socialism (see I, 5).

The particular warning about the use of psychological concepts is part of a general stricture upon the inadequacies and incompleteness of scientific explanation. Father Païssy declares that science has analysed only parts of phenomena, overlooking the whole, and Zossima remarks that science restricts itself to objects of sense, ignoring and indeed deriding other aspects of experience (IV, 1; VI, 3). Dmitri tells Alyosha of Rakitin's materialist analysis of mind in terms of nerve endings and chemical changes (XI, 4); on this view the concept of God becomes explicable by reference to a particular man's chemistry. It is a measure of Dmitri's partial regeneration before the trial that he dismisses the notion with the reflection that without God man cannot be good. We should also take note of the unflattering references to the sorts of evidence characters accept as proof. Dmitri saw as a 'mathematical certainty' that his request to Madame Hohlakova was his last hope of securing a loan, and she herself knew with mathematical certainty that he would call on her (VIII, 3). Like Madame Hohlakova (IX, 1)—the comparison would have mortified him—Ivan was impressed by the cumulative effect of the detail spelled out by Smerdyakov; and the letter produced by Katerina assumed in his eyes the aspect of a 'logical proof' (XI, 6, 7). Although these examples show how Ivan's powers of reasoning were tainted by his desires, they also remind us of his confession to Alyosha that he had a Euclidean mind, one conditioned in its understanding by three-dimensional geometry (V, 3). Ivan added that if he were to find the notion of God intelligible, He must have created the world according to Euclidean principles; such a view, he recognized, made man's comprehension the measure of all things and was little distinguishable from the claim that man himself had invented God. Ivan also declared that even if he were to see parallel lines meet, in accordance with some non-Euclidean notion of space, he would not accept what he saw. In the context this shows his dim recognition of the limits of his comprehension, and of his inability to think beyond those limits. On a more general level, however, they may be taken as the expression of man's psychological inability to cope with sensory evidence which conflicts with his theoretical preconceptions and prejudices, as in the case of well-known perceptual illusions. The Devil (Ivan's *alter ego*) found the realism of the earth, where all is formulated and geometrical, a relief from the indeterminacy to which he was accustomed (XI, 9), and he reprimanded Ivan for requiring material proofs in contexts where only belief or faith are appropriate. He reminds Ivan that Thomas believed, not because he saw Christ, but because he wanted to believe, before he saw—and the reader is reminded of Alyosha's impassioned retort to Rakitin: 'I believed, I believe, I want to believe, and I will believe' (VII, 2). We must say, therefore, that through the consciousness of his other half, Ivan knows what is needed but suffers from a failure of will. According to the positive doctrine of the novel, wanting to believe is a necessary condition of belief; the leap of faith must itself be willed, in full consciousness of what one is doing.

Ivan's insistence on comprehension permeates his demands for proofs and his narrow restrictions on what is to count as proof. In the face of apparently guiltless suffering, he demands justice or retribution here on earth, where he may see it, not in some remote space and time (V, 4). He believed that any attempt to understand such suffering would lead him to be false to the facts. His point is simple. 'Being false to the facts' would consist in 'accepting' them (*prinyat'*—V, 3) in the sense of conceding that either (*a*) what appeared to be suffering, was not really so, according to some unknown criteria; or (*b*) that there was genuine suffering, but that it could be made not only intelligible, but also justifiable, by reference to phenomena at present beyond our experience. Ivan was explicitly unwilling to envisage that what appeared to be suffering was anything other than suffering. In his imaginative Legend, Ivan shows that Christ's response to the Inquisitor's questions was a silent kiss; whether or not Ivan himself, or the reader, considers this to be an appropriate answer to his formulation of the problem of evil, it is a response that conforms to the moral tenor of the novel.

Although the novel is not an allegory, Dmitri, Ivan, and Alyosha may be seen as being under the primary influence of body, mind, and soul, respectively. And in connection with this three-part division we may also speak of three types of response and enquiry in the novel—personal, technical, and metaphysical. Personal enquiry is governed by an individual's psychology—his desires, habits, and mental constitution. All the Karamazov brothers sometimes fail to understand other people because of their own interests and preoccupations. Alyosha's initial impressions of both Katerina and Grushenka are mistaken (III, 10); Dmitri, according to Katerina, did not understand her gesture of a loan to him (ibid.); Smerdyakov did not believe that Ivan failed to understand the implicit arrangement between them over Fyodor's murder (XI, 8). On the comic level we have Madame Hohlakova's responses to Dmitri, Rakitin, and Pyotr Ilyitch, and her readiness to accept the incidence of temporary insanity (*affekt*) as an explanation of everything—in her hands, at least, the notion explains nothing and merely redescribes the problem at issue. Technical enquiry, associated with the dominance of the mind, is illustrated by the methods of science and the law. Here, the conventions of the method may combine with personal foibles to influence reasoning. The investigating lawyers failed to grasp the significance of Dmitri's reference to the 'signals' Smerdyakov had revealed for getting Fyodor to open his door (IX, 5). They were obsessed, as we have seen, with finding single motives to explain complex actions. The prosecutor, as we also saw, was led to invent a hypothetical agent to satisfy his own hypotheses about the murder. Personal traits may thus influence not only the collection and analysis of evidence, and the postulation of hypotheses, but even the selective application of the rules of inference needed for drawing conclusions from premises. Metaphysical enquiry belongs to the highest level of reflection shown in the novel, and it is concerned with spiritual truths, matters often regarded as abstract, but here claimed to have concrete realization in actual life—the theoretical pronouncements of Ivan and Zossima have their embodiment in the despair of Smerdyakov and the loving service of Alyosha, their beliefs and actions enforcing one another.

PRIDE, SHAME, AND RESENTMENT; AND THEIR PASSIVITY

The notions of pride (*gordost'*), shame (*pozor, styd*), and resentment (*obida, oskorblenie*) dominate the novel. We infer other people's attitudes and intentions towards us from their behaviour, and our beliefs about those attitudes govern our own private feelings and public reactions—think of Levin's reactions, discussed in the previous chapter, pp. 82, 101. If pride is seen, most generally, as self-esteem, shame may be seen as a painful emotion arising from a belief that something is hurtful to our self-esteem; we resent what we believe to be causing our shame, even though our beliefs may be completely mistaken. Pride, shame, and resentment thus have intimate reference to the self.

At the outset of the novel we are told that Alyosha did not resent the behaviour of others and we are shown his refusal to be offended by Rakitin (I, 4; II, 7), who himself is deeply offended by Ivan's insults. Zossima takes no offence from the Karamazov invasion of the monastery, and he tells Fyodor not to revel in resentment or indulge in shame and by so doing succumb to his pride (II, 2)... But Fyodor is ready to take offence from anyone, except from Alyosha whom he believes to be alone in approaching him without contempt.

Dmitri saw himself as a martyr to a sense of honour (IX, 3) and his lawyer described him as having a sense of honour which, although often misplaced and mistaken, amounted to a passion (*strast'*—XII, 11). It is characteristic of passions, as we saw in the last chapter, to make their owners their victims. We thus find Dmitri proud of throwing himself wholeheartedly into anything, no matter how degrading—the total commitment is ecstasy (*vostorg*—III, 3). It is important to note that the regenerations of Dmitri and Ivan are indicated by the feeling of joy (*radost'*—XI, 4, 8) which is a necessary stage towards achieving the proper ecstasy referred to by Zossima (*isstuplenie*—VI, 3). Dmitri wanted to revenge himself on Katerina because she had wounded his pride in failing to see what a hero he was (III, 4). And he was deeply ashamed at being required to display his private feelings to the interrogators (IX, 4), largely because he believed (like Kolya—X, 2) it improper to be called to public account for his feelings (IX, 3) except in so far as he had already expressed them. His unwillingness to account for them to others manifested an unwillingness to account for them to himself; simply having feelings, of no matter what quality, seemed to him to be enough. It is in this way that he resembled his father. For Ivan, conversely, simply having ideas seemed enough. He was, of course, equally proud and self-indulgent, caring only about his intellect, as the Devil warned him (XI, 9), failing to examine his motives in relying on it, or the consequences to others of doing so; his intellectual pride suffered greatly under Katerina's reactions to the trial, and over Smerdyakov's insinuations (XI, 7).

Katerina's pride often revealed itself only in her faith in herself (III, 10) but it craved satisfaction when hurt, as when Grushenka insulted her (IV, 5). The moment she achieved her desired revenge, however, she sometimes succumbed to overwhelming shame, as at the trial (XII, 5), and here we see the self-consuming effect of pride—it forced her to revenge, and yet it resents its own success. Both her desire to be revenged on Dmitri and Ivan, and her own self-abasement, stem from her pride (IV, 5; XII, 5). Other characters reveal the same traits—Grushenka resents the merest suggestion of contempt, Snegiryov and Rakitin are ashamed to be seen to welcome money (XII, 4; V, 1; VII, 3).

A man of pride is essentially a passive man at the mercy of his desires and self-interest. Thus, although a man may seek out self-punishment he is nevertheless thereby seeking to surrender himself. In addition to such willed passive states, however, there are unwilled passive states and we are shown in the novel how almost all the characters find themselves sometimes unable to overcome certain states, or discover themselves to be in a state over which they have exercised no control. At the end of his visit to the monastery, Fyodor 'knew' that he could not control himself (II, 8). When Dmitri questioned Fenya over the departure of Grushenka a new determination 'took possession of him' (*ovladevat'*—VIII, 5); but as so often, his head was in a whirlwind, his heart in confusion, and it was a plan of action that had arisen 'without reasoning' (VIII, 6); it had arisen from feeling and had been adopted with all its consequences. In terms of rational appraisal it was little better than hoping that the 3,000 roubles would come to him of itself, as though from heaven (VIII, 1). Alyosha, too, is subject to ideas that seem to force themselves upon him, as when he wondered whether Katerina loved either of his brothers, or when he recounted to the court how Dmitri had pointed to something on his breast (IV, 5; XII, 4). An evil impression of his conversation with Ivan about the Inquisitor forced its way into his consciousness (VII, 2) and shortly afterwards the image of Dmitri rose before his mind: 'but only fleetingly, and although it reminded him of something special that it was impossible to put off a moment longer, some duty, some dreadful obligation, even that recollection made no impression on him, did not reach his heart, and in a twinkling fled from his memory and was forgotten'. We notice here the important distinction between what reaches the mind and what reaches the heart.

Ivan found himself possessed by tormenting thoughts of Smerdyakov (V, 6; XI, 6), by consuming passion for Katerina (XI, 6), and irresistible impulses, such as the impulse to knock Miüsov from his father's carriage or to knock down the drunken peasant (II, 8; XI, 8); he resorts to violence whenever he fails to achieve his ends by more rational means, as in his conversations with Smerdyakov (V, 7; XI, 7). Such cases may be usefully connected with those in which characters are unable to explain their behaviour or reactions. Fyodor claimed that he did not know why he played the fool to make himself agreeable (II, 2); Alyosha did not understand his own embarrassment at Ivan's lack of sympathy towards him (I, 5) or his anxiety about Katerina, or the effect of Grushenka's voluptuousness (III, 3, 10). Again, Alyosha could not understand the significance of his wondering aloud to Lise whether he believed in God (V, 1). Ivan could not explain his feelings on leaving Smerdyakov and before departing for Moscow, nor could he explain his hopes and desires in going there (V, 6)—except that he would be as 'solitary' as ever.

To the examples of the states under which men are merely passive, and those which they do not understand, must be added states which reveal a man's involuntary response. Many characters experience spontaneous thoughts akin to those which occur to a prisoner on the way to execution—to use the favourite metaphor (IX, 9; XI, 9; XII, 5, 9). Dmitri involuntarily declared that Katerina loved her own virtue, not him (III, 5); Rakitin believed Alyosha's confession about the sensuality of the Karamazovs to be of greater importance because it was spontaneous (II, 7); the fact that Ivan's view that 'one reptile will devour another' had escaped him unawares, made it all the more important, in Alyosha's view (IV, 5). Alyosha asks Snegiryov whether he addresses him as 'Sir' on purpose or involuntarily, because he wants to determine whether the Captain is trying to show contempt, or indulging in self-punishment (IV, 6).

SELF-PUNISHMENT AND OTHER NEEDS

Book III 'The Sensualists' is followed immediately by the book entitled *Nadryvy*. Literally, *nadryv* is a tear, but figuratively it refers to overstrain caused by lifting heavy weights. In the context of the novel the notion is best denoted by the family of terms 'self-punishment', 'self-flagellation', 'self-torture'. 'Self-punishment' describes behaviour but does not explain it; it is important, there-fore, to grasp the multiple causes that can bring it about. A victim of self-punishment is characteristically—in *The Brothers Karamazov* —a man beset by despair, doubt, self-concern, and failure of nerve; this failure itself shows the victim to be morally sensitive and struggling towards true freedom from himself. Nevertheless, some people find the pain of the struggle so pleasurable that it suffices, and self-punishment then becomes an end in itself. The two most important aspects of this state are that it is willed by the agent himself, and that it is pleasurable. Self-flagellants maso-chistically indulge themselves in pain; they are, indeed, sensualists of a more refined breed, using their minds as well as their bodies for the furtherance of their self-degradation. But a third feature must also be noted: self-punishment implies both a need on the part of the victim, and a struggle to satisfy that need. The need can in fact be fulfilled only with the help of faith—according to the positive moral doctrine—since it is the need to transcend concern for the self. Even Ivan's heartfelt outburst on the problem of evil, together with the Legend of the Inquisitor, reveal aspects of self-torture of a kind found among intellectuals. Recognizing this fact we can see that the declaration of Zossima's faith in Book VI is an answer to all the previous books: to the largely physical sensualism of Fyodor and Dmitri, to the sensualistic self-flagellation of Fera-pont, Snegiryov, Madame Hohlakova, Lise, Katerina, and Grushenka, and to the intellectual self-torture of Ivan and his shadow Smerdyakov.

Self-punishment is associated with that lying to the self that leads to loss of self-respect, noted by Zossima (II, 2). But when Zossima told Fyodor not to be ashamed of himself, Fyodor asserted that it was 'beautiful' to be insulted, and that, moreover, he had taken offence on 'aesthetic' grounds (ibid.). This admission is powerfully underlined by Dmitri's confession to Alyosha, during which he asserts that for the immense mass of mankind beauty is found in Sodom: 'what to the mind is shameful is without exception beauty to the heart' (III, 3). The narrator himself observes that the lamentations of the peasant women soothe the heart only by irritating and straining it even more (II, 3). And the notion recurs. Madame Hohlakova insisted to Alyosha that Katerina was really in love with Ivan and only deceived herself through self-torture, from some sort of pose. Alyosha himself awoke from a dream about the scene between Katerina and Grushenka shouting 'self-torture' (IV, 5). Later, Ivan asserted that Katerina's feeling for Dmitri was one of self-torture (V, 3). But here a caveat must be issued. Ivan is wrong to think that just because Katerina wilfully tortured herself over Dmitri, she cared nothing for him (ibid.). This would be to conflate self-torture with self-deception. Self-deception is not identical with self-torture, and neither does it completely explain it—or, when it does, it is because self-deception has become for the moment, and perversely, the truth. This obscure remark is illustrated by the passionate confessions of Dmitri and Katerina at the end of the novel, in the chapter of the epilogue entitled 'For a moment the lie became the truth'—the title echoes Ivan's insistence that Katerina's love for Dmitri was a lie (XI, 6): 'Thus they both murmured to each other words that were almost meaningless and ecstatic [*isstuplennyy*], and perhaps not even true, but at that moment it was all true and they both believed each other utterly.' The reference to ecstasy is here exactly right to characterize not only Dmitri and Katerina themselves, but also the effect of behaviour in which *nadryv* has had a part. Katerina adds, indeed, that she had forgotten that she came to accuse herself. And to revert to Ivan, he had himself told Katerina that she really did love Dmitri, for the way he insulted her; this was her self-torture (IV, 5): 'You need him in order to contemplate continually your heroic fidelity, and to reproach him for infidelity. And it all comes from your pride.' The narrator himself surmised that Katerina's sudden moment of revenge at the trial had arisen from her self-torturing love for Dmitri, a love based on her own pride; he also added that perhaps the self-torturing love would have grown into true love and perhaps Katerina herself longed for nothing else (XII, 5).

Ivan's demand for a theodicy is prefaced by his conviction that those who impart charity from a sense of duty are acting from self-punishment (V, 4), and Alyosha conceded the possibility—in such cases, of course, the agent would have succumbed to the self, albeit under the guise of serving others. And Ivan's claim immediately precedes his characterization of the Inquisitor, whose self-deception and, by implication, self-punishment, consisted in taking upon himself the sufferings of the world from love of humanity.

Of the many other incidents of *nadryv* only a few need be listed to aid the reader's memory. Dmitri tells Alyosha how he could have killed himself from ecstasy (*vostorg*—III, 4). The book explicitly devoted to self-punishment shows us Ferapont's self-titillation, no doubt partly induced by fasting, and Captain Snegiryov's buffoonery and self-abasement before Alyosha. Lise's wilfully self-inflicted pain caused by squashing her finger in the door, provides another striking example of *nadryv* (XI, 3). Alyosha visited Grushenka in search of self-punishment in his despair and doubt after Zossima's death; during his visit, Grushenka herself confesses that she had perhaps loved only her own spite, and not the Pole from whom she had been separated for five years (VII, 3).

One notion used repeatedly in association with self-punishment is the bow. The scene of Dmitri's first bow to Katerina, and her deep bow in return (III, 4) is often mentioned. Dmitri sent Alyosha to Katerina with the message that he was bowing out of their relationship (*klanyat'sya*—III, 5), a message repeated four times in as many pages and later referred to by Ivan (*rasklanyat'sya*—III, 9). Katerina herself believed that a great deal stemmed from her first bow to the ground (XI, 5) and obsessively refers to it in each of her statements to the court (XII, 4, 5). Bowing is taken seriously by other characters. Zossima bows down before Dmitri when the Karamazovs visit the monastery (II, 6), a bow explained only later by reference to Zossima's foreboding and his own youthful bow before his servant Afanasy (VI, 1, 2). Grushenka, at Mokroe, bowed to everyone, when drunk, and after the preliminary investigation she bowed before Dmitri, declaring herself for him (VIII, 8; IX, 9). In these bows a person denies himself and submits his will to that of another; it is the recognition that the other person has equal rights to consideration. Such self-denial, however, can be turned by the dedicated masochist into pleasurable self-torture; for it can be adopted as a perverse defence against humiliation by others—he who humiliates himself thus outdoes those who humiliate him. This is the force of Zossima's admonition to Ivan that a self-proclaimed martyr sometimes likes to divert himself with his despair, driven to it, as it were, by despair itself (II, 6). Fyodor, of course, humiliates himself partly in self-defence. But a determined masochist is logically invincible, since he can transform any situation into his own hurt. (Masochist: 'Hurt me!'; Sadist: 'No!'; Masochist: 'Beautiful!') Because of this a masochist is immune to outside help. Self-conquest must come from within.

Self-punishment is only one way in which a character may reveal his need for other people. Alyosha felt that his own and the world's greatest need was something holy before which one could fall down and worship (I, 5). He himself believed that he could not live without Zossima (II, 7), Fyodor craved for someone faithful (III, 1), Dmitri needed someone above him to forgive him (III, 3). It is a measure of Alyosha's successful discipleship that all the major characters need his trust in them or his opinion—Fyodor, Dmitri, Ivan, Katerina, Kolya, Grushenka, Lise (I, 4; III, 3, 9; IV, 5; X, 6; XI, 1, 3). The single and significant exception is Smerdyakov. The need for love is a major theme of the novel. At the outset of the work the narrator tells us that Alyosha had a capacity for making himself loved. Ivan admitted that he could not love his neighbour (V, 4), as Fyodor had already alleged (IV, 2). In contrast, Alyosha tried to follow Zossima's prescription of caring for people as though they were children, or the sick in hospital (V, 1)

—an attitude that would certainly be condescending if it were not accompanied by humility, since it involves treating people as not fully in control. The notion must be primarily connected with that of being responsible for all. Thus, although Ivan declared that he loved life, and passionately loved Katerina (V, 5; XI, 6) he did not accept responsibility for others. He denied that he was Dmitri's keeper or Lise's nurse (V, 3; XI, 5) and only when mentally ill admitted that anyone might administer to him (XI, 9). It should be noted that both Smerdyakov and Pyotr Ilyitch deny that they are Dmitri's keeper or nurse (V, 2; VIII, 5), thus emphasizing the 'childlike' aspect of the eldest brother (referred to by Andrey, the driver—VIII, 6) as well as their own self-centredness.

The most important aspects of Zossima's instructions on the proper sort of loving, are that it is both difficult to acquire, and requires constant striving (VI, 3; II, 4); only by striving can a man transcend bondage to his self-interest. This gives body to the view that 'hell is the suffering of being unable to love' (VI, 3), for hell is the suffering of being by oneself. Thus, in preparing to be 'solitary' by departing for Moscow (V, 6), Ivan was preparing for his descent into hell, from which he emerged only after his mental crisis.

Brief reference should be made to the need for securing the attention of other people. (Cf. the previous discussions of *Middlemarch*, pp. 14, 34, 45–6, and of *Anna Karenina*, p. 82.) There are many occasions on which characters do something largely for effect, and the search for approval is matched by the fear of disapproval. Although he was concerned that others took him for a buffoon, Fyodor claimed that he played the fool in order to make himself agreeable; he constantly exhibited a need to prove himself both to others and to himself (II, 2, 8). It was in the light of this that Zossima urged him not to be concerned about the opinion of others. Miüsov was anxious to dissociate himself from the *bruhaha* at the monastery, Madame Hohlakova sought for Zossima's approval, Grushenka drawled for effect, Kolya was mischievous for effect (II, 6, 4; III, 10; X, 1); Fyodor shouted purely for effect.

Ivan initially spoke stupidly to Alyosha because he was anxious about the effect he was creating, Dmitri hoped that he was not confessing in order to achieve certain effects (III, 3; V, 3; III, 3), and Snegiryov played the buffoon before Alyosha, and was later ashamed at having revealed his need for friendship so openly (IV, 6–7). Alyosha himself explains this buffoonery in terms of the Captain's attempt to protect himself from continual humiliation (X, 4), and adds that Snegiryov's whole life had become exclusively centred on Ilusha; if anything were to happen to Ilusha, the Captain would go mad. This case, like Fyodor's obsession with Grushenka, shows how a man has not transcended self-concern; but it also serves to provide Alyosha with an example of the view that the memory of even a single loving act can serve as the basis of regeneration (Epilogue 3).

IVAN AND DMITRI

At the monastery Ivan discussed his article with Zossima and some of the monks. He had argued that when the Church and State are separate, criminals can compromise with their conscience by claiming that they are not strictly going against Christ—remarks echoed in Smerdyakov's sophistries over the way he could save his soul by denying he was a Christian (II, 5; III, 7). Zossima asserted that the only effective deterrent to crime is a man's own conscience (II, 5), a view consistent with his admonition that Fyodor always knew what he ought to do (II, 2). It may be observed that Fyodor is said to avoid any obscenity that could be legally punished (II, 8) and the implication is that although he happily transgressed the relevant internal sanction of conscience, he was not prepared to transgress the quite irrelevant external sanction of the law. Ivan's Inquisitor, of course, argued that conscience offers only a seductive freedom (V, 5). There are several references to conscience, of the standard sort encountered in *Anna Karenina* and to a lesser extent in *Middlemarch*: the prosecutor holds that a man's conscience throbs incessantly in his mind (XII, 9), the inner uneasiness of Ivan and Pyotr Ilyitch may be taken as the stirrings of conscience (IX, 1; XI, 7), and Grushenka looks upon Alyosha as her conscience (VII, 3). Although Alyosha himself seems to experience the conflicting claims of conscience, there is an implication that the conflict arises only from lack of clarity (III, 10)—a view that few readers would accept. The most important observation upon conscience, however, is made by the defence counsel, who remarks that in order to experience pangs of conscience one must have beliefs about the relevant situation (XII, 12)—Smerdyakov, he argues, may have had no pangs of conscience on committing suicide because he may have felt no remorse or penitence, only despair.

During the discussion at the monastery, Miüsov summarizes Ivan's position as maintaining that without a belief in immortality, both love and the life force in the world would dry up; egoism would be inevitable, nothing would be immoral, the 'moral law of nature' would be changed into the exact contrary of the former religious law, and everything would be permissible (II, 6). Rakitin violently attacks this view, shortly afterwards, assuring Alyosha that humanity will find the power to live for virtue without believing in immortality (II, 7). It is important to note that Ivan himself states much of the positive doctrine of the novel, although he does not practise what he appears to preach. At the beginning of his confession to Alyosha, Ivan declares that he thirsts for life—the affirmation immediately follows Dmitri's attempt to take Fyodor's life—and that at least until he is thirty he will triumph over every disillusionment (V, 3, 5); the reader thus notices at once the conditional nature of the affirmation and its self-centredness. The sort of loving relevant to a love for life, Ivan believes, is not a matter of intellect or logic, 'it is loving with one's inside, with one's stomach' (V, 3). It should be observed that earlier Ivan had told Alyosha that our desires for the life or death of others are not matters of decision or reason, but are issues settled in the heart (III, 9); he does not indicate that such desires either can or should be controlled. One should probably conclude that truly 'loving with one's inside' is incompatible with evil desires.

Alyosha amplifies Ivan's affirmation of loving with one's stomach by asserting that only by loving life, regardless of logic, will one understand the meaning (*smysl*) of it; ironically, this claim immediately precedes Ivan's confession not to understand the world. Ivan in fact begins by claiming to believe in both the order and meaning of life, but on the other hand he does not accept the world—that is, he does not accept that there is a justification for the sufferings he sees in the world. What he means by affirming that he believes in the meaning and order of life is obscure. As a prelude to his diatribe on man's inhumanity to man, Ivan confesses that he cannot understand how one can love one's neighbours, though one might love those at a distance (V, 4). In so doing he is not just revealing his own present inability to love, but he is proclaiming the unintelligibility (and by implication the impossibility) of the actual and possible—loving one's neighbours. This provides the foundation for his assertion in connection with cruelty, that the absurd (*nelepost'*) is only too necessary on earth (V, 4). Since one man can never comprehend the suffering of another, a mother, for example, has no right to forgive the torture of her child—even if she dare (ibid.). And if the price of harmony is such forgiveness, then 'from love of humanity', Ivan declares, he will forgo harmony.

It is necessary at this stage to outline the main points from the Legend of the Inquisitor (V, 5). The Inquisitor holds that since man was created a rebel, a condition in which it is impossible to be happy, Christ had only one way to make men happy. That way was embodied in the three temptations he rejected; the temptations of bread, miracles as proof of divinity, and earthly power. By providing bread Christ would have satisfied the universal need to find someone before whom to bow down—a need on which I commented above. Further, the need for community of worship would have been satisfied also, worship of what was beyond dispute. The secret of man's being, the Inquisitor holds, is having something to live for, for without a firm idea of the object of life, man would not consent to go on living—the reader will recall that Dmitri and Ivan contemplate suicide, and Smerdyakov succeeds, and also that Zossima held that none were more miserable than suicides (VI, 3). The greatest cause of man's suffering, the

Inquisitor continues, is his freedom of conscience, and nothing is at the same time more seductive. He, therefore, who soothes a man's conscience gains possession of his freedom. Three powers were offered to Christ to ensnare the conscience of men—miracle, mystery, and authority, and He rejected them all. But, the Inquisitor maintains, man cannot bear to be without the miraculous, and when he rejects miracle he rejects God (and, presumably, Christ) too. Respecting men less, Christ might have asked less of them, and might have recognized that although they are rebellious like children, men are essentially slaves. Christ offered only what was indeterminate and extraordinary. The Church, therefore, has founded itself on miracle, mystery, and authority, and in so doing is working not with Christ, 'but with *him*' (i.e. the Devil). Freedom, free thought, and science will bring men to such straits that they will turn to the Church in order to save them from themselves. The Inquisitor admits that he has joined the ranks of those who 'corrected Thy deeds', and he has done so out of love for humanity. It will be remembered that the prosecutor accuses the defence counsel of correcting the Gospel and of setting up an Antichrist in the guise of free thought and science (XII, 14).

Ivan admits that the Inquisitor did not believe in God, and that because of this and his incurable love of humanity, he was doomed to suffer. In his old age the Inquisitor had become convinced that millions of men would never be capable of using their freedom and that, knowing this, it was no great moral blessedness to attain freedom for oneself. Only by following the advice of 'the great dread spirit' could one build any endurable life for 'the unfinished, experimental beings fashioned in mockery'. The Inquisitor's deception of the people 'is in the name of Him in whose ideal he had believed all his life'.

Ivan reassures Alyosha that even if his 'senseless poem' reveals a hell in his heart and head, he has not yet lost his desire for life. But the nature of this desire is immediately displayed. He leaves Alyosha, returns to his father's house, meets Smerdyakov, listens to his father downstairs, and prepares to make a new start on the morrow—by becoming solitary again, and by departing: ' "Away with the past, an end to the old world for ever, may there be no news from it and no reference to it; to a new world, new places, and no looking back!" But instead of delight his soul was suddenly filled with such gloom, and his heart began to ache with such grief, as he had never before felt in his whole life' (V, 7). In contrast to Dmitri who rides off to Mokroe to say farewell to Grushenka, and unexpectedly begins a new life and a regeneration aided by her, and in contrast to Alyosha who begins a new life in the world at large after the death of Zossima, Ivan seeks to begin a new life alone, and by avoiding his duties—his *alter ego*, the Devil, is described as having a distinct aversion for any duties that may be forced upon him (XI, 9). It is ironic that Ivan had earlier assured Alyosha that he would always defend Fyodor (III, 9). Of greater importance is his attempt to bring about change by changing his place; in this he is copied by Smerdyakov, whose sole idea of a new life was to go abroad, with money (XI, 8). But moral change, it is implied, takes place only within. In this connection we should note that Ivan's sudden decision not to go to Tchermashnya, thereby pleasing his father and Smerdyakov, but to Moscow, in no way alters his moral stature; as Smerdyakov later points out, Ivan had already decided to leave his father's side, and this gratuitous assertion of freedom is no more than an aesthetic indulgence, associated with *nadryv*, self-punishment—he has partly recognized that he is a scoundrel to leave his father (V, 7), and now he will compound the sin by further thwarting him. It will be remembered that Fyodor and Dmitri spoke of the aesthetic aspects of self-punishment, the beauty of *nadryv*; according to the positive moral doctrine of the novel such aesthetic indulgence is always to be judged unfavourably, especially when, as here, it represents a substitute for a properly moral decision.

Ivan's regeneration is largely dependent upon his three visits to Smerdyakov, akin to the 'three ordeals' of Dmitri during the preliminary investigation. During the third visit Smerdyakov openly charges Ivan: 'you knew of the murder, charged me to kill, and went away knowing all about it' (XI, 8). Smerdyakov taunts Ivan for not daring to confess or to kill him—'for all your former daring, you dare do nothing'—and accuses him of caring too much for his own comfort, being proud, and, above all, being unwilling to turn to others. The verb here, *klanyat'sya*, is a *double entendre*: it can mean 'to seek favours' but, as we saw in connection with Dmitri and Katerina, it also means 'to bow oneself out'. Ivan will bow before no one to seek a favour, and he will also bow out of his responsibilities. After leaving his lackey Ivan becomes conscious of resolution and joy in his heart, and he picks up the drunken peasant who he had knocked to the ground on the way to Smerdyakov's. But, like Zossima's Visitor, he still lacks sufficient strength to go straight to the prosecutor, and with this failure his gladness immediately disappears. For purely aesthetic reasons, for the beauty of symmetry, he decides to leave everything until the morrow; once more, the aesthetic has seduced the moral principle.

On returning to his house, aware that his problem is that of justifying himself to himself, Ivan is confronted with his hallucination of the Devil. It may be deduced from Alyosha's report of Smerdyakov's suicide (XI, 9) that the Devil appeared immediately after the lackey's death; and it should be noted that Ivan feared Smerdyakov was a dream (XI, 8) and addressed the Devil as a 'lackey' (XI, 9). The hallucination is the climax in a series of references to dreams, beginning with Madame Hohlakova's dream of leaving Lise to become a sister of mercy (II, 4), and continuing through Dmitri's dream of 'the babe' and Lise's dream of the demons (IX, 8; XI, 3). Here, the hallucination not only clinches Ivan's acceptance of responsibility, but it also serves to remind the reader—through the device of rehearsing Ivan's youthful speculations—that Ivan had rejected laws, conscience, faith, and the future life. Ivan is even accused of being aesthetically offended that the Devil did not appear in a red glow. To Alyosha Ivan confesses that he fears that not only Katerina, but 'even Lise' and Alyosha himself will despise him for failure to act (XI, 10), and he wonders whether his refusal to commit suicide reflects cowardice or love of life. From Ivan's anxieties about conscience, however,

Alyosha concludes that God was gaining mastery over his brother's heart. It suffices for the reader to recognize that Ivan's regeneration depended upon exorcizing those parts of himself embodied in, or represented by, Smerdyakov and the Devil.

Ivan required an abstract set of principles before engaging in action, and failing to find one, committed himself to nothing and to no one; the principles he had hypothetically entertained nevertheless provided the ground for Smerdyakov's actions, and because they conformed to his own desires, Ivan did nothing to prevent those actions. But if Ivan is not a man of action, neither, in a full sense, is his brother Dmitri. For example, Dmitri's attempts at action are often either bungled, as when he tried to secure loans from Samsonov, Lyagavy, and Madame Hohlakova; left unrealized, as when he failed to bring himself to rape Katerina, beat Grushenka, murder his father or kill himself; or foisted on others, as when he commissioned Ivan to visit Fyodor on his behalf, and both Ivan and Alyosha to deliver messages to Katerina. Alyosha believed that 'the elemental force of the Karamazovs' was an essentially destructive force if left unchecked (V, 1); Dmitri, like Vronsky, succumbs to *passio*, becoming a victim of his passionate states and sudden thoughts.

On his way to join Grushenka at Mokroe, Dmitri recognized that he had come to his present pass of his own free will, and he thirsted for 'renewal'. But like Ivan 'he put his faith in a change of place' (VIII, 1), in the external rather than the internal. In a moment of subdued self-punishment Dmitri looks forward to seeing Grushenka with her Polish lover, and at that thought experiences a new feeling of self-effacement; at the same moment, however, it occurs to him that they might be asleep—and the notion of sleep is associated with inaccessibility, dreaming, proximity and vulnerability to death. It should be observed that Dmitri not only consciously became rougher when humiliated by his interrogators, but in his humiliation felt a perfect right to despise them (IX, 6); it was part of the defence admonition to the jury that by finding him guilty they would ease his conscience, allowing him to believe that he was square with them (XII, 13). Dmitri takes the major step towards his regeneration after his dream of the babe, by accepting responsibility for wanting to kill Fyodor (IX, 9). But in prison he tells Alyosha that he fears the new man within him will disappear; nevertheless he still thirsts for life and accepts that 'all are responsible for all. . . . I am going for all, because someone must go for all' (XI, 4). He asserts, in vehement rebuttal of Rakitin, that one cannot exist anywhere, even in prison or underground, without God, and that he felt he could resist any suffering in order to be able to say 'I exist'—an affirmation immediately following Lise's apparent nihilism and the self-punishment of her squashed finger (ibid.). It is important to note, finally, that Dmitri turns on Grushenka in horrified disbelief that only if Katerina succeeds in saving him, will Grushenka forgive her; at this point Alyosha himself rebukes Dmitri: 'Don't dare reproach her, you have no right' (Epilogue 2). Whatever the reader may feel not only about the naturalness but also the justice of Dmitri's rebuke, Alyosha's rebuke is merely a reassertion of the tenet about not judging. It is mildly obscure how Alyosha can issue such a warning without disregarding it himself.

CONCLUSION

Unconditioned and unconditional faith: that, according to the positive moral doctrine of *The Brothers Karamazov*, must be the ultimate principle of human action. We are shown cases where, in the absence of faith, pride rules, subverting the minds of men to their own egoistic ends, causing them to exercise power over others, and at the same time preventing any understanding of others. In failing to understand others, men thereby fail to understand themselves, and succumb to the ultimately self-induced pain of shame and resentment. A precondition to loving others, however, is loving life—to this extent Fyodor is a stage nearer regeneration than Smerdyakov; a danger of intellectualism is that by substituting hypotheses for actuality, it not only encourages man to act as God, but also discourages engagement in life. Zossima warned Madame Hohlakova of the importance and difficulty of transforming her dreams into reality (II, 4); Kolya, behaving like Ivan, disclaimed responsibility for the peasant's mischief on the grounds that he had merely expressed a hypothetical proposition (X, 5). Zossima asserted that only by recognizing his responsibility does the heart of man grow soft (IV, 1). This is not to say that the intellect has no role to play, only that it is in itself merely a tool at the mercy of good or evil desires. The decomposition of Zossima's corpse, and its consequences, constituted a crisis and turning-point in Alyosha's spiritual development 'shocking but also finally strengthening his mind towards a certain aim for the rest of his life' (VII, 1). He himself had recognized, after his disastrous intrusion between Katerina and Ivan, that sincerity was not enough to ensure responsible action and to secure reconciliation between people (IV, 6). Nevertheless it should be noted that Alyosha wins no one's confidence, and achieves no ends, by means of argument —only by example. It is for this reason that he seems to be so passive; and it is only faith in the ultimate efficacy of 'active love' that secures a man against remorse when it fails to influence those whose time 'has not yet come' (VI, 3). Similarly, it is only by refraining from judging others that men may properly judge themselves, and desist from asserting themselves. Katerina insisted: 'I will be a god to whom he [Dmitri] can pray' (IV, 5); but she ends by asking forgiveness of her bitterest enemy, Grushenka.

We have seen that the novel can be taken to show us several aspects and causes of man's incomprehension of man. The reductionism of specialist technical investigations, like the law or psychology, leaves the 'whole' man untouched. Further, such enquiries work within narrow limits of what are admissible as data, hypothesis, and proof. Ivan knows that it is no comfort to the suffering to know that 'one thing follows another' (V, 4). He sets limits on the nature of justification; in failing to 'accept' the world, he fails to see that love *is* one sort of justification, and that such a view is quite conformable to the general principle that 'every process has its law' (VI, 2). Ivan, like his temporary disciple Lise, fails to see that however widespread are love of crime or the desire to kill one's father (XII, 5; XI, 3; cf. prosecutor, XII, 6), any change must come from within each individual, and that one man can help another only by loving him. But from the fear of seeming ridiculous, men are ashamed of righteous action (X, 6; VI, 2); this fear of judgement has its roots in pride and self-concern. When others stupidly misunderstand us—as when the investigator assumes that to remember an event entails having been fully conscious of it at the time (IX, 5)—we must curb our resentment, for mutual understanding, too, results from 'active love'. Zossima, for example, shows by his advice to Fyodor, Madame Hohlakova, and the peasant woman, that he fully understands the attractions of self-punishment as well as its cause—a behavioural pattern that is recognized by neither of the legal protagonists.

It may be wondered, however, why a man's salvation depends on belief in God and belief in immortality—beliefs, be it noted, that are logically independent of each other in spite of Alyosha's assertion that 'in God is immortality' (III, 8). It may be thought that belief in immortality is a necessary condition for salvation because it can provide a rationale or point for a man's struggle with himself; in other words, the struggle is undertaken for the sake of future rewards. Those who advance such views have been accused—George Eliot made such an accusation—of making fear of consequences the primary motive to action; and since fear of humiliation is the offspring of pride, the goal consists of victory over pride by means which presuppose pride. In *The Brothers Karamazov* we are shown no character who achieved self-realization without the twin beliefs in God and immortality; but readers should recognize that it follows only that for *those* characters such beliefs were a sufficient condition for regeneration. It does not follow that such beliefs are the sole necessary condition for all men. It should be noted, however, that Zossima tells Ivan that if questions about immortality cannot be answered in the affirmative, neither can they be answered in the negative (II, 6). The question, in brief, is not a matter of argument or proof, but of faith—ironically underlined by Dmitri's half-serious suggestion that 'de ideabus non est disputandum' (XI, 4). And a pragmatic justification of such faith could be derived, if need be, from reflection upon the consequences of its absence. Païssy reminds Alyosha that none have been able 'to create a higher image [*obraz*] of man than the image shown by Christ' (IV, 1). It may be objected that the meaning of the articles of faith is far from clear. What does one have to believe, to believe in God or in immortality? Now it is part of the unconditional nature of the faith required that a man must will to believe in what, beforehand, he does not understand; this is why Alyosha asserts that it is only by loving, regardless of logic, that one will come to understand the meaning of the world and thereby, of course, of the articles of faith (V, 3). The meaning, therefore, cannot be set out in a series of intelligible propositions for the benefit of those without faith; what can be done for such people is to characterize the life, thought, and deeds of men with and without faith, in the hope that such a presentation will awaken a favourable response. Although faith cannot be reached by argument there are practical steps that may be taken towards the leap of faith, steps designed to conform to, and mould, the psychological nature of man. Thus Zossima's advice to Alyosha to treat men as one treats children or the sick depends on the recognition that men find it easier to withhold their judgement and resentment of such persons. It is notable that whereas Ivan used the suffering of children for the purposes of accusing his hypothetical God, Dmitri used the dream of the 'babe' as a ground for 'accepting' what his brother could not; and Alyosha's stress on the memory of childhood (Epilogue 3) explicitly embraces the view that no man can ultimately deny to himself his own unselfconscious acts of loving. Such acts form the inner standards that constitute self-respect; but the outward-looking nature of these standards entail that the 'active love' of others is the fundamental practical policy; from it will follow the conditions and states that men mistakenly search for as preconditions of their concern for others. By loving his neighbour before all else a man comes not only to understand him, but also to achieve self-fulfilment and self-knowledge. Some readers of *The Brothers Karamazov* may feel that these tenets of the explicit moral doctrine of the novel are acceptable as ends-in-themselves, without faith in God and in immortality. A secularization of its central doctrine, however, will have consequences for both the understanding and the assessment of the novel as a whole. Upon these each reader must reflect for himself.

CHAPTER 4

Knowledge and Illusion in
A la recherche du temps perdu

In the first two chapters I tried to show, *inter alia*, some of the ways in which a particular novel can be taken to explore the problem of how, and in what senses, a man may be said to acquire knowledge. I emphasize again that I do not imply that this constitutes the major theme of any of the novels I have discussed; such a view would exaggerate the similarities between the texts at the expense of their unique and special aspects. In both *Middlemarch* and *Anna Karenina* we saw how a man's desires can distort the operations of imagination, and hence prevent his acquisition of knowledge; these very same views, together with emphasis on the roles of egoism and habit, reappear in *A la recherche du temps perdu*.[1]

The philosophical remarks in Proust's novel are more evidently interrelated than they are in the other novels discussed; but the narrator's views about the nature of knowledge are both complex and, at first, confusing. If the self-knowledge which the narrator claims a reader should gain from the novel (III, 1035/12.418) depended on the soundness and coherence of the philosophical reflections it contained, Proust's work would not fulfil its declared utilitarian aim. The narrator himself states that he seeks to combat a prevalent form of materialism with a form of subjective idealism (I, 816, 848/4.160, 204); but it would be more accurate to say that

---

[1] References are to Marcel Proust, *A la recherche du temps perdu*, edited by Pierre Clarac and André Ferré, Paris, 1954, in three volumes. I have also given the corresponding references to the English translation in twelve volumes by C. K. Scott Moncrieff (volume 12 translated by 'Stephen Hudson'), entitled *Remembrance of Things Past*, London, 1941. French references precede the English, thus:

(III, 1032/12.415).

In general I have adopted Scott Moncrieff's translations in the quotations, amending them only slightly. My interpretation, of course, is of the French text.

he tries to fuse his epistemological views largely founded on idealism, with the realism he deems essential to his role as narrator. For
his problem is to show how it is possible to give the narration he
gives, with the truth-claims it involves, while subscribing, at least
for some of the time, to the theoretical belief that the objectivity
of the external world is an illusion. I shall show how the narrator
thinks knowledge *is* possible by examining his views about the
nature of knowledge and the difficulties of obtaining it. I declare
my awareness of four immediate objections to my methods in
both this and the preceding chapters. I do not discuss whether, or
how far, the narrator's philosophical pronouncements reflect those
of Proust himself; I do not discuss the metaphorical content and
implications, where present, of the quotations and incidents to
which I refer; I do not examine the literary embodiment of the
philosophical views I abstract from the text, their working-out by
means of the characterization of persons and events; I do not consider the particular contexts within the novel which occasion the
philosophical utterances, and because of these omissions I mistakenly look for the consistency of an argument. In short, I may
be accused of a naive, literalist interpretation of the text of what is,
after all, a novel. To some of these criticisms I shall turn in the next
chapter, but at this stage they are irrelevant. I am concerned with
one aspect of the novel, and my argument is to be examined in
itself. I argue neither that the novel ought to display the consistency of a philosophical discourse, nor that such inconsistencies as
I detect detract from the merit of the novel. A final word about
one of the many apparent omissions from my discussion may help
to clarify my approach. I refer to the concept of 'souvenir involontaire' ('involuntary memory') only briefly, treating it as an
integral, but not a dominant, part of the epistemological structure
I outline. If this treatment is thought to constitute an indefensible
under-emphasis, it should also be accepted as a challenge: if my
account of the epistemological structure is plausible, how could
the concept be assigned a more prominent role than the one I give
it; how could one avoid the conclusion that the narrator's persistent references to 'souvenir involontaire' must be seen as non-

literal and non-epistemological? It may be replied, however, that any account that gives it such an unprominent role must be false. Such a claim, I suggest, would need closer argument and more examples than I have mustered for my own position.

THE FACULTIES OF, AND THE OBSTACLES TO, KNOWLEDGE

The narrator believes that we have three faculties: our senses, our imagination, and our intellect.[1] A fourth faculty, memory, is variously described as oscillating between imagination and intellect, and now as associated with imagination, now with intellect. We attain knowledge when we successfully use our intellect to elicit the true nature of the data provided by our senses; we fail to attain knowledge, and suffer illusion, when our imagination and intellect, unknown to us, operate to prevent an accurate examination of this data. The data provided by the senses are called 'sensations' or 'impressions', and these terms refer to 'ce qu'on a senti' (III, 896/12.248, 'what one has felt'), in the widest sense of 'feel'; they refer to our total response to the particular situation, irrespective of the degree to which we are fully conscious of the nature of our response; to our ideas and to the emotional connotations which invariably accompany them. It is because emotions are regarded as accompaniments that sorrow is described as a 'mode' under which certain ideas come to us (III, 906/12.260). There are two reasons for not identifying the terms 'sensation' and 'impression' with what we normally call visual images. First, our eye is not a simple recording machine (II, 524/6.295), for what we see, in the sense of consciously notice, depends on many factors, including our interests and moods at the time; secondly, 'le monde visible ... n'est pas le monde vrai' (I, 548/3.171, 'the visible world ... is not the true world'). Reality, indeed, is encumbered by properties of invisibility (II, 607/7.9).

The narrator explicitly lists four major obstacles to knowledge;

---

[1] This traditional view, dating back at least to Aristotle (see *De Anima*), is clearly stated in Descartes, *Regulae*, no. XII.

I shall add three more, drawn from his own discussions. His list consists of 'l'amour-propre, la passion, l'intelligence, et l'habitude' (III, 896/12.247, 'egoism, passion, intellect and habit'); each of these has a good and a bad side. The factor which most distorts recognition of the true nature of our sensations or impressions is passion or, more particularly, desire; this fact the narrator claims to have learned from Bloch (III, 610/11.267). The operations of our desire resist our consciousness, let alone our analysis, primarily because they seek above all to be satisfied (I, 614/3.266). Under the influence of desire the primary thought is one of perfection (II, 46/5.53); it is always an ideal person, that is to say an imaginary one, that we love (III, 453/11.51). Just as Swann had been a lover of phantoms (II, 1013/8.218), so the narrator's love for Gilberte, at least initially, was love for an idea (I, 410, 795/2.265; 4.131); indeed, the narrator comes to see himself as having pursued, all along, the abstract notion of 'la jeunesse' (III, 644/11.314, 'girl-hood'). Similarly, just as Elstir found, or thought he found, an ideal beauty in Gabrielle (I, 850/4.208), so it was an ideal of femininity (I, 860/4.223) as conveyed by Botticelli that Swann sought to find in Odette (I, 224/2.8). Because ideals, when recognized as such, are associated with the unattainable, and the unattainable itself causes a desire for its possession, the narrator argues that the thought of an ideal creates the desire for possession of it. Although our desires are initially governed by our perceptions (III, 487/11.98), it is also true that desire for possession may underlie initial curiosity in someone (I, 788/4.122); in such a case, presumably, the desire takes its root from an antecedent perception or thought. Not only is desire a function of the largely unknown (III, 142/3.185), but it increases with the uncertainty of the attainment of its object (II, 726/7.174). The narrator concludes that *we* create the object of our love (I, 858; III, 503/4.220; 11.120); we love only the inaccessible (III, 384/10.245), that which we do not possess (III, 106/9.138); we love only in ignorance of those we love (II, 282/5.388). It is even claimed that if possession is what we want, then possession of the loved object brings greater joy than love itself (III, 496, 51/11.111; 9.59), but much depends on what is meant by 'possession' here;

the long episode in which Albertine is kept physical prisoner, and the narrator becomes his own mental prisoner would otherwise seem to contradict this view. The desire for possession illustrates the degree of egoism in love, which explains why we do not relish the achievement of possession unless the desired object has shown resistance (II, 362/6.73). The narrator even equates the infinite aspects of love with the infinite aspects of egoism (III, 495/11.110). The lover's egoism, as portrayed by the narrator himself, explains his self-indulgence towards his fantasies and fears, and the invariably masochistic pursuit of knowledge about his loved one— knowledge which will reveal that the object of love has been an ideal.

We commonly assume our desire to be reciprocated; we transfer our desire to its object (I, 887/4.260). Even when it is reciprocated we may fail to recognize the signs, as did the narrator on the first occasion he saw Gilberte, near the hawthorns. On the other hand, when there is no reciprocation this may be a result of the operations of our own jealousy (II, 1124/8.374); for jealousy is itself an aspect of the desire for possession; it is the need to be tyrannical (III, 91/9.115). Here again egoism operates; for predictability is a function of our knowledge, and our inability to predict arouses our jealousy for any person in whom we are interested. The jealousy of Swann and Marcel increases in direct proportion to their ignorance of the activities of Odette and Albertine. Having argued that we create the object of our love, the narrator now urges that love is what we feel for the person whose actions arouse our jealousy (III, 61/9.72); we thus become victims of our own mental fabrications. Since the narrator believes, as we have seen, that our desires are governed by our perceptions of the external world, we might say that for him the cause of our desire is in the external world, but that the object of our desire is in our minds. Desire also engenders belief in its objects (III, 511/11.132), as when the narrator felt that he 'knew' which of the three girls who called on the Duchesse was 'Mlle d'Eporcheville' (III, 563/11.203). And this example is doubly instructive, because it shows not only how association of ideas operates in the formation of desires

(I, 196/1.270), but also a case where the facts coincided with an imaginative construction, although there was no means of discovering this at the time.

When we are in love we are unable to talk about our state, even to recognize it (I, 611/3.263); to recognize the state we need separation from the object of our love (III, 506/11.124). Marcel only realized that he loved Albertine after he lost possession of her, and the same may perhaps be said of his relations with Gilberte; on the other hand, they, perhaps, came to love him only after separation from him. Although there are many passages in which the narrator seems to identify desire with love, a reader should not be misled; for desire is essentially a state associated with the present and future which blinds one's perception and conjures up an ideal; love, however, is a state associated only with the past. This retrospective recognition, which occurs also in connection with other states, such as pleasure (I, 872; III, 877/4.240; 12.223), is related to two important points in the narrator's philosophical views. First, realization follows the death of the state, even, in a sense, the death of the self who had the state (I, 671; III, 484, 488, 595, 599, 642, 1038/3.349; 11.94, 100, 249, 257, 311; 12.421)—there is a suspicion that the narrator has here confused temporal and logical priority. What we love, therefore, is in the past (III, 440/11.32). Secondly, this retrospection emphasizes the discrepancy between what we feel and what can be communicated about what we feel (III, 258/10.70). Indeed, the narrator comes to view language, because of its conceptual character and the conventionality which ensures its very utility, as an additional barrier to knowledge (rather in the way Levin did. See above, p. 98); and when in this frame of mind he seems to follow Walter Pater in regarding music as the perfect language for communicating emotions, in the sense of what we feel, precisely because he considers music to lack conventional conceptual aspects. It should not be thought that our desires are effective in achieving their ends; on the contrary, they are powerless: 'nous n'arrivons pas à changer les choses selon notre désir, mais peu a peu notre désir change.' (III, 451/11.48, 'we do not succeed in changing things according to our desire, but gradu-

ally our desire changes'.) Without attempting to impose illusory
order on the narrator's views a number of puzzles must be separated and answered. How are desire and love related, and how is
the object of desire related to the object of love? How is the claim
that we create the object of our love related to the claim that what
we love is 'trop dans le passé, consiste trop dans le temps perdu
ensemble pour qu'on ait besoin de toute la femme' (III, 440/11.32,
'too much in the past, consists too much in the time that we have
spent together for us to require the whole woman')? If what we
desire are largely fictions, and if we can only recognize our states
after the event, can we be sure that we recognize them aright?
What, precisely, do we come to recognize? Do we come to see
that our state has been one of desire, or do we come to grasp the
nature of the external object to which that desire had been attached, however tenuously? It might be suggested that the narrator, far from identifying love with desire, clearly contrasts them;
the relations between his grandmother and his mother, and between them and him is quite different from most of the other
relationships described under the heading of 'love'. He might be
interpreted as saying that most instances of what we take to be
love are in fact instances of egotistical desires. This relatively un-
exciting view is not entirely compatible with the narrator's observations on perception and knowledge; and it is because of his
philosophical position on these latter concepts that he so frequently
and seemingly without thought, speaks of love and desire inter-
changeably. Anticipating my later discussion this much may be
said here. The sense in which the narrator believes that we create
the object of desire is this: we select from our impressions of the
external world only those aspects which are conformable to our
antecedent interests and emotional condition; these antecedents
not only determine the selection but also augment it, so that the
resulting percept resembles the actual object of perception only (if
at all) when the operations of the antecedent elements have been
checked or nullified. Essentially, the narrator believes that when
we are in the emotional state we call love, we confuse the desire
for physical possession with the only true form of possession,

spiritual or mental possession (II, 351/6.57), by which he means 'knowledge'. Desire and knowledge are mutually exclusive.

So far we have sketched only one of the obstacles to knowledge. We have seen how desire deceives us about the true nature of our impressions, and how the object of desire reflects the ex-pression of our internal needs rather than the im-pression of external phenomena. Knowledge is achieved only of past states, and the melancholy claim that love is of the past refers not only to the view that past conceptions operate in the formation of desires for present objects, and not only to the view that one cannot know that it is love that one feels; but also to the view that one comes to long for the 'new' person, the real person, of whose nature one acquires knowledge only when the fabrications are destroyed. The old desires give way to a new love; but it is a love whose only effective outlet is acceptance of the knowledge won. I now turn to two of my additions to the narrator's list of obstacles; imagination and memory.

For Robert de Saint Loup, Rachel was a woman created out of his successive desires (II, 161/5.216); the realm of these constructions is the imagination. Although reality can force us to abandon our musings (II, 13/5.6), the operations of imagination may blind us to features of that reality (II, 159/5.213), primarily because imagination is subject to its own laws of perspective (II, 235/5.322). The imagination is the realm of our hopes and desires for the future (I, 626/3.284), but because it is logically impossible to imagine the unknown (III, 424/11.8), the possibilities it conceives are based essentially on the past; in this respect imagination resembles memory. The association of ideas, itself an intrinsically dangerous activity (III, 574/11.218), takes place in imagination, and arises particularly in connection with the evocative powers of proper names (II, 568/6.355). For names are not only the stimuli to associations, but are also the tokens of our imaginative constructions; as such, they, too, may cause disillusion, when the persons or phenomena to which we have applied the name no longer exist under the forms associated with it (III, 956/12.321). Names are the static representatives of instants in time, labels accorded to particular impressions in memory or imagination (cf. the quotation from G. H. Lewes, p. 60); artists such as Elstir are commended for combating the intellectual notions contained in names by continually re-naming phenomena. 'Les noms qui désignent les choses répondent toujours à une notion de l'intelligence, étrangère à nos impressions véritables, et qui nous force à éliminer d'elles tout ce qui ne se rapporte pas à cette notion' (I, 835/4.187, 'The names which denote things correspond invariably to an intellectual notion, alien to our true impressions, and compelling us to eliminate from them everything that is not in keeping with that notion'). The obstacles to knowledge erected by the operations of and within imagination are many: imagination is as inaccurate as vision (I, 548/3.171); it falsifies because it is based on the past; as the domain of names (II, 524/6.295) it inculcates the errors of habit as well as of fantasy, such that neither Guermantes nor Balbec, neither Swann nor Odette, indeed such that nothing resembles its name (II, 438/6.179); and the operations of imagination bring inevitable disillusion because the world of possibilities is richer than reality (II, 115/5.151). There are only two favourable features to note. There is less egoism in pure imagination than in recollection (II, 754/7.216); for self-esteem is as decisive a factor in limiting our capacities to remember (III, 972/12.342) as in blinding us even to our own physical appearance (II, 272/5.374: see the similar remark in *Middlemarch* (39.288) to the effect that 'even our own persons in the glass are apt to change their aspect for us after we have heard some frank remark on their less admirable points'). Secondly, it is only by an act of imagination that we can isolate phenomena from their environment in order to grasp their essence and their individuality (I, 645/3.310).

Memory, as associated with imagination, is both an obstacle and an essential clue to knowledge. Here, the narrator distinguishes between voluntary and involuntary memory, correlated with which distinction are two senses of the past—the past that we discover afterwards, and the past that we retain in ourselves (III, 87/9.109).[1] In *Middlemarch* there are several references to the

---

[1] Cf. the opening sentences of the Préface to Marcel Proust, *Contre Sainte-Beuve*.

autonomy of memory. Raffles recalled Ladislaw's name as a result of the operations of 'unconscious memory' (53.389), and when Bulstrode's memory was 'set smarting' he came to realize that 'a man's past is . . . still a quivering part of himself' (61.450). In *A la recherche du temps perdu* the narrator holds that voluntary memory does not preserve the past itself (I, 44/1.57), but only isolated instants from the past, the record of which may be doubly distorted; first, by the initial perceptions, themselves a function of our interests at the time, secondly, by our interests in remembering them now (I, 949/4.348). Even groups of memories of instants would be inadequate (II, 1021/8.230), because the aim is not to remember *that* something occurred, but to recall the actual experience from the past, to have it again, but as if for the first time (III, 873/12.218). Such a process is involuntary, and the narrator asserts that we have knowledge only of involuntary sensations (III, 166/9.220)—he presumably means involuntarily recalled sensations. Conscious memories are unreliable as a basis for knowledge because, although memory is powerless to invent (III, 555/11.190), not all memories are genuine (III, 593/11.245); for example, there is no distinguishing difference between a memory of a dream and one of reality (III, 651/11.318), just as there is none between the memory of a dead person and that of a fiction (III, 508/11.130). The point here is that it would be impossible to distinguish, by examining the memory-content alone, a memory of a fiction from a memory of a dead person. An analogous point was made in *Middlemarch*, as we have seen; the mere possibilities of imagination carry no mark and exhibit no criterion, by means of which one can know which possibilities are actualized in the world and which are figments of the mind.

Passion, imagination, and conscious memory are not the only obstacles to knowledge, and brief mention must now be made of two others, the intellect and habit. The intellect issues false judgements because, forming general notions by abstraction from particular cases, it treats the essentially transient as permanent, by applying categories that blind us to individuality (III, 66/9.80). Reason, in fact, joins with desire as an opponent of the truth

(II,1117/8.365). This feature of the intellect is to be associated with the heavy curtain of habit (III, 544/11.175). Habit is a force which suppresses the originality and even the consciousness of our perceptions; at the same time, it is a deity which, if detached from us, can inflict upon us the most cruel suffering (III, 420/11.3). Habit is most apparent in conventions such as language; thus habit explains the mispronunciations of Françoise and the lift-boy. Habit is the residue of outmoded convention, whether at Combray or Balbec, *chez* Guermantes or *chez* Verdurin. The habit of thinking may make us immune to reality, may prevent us from feeling it (III, 602/11.256)—we should remember that the distinction was drawn in *Middlemarch* (42.311) between merely knowing that something was the case, and 'feeling the truth' of something. Habit obscures the present, which explains how we may live with evil, as in war time, unconcerned about, indeed unconscious of, its presence (III, 535/11.163). But we cannot live without habit, for it secures us against perpetual bewilderment at the new and the transient. 'Si l'habitude est une seconde nature, elle nous empêche de connaître la première, dont elle n'a ni les cruautés, ni les enchantements' (II, 754/7.215, 'If habit is a second nature, it prevents us from knowing our original nature, whose cruelties and enchantments it lacks').

THE NATURE OF REALITY

Brief reference has now been made to six of the factors which prevent us from grasping the nature of our impressions: egoism, passion, intellect, habit, imagination, conscious memory. To the seventh factor, time, I shall refer later. The account so far has been almost entirely negative, and since it is a mistake to suppose that we ordinarily perceive reality (III, 573/11.217), we need to ask: what is the nature of reality and the nature of our knowledge of it? The narrator regards the self as a composite of its own modes of perception (III, 430, 466ft/11.17); and he regards other persons as composites of the series of emotions we have experienced in the past in connection with them, and which habit has attached to them (III, 433/11.21). It is thus not only because of our desire that he claims the woman we love is created by our own nature (I, 585, 858/3.225; 4.219), for all persons are constructions out of our thoughts and emotions (I, 84, 797/1.111; 4.134). This is the sense in which knowledge of others is deemed impossible (I, 874/2.242); we understand only the characters of those who do not interest us (I, 895/4.271), those, that is, of whom we have received impressions involuntarily and perhaps unwittingly. (Compare this view with the view I inferred from *Middlemarch*, above, pp. 23, 30.) And it is with this implicit reference to the agent's activities in seeking knowledge that the narrator asserts that one has no means of determining reality (II, 799/7.278). He concludes from this that the only reality there is for us lies in the domain of our own sensibility or feeling (III, 884/12.233). What we *call* reality, he says, is a relation between those sensations and memories which simultaneously encircle us (III, 889/12.238); 'la véritable réalité n'étant dégagée que par l'esprit, étant l'objet d'une opération spirituelle, nous ne connaissons vraiment que ce que nous sommes obligés de recréer par la pensée' (II, 770/7.237, 'true reality being discoverable only by the mind, being the object of a mental operation; we truly know only what we have been forced to recreate by thought'). If it is correct to say that 'tout est dans l'esprit' (III, 912/12.271, 'everything is in the mind'), then there is a sense in which truth may be thought to be relative to one's point of view. 'On ne reçoit pas la sagesse, il faut la découvrir soi-même après un trajet que personne ne peut faire pour nous, ne peut nous épargner, car elle est un point de vue sur les choses' (I, 864/4.228, 'Wisdom is not given to us; we must discover it for ourselves, by means of a journey that no one else can make for us and from which no one can absolve us; for wisdom is a point of view'). It is not that the narrator denies the existence of the external world; on the contrary, he is at pains to contrast objective reality with our subjective reactions to it (III, 912/12.271). But he seeks to stress two points, the first of which is the difficulty of sifting the evidence about reality. For example, when we realize that the truth is not always conveyed directly (II, 65/5.81), we may then mistakenly look for and accept only indirect evidence (III, 88/9.111); thus, the narrator, having failed to grasp how Françoise conveyed the truth indirectly, also failed to grasp later how Albertine conveyed it directly. Secondly, he wishes to emphasize the sense in which even the knowledge we achieve remains 'subjective'. 'Ce que nous n'avons pas eu à déchiffrer, à éclaircir par notre effort personnel, ce qui était clair avant nous, n'est pas à nous' (III, 880/12.227, 'What we have not had to decipher, to clarify by our own personal effort, is not ours'). This is the true spiritual possession to which I referred above, and which is to be equated with knowledge. But how is knowledge achieved, and who best achieves it? The narrator's answer to these questions is best given by reference to what he says about the role of the artist; and this account itself may be usefully prefaced by noting the positive role of the intellect in the acquisition of knowledge.

'C'est la vie qui, peu à peu, cas par cas, nous permet de remarquer que ce qui est le plus important pour notre cœur, ou pour notre esprit, ne nous est pas appris par le raisonnement, mais par des puissances autres. Et alors, c'est l'intelligence elle-même qui, se rendant compte de leur supériorité, abdique, par raisonnement, devant elles, et accepte de devenir leur collaboratrice et leur servante. Foi expérimentale' (III, 423/11.7, 'It is life which, gradually and case by case, allows us to pick out what is most important to our heart or our mind; for this cannot be learned by reasoning, but only by other means. And then it is the intellect itself which, taking note of the superiority of those other means, abdicates in their favour, on rational grounds, and consents to become their collaborator and their servant. "Applied" faith'). (Compare this view with George Eliot's quotation from Mackay, cited above, p. 57.) But when experiment confirms faith, what are the criteria of verification? How do we know when reality matches our ideal? Such an occasion arose when Mme Swann told the narrator that Gilberte regarded him as her favourite (I, 537/3.155); but the reader is informed that in such a situation one is unable to construct one's former state of longing in order to compare it with, and savour, its present realization. And yet it is hard to see why it follows from this inability alone, that our ideal has been realized.

In any case it is likely that the narrator takes truth to be its own guarantee, without need of any criterion; for otherwise it would be possible to doubt whether the narrator's experiences at the final Guermantes matinée, for example, were instances of genuine recall. I postpone further discussion of the intellect in order to return to the narrator's views about the artist.

THE ROLE OF THE ARTIST

He who best achieves knowledge is the artist who follows his instinct (III, 880/12.226). Fortuitousness is the guardian, the narrator believes, of the truth of the series of impressions we re-call. The artist's task is to find mental (*spirituel*) equivalents for his involuntarily recalled sensations, in order to convey them to others (III, 879/12.225); equivalents which express the individual-ity and essence of the phenomena (III, 885/12.233). The distinction to bear in mind, as always, is between having sensations and think-ing about them (III, 869/12.213); and the warning to heed is that the present may not be captured by our senses, nor the past by our intellect (III, 872/12.217). The artist's problem is to avoid both the conscious resurrection of memory material and the conscious manipulation of whatever unconscious material presents itself (III, 870/12.215). At the end of the novel the narrator strives to show the sense in which we retain the past within ourselves, and the consequences of this retention (III, 1047/12.432); he believes he can show this only by transcribing life in a way other than that conveyed by our erring senses (III, 1045/12.430), and that involves grappling with the problem of Time. We shall return to these matters shortly. For the moment we need note only that for the required transcription description is said to be inadequate, because it necessarily uses old concepts for new phenomena; what is needed is a detailed comparison and contrast of the same and different phenomena from different standpoints (III, 885/12.233), and the resulting picture will be highly complex. 'Car nous sen-tons que la vie est un peu plus compliquée qu'on ne dit, et même les circonstances. Et il y a une nécessité pressante à montrer cette complexité' (III, 916/12.273, 'For we feel that life is rather more complex than is generally thought, and so are particular circumstances. And there is a pressing need to show this complexity.'). A similar reference to making 'the mind flexible with constant comparison' occurred in *Middlemarch* (22.157).

We have seen how the data of knowledge, our impressions, are distorted by the operations of various factors such as desire and habit, imagination and intellect, so that we are unable to determine their true characteristics. We noted the narrator's view that since reflection presupposes its objects, conscious knowledge is always of the past; the only present knowledge was said to be involuntary memories of past sensations. He holds that the living past, that which we involuntarily recall, is present; the consciously past is dead. But clearly even the knowledge of the living past is knowledge of the *past*. Reality is something created by each of us in our own minds, and this creation is intimately related to genuine knowledge, or spiritual possession. In this creation the artist plays a crucial role. The over-all impression of the account so far is inescapably negative; the positive side of the narrator's epistemology must therefore be examined, in order to redress the balance. For although he stresses the difficulty of, and the obstacles to, attaining knowledge, he also stresses that, in spite of everything, we can and sometimes do succeed (I, 949/4.348).

The all-pervading influence of man's memories, whether in the form of habits or concepts or whatever, together with the pain and illusion they bring, are simply consequences of the fact that we all seek to cope with the unknown and apparently unassimilable in terms of the known and already assimilated; we all see the new in terms of the old. The narrator argues that it is the suffering thus engendered which alone enables us to conquer the inertia of thinking (III, 908/12.263); and it does this because pain is a phenomenon that admits of no argument, only obedience (II, 744/7.199). It is in this sense that 'la souffrance est la meilleure chose qu'on puisse rencontrer dans la vie' (III, 909/12.264, 'suffering is the best thing one could meet with in life')—to which Ivan Karamazov might have retorted that such a view does nothing to justify the amount of suffering actually experienced in the world. Suffering develops the power of the mind because it forces us to look again at phenomena, unhampered by habit (III, 906/12.260): it forces us 'à prendre les choses au sérieux, arrachant chaque fois les mauvaises herbes de l'habitude, du scepticisme, de la légèrité, de l'indifférence ('to take things seriously, pulling up the weeds of habit, scepticism, frivolity and indifference'). The narrator postulates the following model: without happiness, of which hoping is a form, there would be no suffering (III, 907/12.261); for when we are happy we form attachments whose rupture causes sorrow: 'quant au bonheur, il n'a presque qu'une seule utilité, rendre le malheur possible' ('happiness serves hardly any purpose other than to make unhappiness possible'). The happiness associated with an ideal will give way to suffering when we realize that our ideal is an illusion; the pain we then feel will force us to grapple with reality. The major hazard to avoid at this stage is the assumption that the degree of pain we feel is equatable with the degree of truth we attain (II, 834/7.326). It appears that suffering is not only a sufficient condition for most of us to re-examine our experiences, but also a necessary condition; because suffering plays a crucial role in the life of him who, above all, achieves knowledge, namely, the artist (III, 896, 905/12.248, 259). There is a sense in which the artist, because he is speaking for all men, transforms felt sorrows into ideas while he is at work, and in this way fuses the particular with the general (III, 904–6/12.257–60).

Elstir the painter, it will be remembered, is praised for having stripped himself, when confronting reality, of every intellectual concept: 'L'effort qu'Elstir faisait pour se dépouiller en présence de la réalité de toutes les notions de son intelligence était d'autant plus admirable que cet homme qui avant de peindre se faisait ignorant, oubliait tout par probité (car ce qu'on sait n'est pas à soi), avait justement une intelligence exceptionnellement cultivée' (I, 840/4.193, 'The effort Elstir made, when face to face with reality, to cast aside all intellectual notions, was all the more admirable in that this man, who before sitting down to paint made himself ignorant, forgetting everything, in the integrity of his purpose (since what one knows ceases to exist in itself), in fact had an exceptionally cultivated mind'). Elstir is credited with showing us things not as he knew them to be, but according to the optical illusions of which our first sight of them is composed: 'ne pas exposer les choses telles qu'il savait qu'elles étaient, mais selon ces illusions optiques dont notre vision première est faite' (I, 838/4.191). Further, Elstir is compared with Dostoevsky in presenting things not in their logical sequence, beginning with the cause, but in the reverse order, beginning with the effect, the illusion that strikes us (III, 379/10.238). Now what does 'illusion' mean here, and why is Elstir praised for showing us illusions? At this stage the tension to which the narrator subjects such terms as 'reality', 'illusion', 'impression', can no longer be disguised.

THE NATURE OF IMPRESSIONS AND OF KNOWLEDGE

It is 'en présence de la réalité' ('when face to face with reality') that the artist, such as Elstir, seeks to disabuse himself of the blinding operations of intellectual concepts. Reality is indeed things as they are, but it is not what we think we know it to be ('telles qu'il savait qu'elles étaient'), for we generally take our first impressions to be illusory. Paradoxically, the illusion is what we believe we know, and what we believe to be illusory is true; every impression is 'singulière et pourtant vraie' (I, 838/12.191, not translated: 'unique and yet true'). On the other hand, as we have already seen, reality is said to be in the mind, not things as they are; it is nothing other than a construction either by or of our sensations; in this case illusion consists simply in a general and inadequate grasp of the nature of our sensations. But in this second sense of 'reality', which exists in the mind, one is inclined to ask: of what are the sensations sensations? It has often been argued that whereas sensations cannot have, perceptions must have, external objects.[1] Proust's narrator seems not to make this distinction which, in any case, is likely to be obscured if a single verb 'to feel' covers both sensations and perceptions; we saw just this conflation in *Anna*

[1] e.g. Thomas Reid, *An Inquiry into the Human Mind*, (1764), Ch. 6, section 20. Aristotle, *De Anima* is one of the primary sources of the view.

Karenina. What, then, are the objects of one's impressions? In the first sense of the term, reality is that of which one has sensations; in the second sense reality just consists of those sensations. If all our first impressions are illusory a number of difficult questions arises; such as how we would correctly identify the object of which our first impression was necessarily illusory. Indeed, one might wonder why artists should be praised for preserving illusions, since, according to the narrator, we most of us suffer from these most of the time. Such comment would be unjust, because the narrator's view may be paraphrased thus: we often think our first impressions are illusory because our subsequent ideas do not, and cannot, fully incorporate them; but, in fact, it is our first *ideas* that are illusory, not the primary impressions which are their foundation.

An artist such as Elstir makes two truth claims in his work. He says, first, 'My impression was this', and secondly, 'In some sense one can be misled by it.' The sense in which the impression misleads is the sense in which our intellect mistakes, initially, the nature of the relations, whatever they are, between impressions and their objects. It is not our impressions that are illusory, but their initial interpretations by our interpreting mind. That is, the nature of our first impressions cannot be specified, even to ourselves, without some form of interpretation or intellectual operation: 'nous n'identifierions pas les objects si nous ne faisions pas intervenir le raisonnement' (II, 419/6.153, 'we should never identify objects if we did not make some process of reasoning intervene'). But this very act, albeit logically unavoidable, destroys the uniqueness of the present experience by applying to it terms or concepts which have been applied in previous cases: 'Les surfaces et les volumes sont en réalité indépendants des noms d'objets que notre mémoire leur impose quand nous les avons reconnus' (II, 419/6.154, 'surfaces and volumes are in fact independent of the names of objects which our memory imposes on them after we have recognized them'). Underlying the narrator's view is the doctrine that there are no percepts without concepts; for one cannot talk of mistakenly seeing something *as* something else, without implying the application of concepts. The narrator's terse comment that the effect which strikes us is an illusion may be unwrapped, perhaps, in the following way. If we subscribe to the universality of the causal law, to describe an event as an *effect* is vacuous, since all events are effects. But *a priori*, as Hume observed,[1] anything may be the effect of anything else; in ignorance of the particular cause we are likely to be deprived of descriptions essential for the designation of the 'effect' in question. And since we rarely, if ever, have impressions of the cause simultaneously with impressions of the effect, to assign a cause to the event of which we are having present impressions necessitates the intervention of the intellect, at least under the guise of memory. To be of use, impressions must be interpreted; generally, the most practically valuable descriptions will be, at some stage and in some form, causally referential, and hence backward-looking. Here, once more, we see a sense in which the narrator believes that our knowledge is essentially of the past: 'à peine l'impression reçue, nous descendons insenbilement la pente du souvenir' (I, 917/4.302, 'no sooner is the impression received, than we begin insensibly to descend the slope of memory'). The narrator provides numerous examples of occasions on which, ignorant of the causal story behind the phenomena of which he is having impressions, he fails to find a description adequate to the phenomena; or, to put the point differently, the appropriate description which will issue in one's realization of the situation, itself depends on knowledge about the connections between this event and others. Thus, ignorant of the name and character of the sitter, the narrator failed to grasp the nature of the ambiguity in the early Elstir portrait of *Miss Sacripant*, alias Odette (I, 849/4.207). It is undeniable, however, that the narrator occasionally reiterates his inconsistent views that our initial impressions are themselves illusory, and that they them-

---

[1] David Hume, *A Treatise of Human Nature*, (1739), Book I, Part IV, Section 5; and *An Inquiry Concerning Human Understanding* (1748), Section XII, Part 3. Mention of Hume in this context is not inappropriate; the narrator refers to Hume's observation that the mere association of ideas can give to phenomena the illusion of causal necessity (III, 504/11.121), and he uses the view to account for a common tendency to see whatever good or evil occurs as having been inevitable.

selves are not illusory but that only our first interpretations of them are.

But why, in any case, is so much importance attached to first impressions? The narrator's view is that all our subsequent thinking about a thing depends on what we take our initial impression to be; the impression is the foundation of all we know, and it dominates even if it does not also determine the nature of our subsequent impressions of the same thing. (Compare the discussion of 'feeling' as a basis of knowledge in *Middlemarch*, above, p. 46.) Thus the narrator's first impression of Albertine on the beach remains with him throughout his subsequent experiences of her: 'je ne peux pas lui conférer rétrospectivement une identité qu'elle n'avait pas pour moi au moment où elle a frappé mes yeux' (I, 846/4.202, 'I am unable to confer on her retrospectively an identity which she did not have for me at the moment she caught my eye'). If things are mental constructions out of our impressions, the essence we confer on those things will be inseparable from the impressions; this, indeed, is the sense in which the narrator claims that impressions may be said to be the essence of things; to get at the essence of a thing we therefore need to grasp the nature of our first impression, and it is only the difficulty of the latter task, the primary task, that entitles him to speak of 'l'essence permanente et habituellement cachée des choses' (III, 873/12.218, 'the permanent, yet characteristically hidden, essence of things'). Before turning to some of the more obvious puzzles in this account it is worth trying to unravel the narrator's claim that sometimes one's first glance reveals the true proportions of something or somebody, as he felt his own initial glance at Albertine did (III, 609/11.266). If the essence of Albertine, or anyone else, is founded on the first impression, we may wonder how he can speak of this essence as true or false; for the notion of truth here presupposes an independent something against which one is measuring one's first impression; but, by definition, this independent thing will be mediated by our impression of *it*, and so on. It is as if the narrator postulates two worlds; the world independent of our impressions, which is the ground of them, that is, that *of* which they are impressions; and the world built of our impressions. There is an Albertine independent of us, and there is our Albertine, existing only in the mind and built out of our impressions of the external Albertine. Now this view need be nothing more exceptional than the commonplace that concepts are distinguishable from their objects; for example, that the narrator's concept of Albertine is to be distinguished from Albertine herself. And it may be that this is all he means; in spite of the fact that he seems to accord a peculiar ontological status to the construction out of impressions, to what I have called concepts. It is unlikely that this is all of the narrator's meaning, however; for although he accepts that even our first impressions of a thing must be interpreted, he also wants to stress the importance of their pristine, uninterpreted states. On this account he would have to postulate at least three Albertines, a move to which he is not averse, as we shall see: the first is the person in the external world called Albertine; the second is she who is epitomized in, or represented by, one's first, immediate, unmediated impression of her; the third is she who is represented by one's concept of her, which concept is a construction out of one's several impressions. The narrator holds, we should remember, that 'nous sentons dans un monde, nous pensons, nous nommons dans un autre, nous pouvons entre les deux établir une concordance mais non combler l'intervalle' (II, 50/5.58, 'we feel in one world, we think, we give names, in another; we can bring the two into harmony, but never fill in the gap'). One might thus distinguish between the 'felt' Albertine of one's first impression and one's concept of her. Before developing this point it may be helpful to take our bearings on the discussion so far.

The basic data of knowledge were said to be sensations or impressions; and the artist was said to be best able to convey to us the nature of this data, because he is able to combat the distorting operations of concepts and passions. He is able to show us that it is itself an illusion to suppose our first impressions are illusory, for they are, in fact, true; and he does this by presenting to us again the very impressions we had thought were illusory. Initially, it was unclear whether the narrator held that the impressions themselves were in some sense faulty, for this common view to obtain, or whether it was what we did to them in the way of interpretation that was faulty. Secondly, recalling what he said of reality as a creation of our mind, it was unclear how reality could also be that in the presence of which the artist sought to disabuse himself of outworn concepts in order to present the truth about it. In other words, it was unclear whether phenomena were held to be independent of, or dependent on, our perceptions; and how, if the narrator wished to fuse these tenets, he would do it. He could argue, and at times does (III, 191/9.255), that the so-called external reality is best defined in terms of the sum of all actual and possible perceptions of it; but that each one of us only has a contingent selection of these perceptions, in terms of which our own concept of reality must be necessarily interpreted; and that the object of our perception, what our impressions are of, must itself be analysed in terms of impressions, whether ours or others. On such a view impressions are the atoms of knowledge, and our knowledge of all things is mediated by our impressions of them. Now even if our acts of apprehending are mental operations, and even if our knowledge depends on such operations, this would not put the objects themselves, which we perceive, in the mind. And it is important to note that the narrator, for all that he tends to subscribe to the view I have just outlined, constantly reminds himself of the independence and reality of the external world. Indeed, that of which we are having impressions can only be specified by reference to the external world; because, if we say that here again impressions intervene, not only does a perpetual regress ensue, but an unbridgeable gap opens between objects and our impressions of them. All these comments are entirely commonplace, of course, and will be familiar, in any case, from my discussion of them in the chapter on *Middlemarch*; but they are worth repeating because of the importance the narrator attaches to impressions, particularly first impressions. An explanation of his claim that our initial impressions of someone are sometimes accurate may now be attempted. Sometimes our first impression will catch the quintessence of someone, but whether it does or not can be determined only subsequently. Only comparison with other impressions will establish the coherence, consistency, centrality, or eccentricity of the first impression. But in any case it forms the first step to forming our concept of the person, because it is in the light of previous experience, in this case the first impression, that we interpret subsequent impressions.

There should now be less difficulty in reconciling the narrator's view that, in one sense, our concepts of other people are constructions out of our impressions of those people, and his view that from learning the nature of other people's passions and desires and defects, we come to recognize our own. It is only failure to remember that it is our concept which is the construction, not the people themselves, that obscures the situation. There is, nevertheless, an issue to be unravelled. We learn about ourselves from others in the ways mentioned (I, 129; II, 65/1.175; 5.81) only when our perception of them is not blurred by passion and interest; in other words, from people who do not at the time greatly concern us (I, 895; III, 519/4.271; 11.143). To these people alone are we able to apply our dispassionate attention; but the knowledge that we thus gain is likely to induce a shocked scepticism. For example, it was the realization that Françoise did not think as highly of him as he supposed, that led the narrator to speculate 'que toute réalité est peut-être aussi dissemblable de celle que nous croyons percevoir directement et que nous composons à l'aide d'idées qui ne se montrent pas mais sont agissantes' (II, 67/5.83, 'that all reality is perhaps quite different from what we believe ourselves to be directly perceiving, and that we construct with the help of ideas that do not show themselves, but are nonetheless influential'). He is careful to stress, however, that if noticing largely depends on expectation, expectation itself is invariably the offspring of habit; and, as such, operates fatally against the recognition of the unique and previously unexperienced. Indeed, of the unique there literally can be no recognition; even if we can, as it were, immediately sense that it is unique. An anticipatory suspicion was a necessary condition for Swann to form the belief that Odette was lying to him (I, 297/2.110); and it was precisely the operation of expectation, in the form of pre-formed notions of what constituted theatrical excellence, that prevented the narrator from appreciating Berma (I, 481/3.74), even if he was also, in a sense, aware of the excellence (II, 47/5.55). But if habit, imagination, passion, and intellect operate on our perceptions without our consciousness of them, it is also the case that a further barrier to obtaining knowledge is our own self-consciousness, which interposes between us and its objects (I, 87/1.116). A reader may wonder how the narrator is entitled to claim that knowledge of some people is possible, albeit of those who do not interest us at the time, and also that no knowledge of others is possible. One reason for this latter, total scepticism, is to be found in his views about Time.

KNOWLEDGE OF PERSONS

The narrator contends that while our original impression of a person undergoes correction, the person himself changes. It is always and only the old impressions, which we have already formed that we clarify, but which also no longer represent him: 'tandis que se rectifie la vision que nous avons de lui, lui-même, qui n'est pas un objectif inerte, change pour son compte, nous pensons le rattraper, il se déplace, et, croyant le voir enfin plus clairement, ce n'est que les images anciennes que nous en avions prises que nous avons réussi à éclaircir, mais qui ne le représentent plus' (I, 874/ 4.242, 'while our original impression of him undergoes amendment, he himself changes, since he is not an inanimate object; we think we have caught him, he moves, and when we imagine that at last we are seeing him clearly, it is only the old impressions which we had already formed of him that we have succeeded in making clear, but when they no longer represent him'). Here, then, the changes brought about by the operation of time, together with the passage of time during which one strives to clarify one's first impression, combine to preclude anything but knowledge of the past. Now this thesis seems to be a temporal one about what follows what in the course of time, whereas the former version, which he often holds simultaneously, was a logical thesis, namely, that knowledge requires the logical priority of its objects. To the objection that on the temporal thesis one could at least attain knowledge of inanimate objects, or of any phenomena not subject to the specified ravages of time, it is not unlikely that the narrator would retort by making use of the logical thesis, arguing that our knowledge of anything presupposes our experience of it. This aside, he neither precisely characterizes the nature of the clarificatory activity which operates on impressions, nor does he indicate the nature of the assurances which indicate genuine clarification.

We have noted already the sense in which our concepts both of the self and of others are constructions from our impressions; but it is not clear whether the constituent impressions play their role in the constructed concept before or after they have been correctly interpreted. The following passage does not settle the issue, but it shows the narrator's temptation to abandon the notion of a concept as a complex construction in favour of the view that there is one concept for each impression; and, further, a presupposition of the passage appears to be a notion of the basic data of knowledge, impressions, as true and unquestioned reports which are to be simply accepted.

C'est peut-être parce qu'étaient si divers les êtres que je contemplais en elle à cette époque que, plus tard, je pris l'habitude de devenir moi-même un personnage autre selon celle des Albertine à laquelle je pensais: un jaloux, un indifférent, un voluptueux, un mélancolique, un furieux, recréés, non seulement au hasard du souvenir qui renaissait, mais selon la force de la croyance interposée, pour un même souvenir, par la façon différente dont je l'appréciais. Car c'est toujours à cela qu'il fallait revenir, à ces croyances qui la plupart du temps remplissent notre âme à notre insu, mais qui ont pourtant plus d'importance pour notre bonheur que tel être que nous voyons, car c'est à travers elles que nous le voyons, ce sont elles qui assignent sa grandeur passagère à l'être regardé. Pour être exact, je devrais donner un nom différent à chacun des moi qui dans la suite pensa à Albertine; je devrais plus encore donner un nom différent à chacune de ces Albertine qui apparaissaient devant moi, jamais la même, comme—appelées simplement par moi, pour plus de commodité, la mer—ces mers qui se succédaient et devant lesquelles, autre nymphe, elle se détachait. Mais surtout—de la même manière, mais bien plus utilement, qu'on dit, dans un récit, le temps qu'il faisait tel jour—je devrais donner toujours son nom à la croyance qui, tel jour où je voyais Albertine, régnait sur mon âme, en faisait l'atmosphère, l'aspect des êtres, comme celui des mers, dépendant de ces nuées à peine visibles qui changent la couleur de chaque chose par leur concentration, leur mobilité, leur dissémination, leur fuite (I, 947/4.345 'It was perhaps because they were so different, the persons whom I used to contemplate in her at this period, that later on I acquired the habit of becoming a different person myself, corresponding to the particular Albertine to whom my thoughts had turned; a jealous, an indifferent, a voluptuous, a melancholy, a frenzied person, created anew not merely by the accident of what memory had risen to the surface, but in proportion also to the strength of the belief that was lent to the support of one and the same memory by the varying manner in which I appreciated it. For this is the point to which we must always return, to these beliefs with which most of the time we are quite unconsciously filled, but which for all that are of more importance to our happiness than is the average person whom we see, for it is through them that we see him, it is they that impart his momentary greatness to the person seen. To be quite accurate I ought to give a different name to each of the "me's" who were to think about Albertine in time to come; I ought still more to give a different name to each of the Albertines who appeared before me, never the same, like—called by me simply and for the sake of convenience "the sea"—those seas that succeeded one another on the beach, in front of which, a nymph likewise, she stood apart. But above all, in the same way as, in telling a story (though to far greater purpose here), one mentions what the weather was like on such and such a day, I ought always to give its name to the belief that, on any given day on which I saw Albertine, was reigning in my soul, creating its atmosphere, the appearance of people like that of seas being dependent on those clouds, themselves barely visible, which change the colour of everything by their concentration, their mobility, their dissemination, their flight').

It is clear from this passage and others that to say that everyone may be seen as a Janus, depending alone on whether they attract or repel us (III, 181/9.241), is an over-simplification. For such a view would not explain the variety of states the narrator comes to recognize: 'la complexité de mon amour, de ma personne, multipliait, diversifiait mes souffrances' (III, 489/11.101, 'the complexity of my love and of my person, multiplied and diversified my sufferings'). We must return to the question whether the narrator can fuse satisfactorily his views that no knowledge of others is possible and that knowledge is possible of those who do not interest us. One might be tempted to suppose that the narrator holds a view such as this: the person-in-himself, like things-in-themselves, are unknowable; our impressions of persons are not passively received data, but are composites formed of independent, incoming data by our conceptual machinery which sorts and moulds this information; the nature of the concepts that are formed from these aggregates of impressions are thus partially conditioned by the incoming data, and partly by our own sorting processes; the more we are conscious of and in control of the intellectual machinery, the more we are likely to grasp the nature of our incoming impressions; and the more we do this, the more we are entitled to assume that the impressions give reliable information about aspects of things-in-themselves. Our concepts of persons, then, are never more than reliable guides to the nature of persons-in-themselves; they are reliable to the extent that the constituent impressions cohere adequately, after having been consciously processed; we could always be wrong. We have already encountered a paradigm case of someone who made a comprehensive, yet internally consistent, error: Anna Karenina. As an account of concept-acquisition this view suffers from some of the same inadequacies I discussed in the first chapter, when considering presuppositions in *Middlemarch*; and that is not surprising, since the theory of knowledge, whether explicit or implicit, is much the same in both novels.

This is, perhaps, an exaggerated attempt to conjure order out of confusion, but it may enable us to grasp the tension between the narrator's thoughts and actions, between his views and what he does in his narration; for the philosophical scepticism about knowledge contrasts markedly with the nature of the judgements made about the characters portrayed. Certainly, the unreliability of the narrator's concepts based on subjective impressions is revealed, but it is revealed precisely by being contrasted with apparent accounts of the things-in-themselves of which his own concepts are inadequate; it is by reference to reality that the narrator shows the inadequacy of his own concepts of it. By reflection upon the nature of his own concepts the narrator deems knowledge of other persons impossible: 'une personne n'est pas, comme j'avais cru, claire et immobile devant nous avec ses qualités, ses défauts, ses projets, ses intentions à notre égard . . . mais est une ombre où nous ne pouvons jamais pénétrer, pour laquelle il n'existe pas de connaissance directe, au sujet de quoi nous nous faisons des croyances nombreuses à l'aide de paroles et même d'actions, lesquelles les unes et les autres ne nous donnent que des renseignements insuffisants et d'ailleurs contradictoires' (II, 67/5.83, 'a person does not, as I had believed, stand motionless and clear before our eyes, with his merits, his defects, his plans, his intentions with regard to us . . . but is a shadow which one can never succeed in penetrating, of which there can be no direct knowledge, about which we form countless beliefs based on his words and deeds, although neither gives us anything but inadequate and, as it turns out, contradictory information'). And yet, if it is ever correct to talk of recognizing someone, if it is ever correct to argue for the re-applicability of our concepts, there must be steps we could take towards attaining knowledge. 'En effet, "reconnaître" quelqu'un, et plus encore, après n'avoir pas pu le reconnaître, l'identifier, c'est penser sous une seule dénomination deux choses contradictoires, c'est admettre que ce qui était ici, l'être qu'on se rappelle n'est plus, et que ce qui y est, c'est une être qu'on ne connaissait pas' (III, 939/ 12.301, 'Actually to recognize someone, more still to identify someone you have been unable to recall, is to think two things under a single denomination; it is to admit that he who was here is someone we no longer recall, and that he who is here is someone we did not know'). The only way we come to realize the imperceptible but relentless march of time, the only way we grasp that other people never cease to change in relation to ourselves, is when we select and compare from our memory two pictures of the same person taken at different times (II, 1021/12.400). Constant and uninterrupted experience of anything precludes recognition of this basic fact—the continual change in both observer and observed (III, 489/11.101). On this view, it should be noted, the compared memories will consist of impressions in their subsequently clarified state, not in their initially misinterpreted one; the knowledge deriving from the comparison will thus refer to the past. It is doubtless a justified inference by the narrator, however, that the march of time continues to distort our present judgements, the true nature of which we shall not determine until the future.

CONCLUSION

We may now gather the threads of my argument. I have isolated seven major barriers to knowledge, the perpetual presence of which, coupled with general ignorance of their presence, combine to ensure that much of what we take to be knowledge is really illusion. The barriers are constructed from the debris of the operations of egoism, passion, imagination, memory, intellect, habit, and Time; other factors can be subsumed under these headings, factors such as association of ideas, self-consciousness, and the narrator's confessed lethargy,[1] which showed itself in the common but misguided wish for the truth to be revealed by novel and unmistakable signs (III, 602/11.256). Although the narrator believes these barriers can be surmounted he does not argue that life as we know it would be possible without them; rather, he takes them as features to be accepted, but also to be seen for what they are; indeed, they constitute utilitarian means to our desired ends as well as the ultimate justification of art, for art alone shows us their presence and their effects (III, 895-6/12.248). The realization that we have been pursuing an unattainable ideal produces the stimulus of pain necessary for the attempt to grasp reality. When we

[1] Cf. Marcel Proust, *Pastiches et mélanges*, Paris, 1921, p. 251: 'il existe certains esprits ... qu'une sorte de paresse ou de frivolité empêche de descendre spontanément dans les régions profondes de soi-même où commence la véritable vie de l'esprit'. ('There are people who are prevented by a sort of indolence or flippancy from spontaneously plumbing the deepest regions of the self where the true life of the spirit begins.')

recognize that we invariably misinterpret our first impressions, we come to see that our knowledge will be of the past; for by the time we have rectified our first interpretation, the impressions we then had no longer accord with the present state of the object; by the time we have grappled with the inapplicable aspects of our old concepts, that to which we were trying to apply them is already in the past. The ineluctable presence of concepts or ideas, and thus of intellect and habit, in the operation of our perception is a consequence of the premise that we can only cope with the unknown in terms of the known; this is part of what is meant by saying that the past remains present (II, 418, 985/6.151; 8.180). It is important to note that clarification of the nature of our first impression does not necessarily issue in clarity; for some impressions just are vague, some phenomena obscure, and the difficulty is to distinguish genuine vagueness from incomplete or erroneous analysis (III, 381/10.242).

There are several reasons for the importance attached to first impressions. As the basic constituent of knowledge they also serve as the primary elements in the formation of our concepts; the accuracy with which our concepts reflect their objects thus depends on the accuracy with which our impressions reflect their objects—and there is no independent check on their success as representations. Our concepts of other people, or other things in general, are mental constructions out of our complex perceptions of them through time; this is the sense in which the narrator urges that we exist alone: 'l'homme est l'être qui ne peut sortir de soi, qui ne connaît les autres qu'en soi' (III, 450/11.47, 'man is the being that cannot escape from itself, that knows others only through itself'). But further, it is only in virtue of his present impressions that a man can reassure himself of his self-identity; we fully exist only to the extent that we grasp the nature of these immediate perceptions: we exist only by virtue of what we possess, and we possess only what is really present to us (III, 488/11.99, 'on n'est que par ce qu'on possède, on ne possède que ce qui vous est réellement présent'. Compare the narrator's attempt to 'possess' the Vinteuil sonata I, 530/3. 145). 'Sans doute, c'est seulement par la pensée qu'on possède des choses' (III, 552/11.186, 'No doubt, it is only by thought that we possess things'). It will be noted that the narrator at times draws no distinction between the first and subsequent items in a sequence of impressions. This becomes apparent when we note the narrator's insistence on trying to establish 'ce que nous avons réellement éprouvé' (III, 895/12.246, 'what we have actually experienced'), for emphasis upon what we feel refers, not to what we felt on only one occasion, the first, but to what we feel on any occasion. The task is to establish the nature of any or all impressions, not just the first. We have seen how the narrator stresses the independence of reality from us, as well as the dependence of our concepts on our impressions of that independent reality; we have also seen how the veracity of the impressions can be established only by comparing them in some way with the reality which stands over against them, and that this reality must not itself be mediated by impressions. Because the narrator is partly concerned to emphasize the divergence between the objective world and our subjective reactions to it, and to suggest ways in which we may seek to close the gap, he cannot and does not consistently maintain his phenomenalist views. Again, although he aims to show errors which arise from the view that there are no percepts without concepts, he nevertheless accepts this philosophical view; on the other hand, the errors which can and do arise, but need not, sometimes encourage him to adopt the view that in some way we are entirely passive about the impressions we receive and that they are in themselves entirely reliable as to the truth, if only we could lay aside our intellectual tendencies to process them (III, 880/12.227). A conflict that we observed in *Middlemarch* thus re-emerges: between active and passive theories of perception.

I claimed at the beginning of this chapter that each of the obstacles to knowledge also had a good side; the goodness, it should now be remarked is entirely utilitarian. Passion distorts our knowledge because it substitutes an ideal world for the real world; but its favourable aspect is that the suffering occasioned by our shattered illusions, and thus indirectly caused by our passion itself, forces us to look anew at the data ever ready to hand, our impressions. The good aspect of imagination is that by it alone may one grasp the individuality of phenomena; and that of memory is that by it alone may one recall the past; it may be added, however, that the claim that the past remains present refers not only to the notion of involuntary recall, but also to the presence of past concepts in the interpretation of present perceptions (II, 418, 985/ 6.151; 8.180). The good side of habit is that it secures us against perpetual bewilderment, and of Time that it annihilates pain, even if it also annihilates everything else. The good side of egoism is perhaps the fact that our concepts and their veracity are necessarily, and literally, what we make of them; it is only from our impressions that we can make our own concepts. The favourable aspect of intellect is seen whenever it operates properly, and art is the means to this awareness. It will be remembered that only by art can we consciously get outside ourselves (III, 896/12.248), for art reveals the qualitative differences in the way each of us looks at the world; and in showing us another's view it is, of course, *ipso facto* showing us something independent of us. (Dreams sometimes convey unconscious impressions to us (III, 914/12.270), but we have as little control over dreams as over involuntary memory.) Whereas most of us are wedded to the practical needs of everyday living (I, 949; III, 872/4.348; 12.217), the artist, for some unexplained reason, is able to follow his instincts, and to capture the nature of our impressions before they were misinterpreted by intellect. Art is gratuitous (II, 45/5.52) in the sense that it is concerned to establish the initial item of knowledge in its uncontaminated purity; for only the impression is a criterion of truth:

Les idées formées par l'intelligence pure n'ont qu'une vérité logique, une vérité possible, leur élection est arbitraire. Le livre aux caractères figurés, non tracés par nous, est notre seul livre. Non que ces idées que nous formons ne puissent être justes logiquement, mais nous ne savons pas si elles sont vraies. Seule l'impression, si chétive qu'en semble la matière, si insaisissable la trace, est un critérium de vérité, et à cause de cela mérite seule d'être appréhendée par l'esprit, car elle est seule capable, s'il sait en dégager cette vérité, de l'amener à une plus grande perfection et de lui donner une pure joie. L'impression est pour l'écrivain ce qu'est l'expérimentation pour le savant (III, 880/12.227 'The ideas formed by the intellect have only a logical truth, a possible truth; their selection is arbitrary. Our proper book is one in which the characters represented have not been sketched out by us. It is not that the ideas we formulate may not be logically proper, but that we do not know whether they are true. Only the impression, however slight in substance, however imperceptible in outline, is a criterion of truth; it alone deserves to be apprehended by the mind, because it alone is capable, if it succeeds in extracting the truth, of bringing the mind to greater perfection and of giving it unalloyed joy. The impression is for the writer what experiment is for the scientist').

We cannot do anything with uninterpreted impressions; and the tautology which underlies this claim is simply that of the present we have only present impressions. But having stressed the gratu-itousness of art, which is guaranteed by its fortuitousness, the narrator also emphasizes its important role and consequences; there is no contradiction here because the gratuitousness refers to the motive and to how art comes about, whereas it just happens that art has useful consequences. Although each one of us must clarify our impressions by our own effort, the artist shows us how to combat the unseen work of our intellect; as such, art is a means to knowledge. This is not to say that we must not use our intellect; on the contrary, we must learn to use it aright. Whatever hypotheses or interpretations we bring to our impressions must be based on reason, backed by what we already know (III, 423/11.7); for the purposes of placing things in relation to other things and specifying their distinguishing characteristics, intellect is indis-pensible: 'on ne sait pas ce que c'est tant qu'on ne l'a pas approché de l'intelligence. Alors seulement quand elle l'a éclairé, quand elle l'a intellectualisé, on distingue, et avec quelle peine, la figure de ce qu'on a senti' (III, 896/12.248, 'One does not know the nature of one's feelings until they have been submitted to the intellect. Then only, when the intellect has illuminated them, has intellectualized them, does one distinguish, and with what difficulty, the outlines of what one has felt').

The narrator holds, then, that knowledge is possible, even if it is, in a sense, always knowledge of the past; but its presentation is as difficult as its attainment. The synoptic view necessary for the presentation will be of the utmost complexity, compounded as it will be of the most careful comparison and contrast between particular cases. Many readers believe that this affirmation, explicitly set out in the coda to the novel, has been realized and enacted within the novel itself.

cet écrivain, qui d'ailleurs pour chaque caractère en ferait apparaître les faces opposées pour montrer son volume, devrait préparer son livre minutieusement, avec de perpétuels regroupements de forces, comme une offensive, le supporter comme une fatigue, l'accepter comme une règle, le construire comme une église, le suivre comme un régime, le vaincre comme un obstacle, le conquérir comme une amitié, le suralimenter comme un enfant, le créer comme un monde sans laisser de côté ces mysteres qui n'ont probablement leur explication que dans d'autres mondes et dont le pressentiment est ce qui nous émeut le plus dans la vie et dans l'art (III, 1032/12. 415, 'This writer—who, to indicate the solidity of each character, must display its differing facets—would have to prepare his book meticulously, perpetually regrouping his forces, as in an offensive battle; and he would have to accept his book as a burden, a discipline, and build it like a church, follow it like a diet, overcome it like an obstacle, win it like a friendship, nourish it like a child, create it like a world but without neglecting those mysteries whose explanation is probably to be found only in other worlds, and of which the presentiment moves us most in life and in art').

A la recherche du temps perdu is not a philosophical treatise; the views I have extracted and abstracted from the novel have their literary embodiment in the characterization of persons and events portrayed, just as much as in the narrator's own, sometimes laboured, philosophical reflections. The following out of this literary embodiment is a task that each reader must undertake for himself. For part of the fascination of this novel, as of most novels that are concerned with problems of knowledge, lies in the contrast between the presentation of what was to be known, and the presentation of what was known.

CHAPTER 5

Philosophy, Criticism, and the Novel

A THEORY OF INTERPRETATION OUTLINED

I shall now outline in untechnical terms the theory of interpretation applied in the preceding essays. I hope to show why many novels are interpreted differently at different times, why works go out of fashion, why we seem to experience greater emotional impact from texts classified as art, what it means to learn something from a novel, what it means to understand a novel. I claim that my interpretations are in a sense creative and, like all interpretations, aspectival. The term 'aspect', as used in the sub-title of this book, should be taken to embrace the act of consideration, the viewpoint from which something is seen, and the appearance or face of the object perused. Creative interpretation requires the postulation of purposiveness without actual purpose; because of this, one way in which a novel may be described, justifiably, as philosophical is if it displays philosophicalness without philosophy. Reasoned, creative interpretation cannot be branded as merely subjective.

To ensure that disputants are talking about the same thing we need a common referent. Writers create texts, and the text of each novel is the primary referent of my interpretations. Texts must be conceived not as physical objects, but as sets of symbols having meaning; and not just any meaning. We must be able to distinguish between accounts which are, and those which are not, interpretations of a given text; between, for example, an interpretation and an inspirational departure.

Terms such as 'novel' or 'philosophical treatise' represent the classification of a text in one way rather than another; the text of a novel is not separable from the novel. I shall avoid the misleading sense in which 'novel' is sometimes used, perhaps unwittingly, to denote an interpreted text. The classifications we make of the language uses we encounter are important, because they are attended by conventions, which themselves reflect our interests. It is a contingent fact which conventions we have at any one time, of course, just as it is contingent what our interests are; but such conventions may be said to be about the logic of the classifications made. I claim that it is one of our conventions that when a text is classified as a novel, readers are accorded a certain degree of freedom in its interpretation. In brief, the freedom is exercised in redescribing the context in such a way that the relatively severe conditions governing significance that I shall mention shortly are preserved. Two points should be emphasized, however. First, such freedom is only one feature of this concept of a novel; secondly, we can exercise such freedom elsewhere.

Writers create texts: readers interpret texts. My essays are accounts of how I have taken the texts, from a certain viewpoint. All interpretations are takings, and all are from viewpoints. Disputes arise over the legitimacy of certain viewpoints, and of the interpretations dependent on them. Interpretations reveal what significance or import of a text a reader has determined, and the notion of determining here suitably covers the patterns he finds as well as those he forms. Interpretation is the business of making sense of the text, rendering it coherent; this is achieved by placing emphases, drawing connections, suggesting presuppositions and implications. In the previous chapters, characterizing the philosophical aspects of the texts involved suggesting which sentences, ordinarily understood, could be taken from a philosophical viewpoint, to have philosophical import. Philosophers often claim that if a man asserts P, and if P entails Q, then he is logically, if not psychologically, committed to Q, even though he did not assert it and in fact may be ignorant of the entailment. I do not hold that all types of significance attributable to literary texts have the character of logical entailments; nevertheless, if qualified judges accept the description of the implications and presuppositions of a given text, against a specified background, those implications may be said to be properties of the text. Entailments and implications hold, of course, independently of a speaker's awareness of them. Similarly, independently of his awareness, a man's behaviour may reveal signs and symptoms of illness or attitude to qualified observers. Such observers may notice these features immediately and non-inferentially; the rationalist vocabulary of a man may be as obvious to a philosopher as his heart condition is to a doctor, or his egoism to most laymen. I shall return to this notion of immediacy.

I shall assume the intelligibility of a rough and ready distinction between the linguistic meaning of sentences and the various ways in which they may be taken. It is, of course, their significance or import that concerns us here. Because semantic and syntactic rules, and the conditions under which language is learnt, ensure that sentences cannot mean just anything, discussions of their significance presuppose agreement over their normal linguistic meaning —which is not to say that there cannot be puzzles about the linguistic meaning. The significance of a particular utterance is determined partly by the social and linguistic context in which it occurs, partly by conventions for making utterances of that type, partly by what the speaker is doing in uttering it and what he wishes to achieve by its utterance. A presupposition of social communication is that a speaker intends the significance that is normally intended by sentences with that meaning. The notion of 'crying "Wolf!"' rests on such a presupposition, and one can successfully deceive others, by lying, only if the meaning of one's sentences is the same as when one does not aim to deceive. For this reason it is useful to distinguish between what the speaker means and what his sentences mean. 'Whatever did he mean by that?' expresses doubt over how to take what he said, rarely over its linguistic meaning: and to resolve such a doubt we may have to decide what the author meant. To render coherent in appropriate ways the language uses we encounter, we have to assume that those uses represent purposive human agency. But the purposiveness is treated as a property of the form of the text or utterance, not as their cause or causal accompaniment; in this context, intentions and purposes are generally not taken to be the speaker's antecedent plans, inner psychological states or prior musings. For this reason, and despite any of his avowals of intention, a speaker is not the sole arbiter over what import his utterances have; communication is a public, social affair and he is not exempted from responsibility for aspects of his performance he failed to notice.

These familiar points are of great importance in the discussion of literature.

We always assume that novels are consciously conceived products, and that they were intended to be understood; to this extent the artist is held responsible for everything done. The central question for the interpreter is how a given work is to be taken, and this includes deciding what has been done. Interpretations tend towards one of two extremities on a continuous scale. Either one is interested primarily in the historical question of how the author actually conceived the significance of his text, in the light of the precise context in which he saw himself; or one is more interested in the significance of the text against the background of other contexts. It might be thought that two considerations support the former approach. First, if actions, generally, can be seen as the actions they are only against the background of circumstances in which they are performed, then perhaps works of art, too, can be seen as the works they are only against such a background. Secondly, if sentences carry their linguistic meaning only under normal conditions, then perhaps a contemporary viewpoint of any utterance must be especially privileged for determining both the proper linguistic meaning and the proper significance. I shall consider later how these points bear on the question 'What can I make of this text, now?' Obviously there cannot be sharp boundaries between the historically oriented and the non-historically oriented interpretations, because to understand any utterance at all we have to make use of some historical knowledge, if only in a relatively trivial way; and, on the other side, to understand any utterance we cannot avoid being influenced by factors in our present context which help determine, also, the emphases we place. The purposes and context of a reader govern the extent to which he may wish to locate a text in its historical setting, and the context here must include his knowledge or decision that the text may be classified as a novel, and his beliefs about the roles this class plays in his 'form of life', to use Wittgenstein's phrase. Historically oriented critics seem curiously reluctant to follow the lead of most historians, who expect to reinterpret the past and its works for each generation. A published text is as independent of its author as it is of its reader. No author can control the contexts in which diverse readers will approach his text, and many of its effects will be unforeseen and even undesired; but novelists usually try to incorporate as many guides to, and constraints upon, interpretation as they think necessary, for, unlike speakers, they cannot modify their utterances in the face of misinterpretation. But the significance of a text is not worn on its face, as it were, and a reader may decide that he does not wish to know the author's prior plans or preferred interpretation. A reader's attempt to see what he can make of the text presupposes the same basis as the historical approach, namely, that for any text to function as communication, it must be backed by purposes, conventions, presuppositions. But the difference is that he postulates his own purposes, or those familiar from his own context, rather than those which actually operated in the past. A reader has to examine the text in the light of possible, if not actual purposes, and the possibilities will be determined by his knowledge and interests. This is the sense in which a reader treats a novel as possessing the property of purposiveness without actual purpose. Vacillation between taking a given novel as the expression of the author's views, for example, and as a text over which some freedom has been exercised in its interpretation, accounts for a pervasive ambiguity in much literary criticism, because the mere use of the author's name may be no guide as to which approach has been adopted. Indeed, the proper name may denote no more than 'the author of the text-as-I-have-taken-it', and such hypostatized authors should not be confused with historical persons. It makes little sense, however, to ask of every sentence in an interpretation whether it reflects an historical or non-historical viewpoint. Such descriptions are of trends discernible only in an interpretation as a whole. If interpretation is needed even to determine whether or not the stance of a particular discourse is historical, then it may be impossible to break out of the hermeneutic circle.

Purposiveness, then, is a condition of intelligibility in a text, but a man's ability to make sense of what he reads reflects his competence as a language user in a particular domain. Not everyone interprets what he reads, because not everyone succeeds in acquiring competence. But there is a necessary connection between being a competent language user and trying to determine the significance of the uses one meets; and the connection is recorded in the fact that interpretation is incorporated in the notion of 'proper reading'. It is justifiable to describe attempts to render a text coherent as 'immediate' or 'natural' only if one also remembers that the competence they presuppose is neither innate nor unlearned. It is, of course, quite contingent what methods a reader adopts in his attempts, and how self-conscious he is about them; he is most likely to be conscious of his methods when they fail to yield results, and alternatives are called for. A critic differs only in degree from other readers when he reflects, say, on the implications and presuppositions of a text. By calling some interpretations 'creative' I have drawn attention not only to the coherence-enabling assumptions which are necessary conditions of any interpretation, but also to the particular freedom in these assumptions that we have in the realm of art.

The background against which, or the viewpoint from which, we interpret a text generally provide the most interesting differences between interpretations, between the patterns of coherence different critics determine. If we recognize the permanent possibility of other viewpoints, we can see why our own interpretations could not be final or exhaustive; this is the main reason for the continual reinterpretation of many works, not their undeniable complexity or resistance to a single, unified and coherent interpretation. The passage of time enables readers conditioned by different sociological and historical factors to derive new implications; translation opens the gates to inferences determined by new cultures, languages, and concepts. Just as the inferences a modern English reader will make from the text of *Middlemarch* will differ from those of a reader in 1873, so a French translation made in 1873 will differ from one made now, and be differently interpreted. Translators, while sensitive to considerations present to an author even if not evident in the text, are often also constrained to help a modern reader by removing what they believe to be obstacles to comprehension.

Because we commonly talk about a text whose significance we have already decided upon, we are commonly talking about something we have created in part ourselves. To this extent it may be said that my essays, although they are about texts written by George Eliot and Tolstoy, nevertheless present Peter Jones's *Middlemarch* and *Anna Karenina*. There is a superficial analogy here with performances of music, where we speak of Kleiber's *Marriage of Figaro* or Klemperer's *Eroica*; but in the literary case not everything from the original text will appear in the presentation, and paraphrase, rediscription, and reformulation occur without being branded as transcription or reduction. Further, unlike the performer of a musical score, a critic cannot be said to 'complete' a text by interpreting it.

We should no longer be surprised that many novels, and works of art in general, are interpreted differently at different times. On the view I have just sketched we might be more surprised at the occasional similarity of interpretations at different times, for, I have claimed, although it is the ultimate referent of our critical discussion, the text is also the source of our creative engagement. Countless reasons, including boredom with old interpretations, may induce us to seek for new viewpoints; in general we do not re-read major texts in the hope or expectancy of arriving at the same interpretation as before. We value works which yield to new interpretations; but we should remember that new experiences, including experiences of other works of art, together with new knowledge and new interests, are all influential factors here. It is always possible for anyone to reinterpret a text, although we are often more conscious of the fact when we witness the accounts of new generations. Novels such as I have discussed can drop out of fashion and return to fashion because readers find they reward

scrutiny and reflection under different conditions; and a judgement on whether a particular work 'speaks' to a particular reader
in a given context sometimes depends upon its being judged a
valuable stimulus towards perceiving the world, and thinking
about it, in certain ways. To this extent, we may say that fashion
in art is explicable by reference to the *use* to which interpreters
find they can put particular works. Any community of readers
can modify the conventions for understanding the text of a novel.
The view of a reader as creative interpreter illuminates why we
need not ignore art of the past in order to pay exclusive attention
to art of our own time, and it also helps to explain how we come
to believe that past works in some way throw light on our present
situation; for it is we who are using past works to see what we can
get out of them, and since this use reflects our present knowledge
and interests, there is a strong possibility that we shall be able to
construct a contemporary reference for those works. It must be
stressed, however, that 'what it means for me' and 'how I take it'
do not mean 'wherein I believe it to be true'. Intelligibility is
separable from assent, and both are separable from truth: several
times in the earlier chapters I declared my own disagreement with
the views implied by the texts.

Consider one feature of a large-scale interpretative pattern: no
one argues that it is necessary for George Eliot, Tolstoy, or
Dostoevsky to have thought of the Freudian interpretations of
of their novels which some people now feel entitled to use. It
might be urged, however, that we have no interest in Freudian
interpretations of a novel if Freudian theory is itself wrong in its
basic tenets, just as we have no interest in a Christian interpretation if the Christian claims are mistaken. But there are difficulties
in conclusively establishing that such theories and claims are mistaken, and some people may judge explanatory models such as
those provided by Freud to be useful even in the face of admitted
counter-evidence. Further, it is not clear that our interest in the
application of Freudian theory to works of literature would be
altogether diminished if Freudian theory were generally accepted
as discredited, although it is unlikely that many readers would

attempt its application in such a case. To adopt a mode of interpretation, such as a Freudian mode, which was not actually part of one's own critical apparatus, would be to engage in a primarily historical approach to the text.

My theory of creative interpretation helps to explain why the work of recently dead authors so frequently drops out of fashion, and why we often feel less freedom (not to be confused with the bewilderment we may also feel) in interpreting contemporary art than we do in interpreting past art. We generally know the social context in which present-day art in our community is created, and generally know the ideas in the air. We forget that it is purely contingent that some art is contemporary with ourselves, and we tend to treat the present as an essential aspect in our interpretation of the work. We forget the range of interpretations that later on we shall seek and welcome, and may even adopt the view that such diversity is an inferior substitute for contemporary response. Frequently we know something about the living artist, and there is a strong tendency, often actively encouraged by the artist himself, to take his works as public utterances over which he retains speaker-purpose jurisdiction. The mere empirical refusal of a given novelist to allow readers freedom of interpretation does nothing to destroy that freedom although, contingently, it may discourage them from asserting it.

The death of an author releases the public from the possibility of consulting him about anything, and throws them upon themselves. But the renewed consciousness of freedom may be felt as a burden. Even more importantly, with the passage of time, the author's works are bereft of contemporary reference they may be thought to have had at the time of their creation, and the reader is left to his own creative interpretation. But the reader who has so far always taken those works to have a specific reference may have fallen into a habit of uncritical response, and deprived of habitual assumptions about the context, may feel little inclination to look for a new use to which he can put the work. Without either its old original setting or a new use the work may lose popularity, and only after a further passage of time, when the memory of the author and his times has faded, will new readers consider the work, and encourage old readers to look afresh. From these remarks it may be seen why some readers treat some texts as works of art only when they are in the past, and treat all current texts as public-discourse utterances. All this goes to suggest that frequently, but perhaps unwittingly, we have two concepts of art, or at least two attitudes towards it, at any given time—one for art of our own time, under which we feel constrained in our interpretations, and one for works of the past, under which we feel greater freedom. Works receding into the past thus make us uneasy when we have not yet become accustomed to the responsibilities of a freedom we can no longer deny.

The notion of creative interpretation also illuminates why we generally experience a greater emotional impact from works of art than from texts not so classified: we have engaged in the intentional act of interpretation, and are thereby in part committed to what we ourselves have done. It may seem paradoxical to urge that the impact or effect of a work on us is explained by our own active involvement with, and attitude towards, it; but this is only because it is often unclear what is designated by the term 'work'— it may refer to a text, in my sense, or to the interpreted set of elements from the text which represents a particular response. A related point may be made about our reactions to detailed interpretations of a text. Detailed comment challenges a reader to take a stand on the issues mentioned and is thus a constraint upon unfettered freedom. For this reason many readers prefer criticism which seems to leave them greater freedom by demanding less of them.

Creative interpretation, as I have sketched it, does not merely reflect one's subjective opinion, reduce a text to the status of a Rorschach test or of an *objet-trouvé* whose genesis and previous history one disregards. The text of a novel is publicly available: many of its elements are open to sense-perception, and their description may be publicly agreed or challenged. The question 'Are not some interpretations of a particular text just plainly wrong?' can often be answered readily. Accounts of sentence-

meaning (whether or not such accounts should be called 'interpretations') can be wrong if they ignore the semantic and syntactic
conventions which secure such meaning; historical accounts of an
author's prior plans, enacted purposes, or preferred interpretation
can also be wrong; but because there are no formal limits to the
ways in which texts may be taken, or the uses to which they may
be put, it is reference to convention or tradition and practical in-
efficacy in the context which lead to the properly reasoned dismissal
of some interpretations as 'implausible', 'pointless', 'far-fetched'.

It is precisely because the relation between a text and an interpretation is not merely causal, that creative interpretation cannot
be said to be objective in the way that judgements about colours,
say, are objective. We protect our judgements about the real
colours of objects from accusations of subjective relativity by
defining the real colour in terms of conventions which cover the
standard conditions for observing the object in question. But if
creative interpretations are not in this way objective, it does not
follow that they are therefore subjective. Conventions still play a
role. Some interpretations are accepted within a specifiable peer-
group, and some are not; agreement over reasons is the basis for
such acceptance. Appeal to the text and to the contingent conventions and traditions for interpreting it enable us to distinguish
between a legitimate interpretation of a given text and a mere
effect of reading it due, say, to free association. Similar appeals are
made, of course, in everyday conversation. In presenting his interpretation to the public a critic invites their agreement on the
interest and legitimacy of his account; he describes a publicly
available text, and suggests viewpoints of it that are publicly available to those who approach it in the way he indicates. Of course,
the endorsement he requires is one based on the genuine response
of others, not on mere imitation of his own; but the fact that
others ultimately have to determine their own viewpoint of the
text, devalues his account no more than it devalues theirs. Neither
account is justifiably described as viciously subjective. In this
domain there is no timeless truth, and public accord determines
what is accepted. The readers to whom implicit appeal is made by

an interpreter do constitute an ideal group, in a sense, because they consist of those who, in the eyes of the plaintiff, read the text as he believes it should be read from his viewpoint. This is one reason why membership of the group is indeterminate, and why an interpreter may reject rejection by his peers. Familiarity with the text, and scrutiny of the interpretation are among the minimum necessary conditions for assessing the interpretation. But two interesting factors in the relationship between an interpreter and his peers here emerge. First: an interpreter may not accept counter argument as requiring amendment to his account, either because he has no substitute, or because of the practical or theoretical advantages of his original interpretation in other contexts: an interpretation may not be an end in itself. Such recalcitrance is familiar in the domain of science, where theories are often formulated and maintained in the face of known counter-evidence. Second: acceptance by others of one's account may not outweigh one's own subsequent dissatisfaction with it. Neither the agreement nor the disagreement of others can be decisive factors, because usually one aim of the interpreter has been to work out what he can make of a given text, what it means for him. One cannot be a member of a community of language users, however, without substantial agreement in judgements, and constant and extensive deviation from the judgement of his peers serves only to isolate an individual. But however persuasive a reader may find my own interpretations, they are ultimately dispensable, for nothing is achieved by adopting uncritically the interpretation of others. Yet there is nothing special about such dispensability, since it is shared by all attempts to get others to reach their own judgement; one must remember only that no type of interpretation is immune from it. There is, therefore, a causal relation between a text and an interpreter; but there is also more than a causal relation. Criticism may be felt to be invaluable; it is not indispensable.

It is logically possible, although in practice unlikely, that a reader will be able to construct alternative interpretations from precisely the same elements of a text. Because of the indefinite number of implications that can be drawn from a text, and the indefinite number of suggestions it may arouse, critics rarely clash head-on. Moreover, they rarely base their accounts on the same set of textual elements. It is partly because of this fact that different interpretations of the same text are often accepted simultaneously as plausible. Peer-groups generally regard critical questions raised within the group as more interesting than those raised by outsiders, and this explains why views usually evolve only gradually within a moderately stable tradition. A variety of interpretations is encouraged, additionally, by the professional interest critics have in differing from others. Further, of course, to accept the creative interpretation of another person involves either restraint upon, or suppression of, one's own freedom to create an interpretation—to this extent it is to submit to another. We value criticism not only for the knowledge of other possible points of view, but also because of the shared commitment to the text; but the knowledge of the commitment of others cannot release us from the need to make our own decisions. In this context it is useful to preserve a distinction between seeing an object (the text) differently, while recognizing it is the same object as before, and seeing a different object. My theory allows the distinction. When talking about the interpreted-text constructed by each reader we are talking about different objects; but different readers themselves talk about the same fundamental text, from which they may select the same or different sets of elements for their interpretation. We see an object differently when we select and emphasize different aspects of it. Criticism is, indeed, necessarily aspectival—for it is always *from* a viewpoint, and *of* a selection of properties. And some properties, such as significance, are neither literally seen nor determinate, but are created by the critic. The notion of trying 'to see the work as a whole' refers to the unity of a given interpretation of the work, according to some criterion of unity, not to the impossible feat of seeing all its properties, determinate and indeterminate, perceptible and inferrable, at once.

On such an account, how may we be said, legitimately, to learn from a particular text? The answer is that although our interpretation of, and inferences from, a text are determined by our own experience, knowledge, context and interests, the construction we make is itself referrable back to the world we live in; in this way our construction may modify our extant beliefs and attitudes. Only occasionally does a work induce in perception of our world something like a *gestalt*-switch. Since there is an overwhelming case for holding that learning largely consists in the modification of current behaviour and attitude, we can say that we learn from those texts which enable us to construct modifying views of our world. Although what we detect is always a function of our present state of knowledge, this does not imply that we can only get out of the text of a novel exactly what we ourselves put into it; to think this would be a case of confusing the conditions for perceiving with the objects perceived. By providing us with a text that can be interpreted a novelist provides us with raw material enabling us to see things differently; or, to put it another way, we can learn from texts by using them for the construction of propositions applicable to the world we live in. My own interpretation of *Anna Karenina* might thus be summarized: '*if* we select these items from the text, *and* interpret them in this way, we may use the interpreted set as, say, an account of various factors which impede human agency.'

I have been careful to draw no analogies between my theory for interpeting these four novels and notions of interpretation applicable in other art forms—with the one exception of a superficial analogy with musical performance. But a remark by the pianist Alfred Brendel (B.B.C. Radio Three, 31 October 1970) deserves quotation because of its application also to literary interpretation. He declared that he considered his role as a performer to embrace three aspects. As a museum clerk he needed to establish the text; as a solicitor he engaged in the moral activity of doing the best he could for his client; as a midwife he assisted at the birth of a new creation, even though he had done similar things before.

UNDERSTANDING A NOVEL

I have claimed that interpretation, in literature, is based on an assumption of purposiveness in the text, and this assumption enables a reader to search for coherence of some sort. By interpreting a text we determine its significance. I claimed that we are interested in postulating actual or possible purposes because we are interested in deciding how to take apparent attempts to communicate. We postulate purposes in order to determine possible uses of the language we encounter. To this extent we may say that the significance we attribute to a text presupposes its actual or possible purposes. The creative role of the interpreter appears in the postulation of possible purposes and in the nature of the import assigned to the text in the light of the possibility. When the possibility itself rests on using the text in some way, we may say that the significance of the text is then a function of our use. A lament that one does not 'understand the significance' of a given text refers to one's inability to do something, namely to postulate purposes which allow one to find or create coherence in the text. The briefer lament that one does not understand a text likewise refers to one's failure to know 'how to take it'. I claimed that in classifying a text as a work of art one is accorded some degree of freedom in its interpretation. Throughout I have been using the notion of 'taking', which is one of the terms used by *The Oxford English Dictionary* to define the verb 'to understand' ('to take, interpret, or view in a certain way'). To the extent that a text is always open to different takings, given a suitable background, one's understanding of a text, in so far as it refers to takings, is always logically incomplete; but to the same extent it is logically inappropriate to lament this fact. To show how I have taken a text is to show how I have understood it, and if one's interpretation involves 'using' the text in any of the ways I considered earlier, then showing how one takes it will be showing how one uses it. Not all interpretations involve use, however, and not all senses of understanding refer to interpretation of the sort I have discussed. But it is important to recognize the variety of the phenomena in connection with, or aspects of, a given work of art, that may be said to be objects of understanding. In general, the object understood determines the possible senses of understanding it; that is, an analysis of understanding-X depends on the X, and an elucidation of what it is that one understands clarifies what it is to understand it. In this sort of context analogies reward scrutiny. For every analogy, of course, there is disanalogy, and in a given enquiry one point of difference may be more important than all the points of similarity. Nevertheless I shall compare understanding-a-novel with understanding-a-person and understanding-an-argument. Understanding-a-situation is a less linear process than understanding-an-argument, but I refer readers to my discussion of the notion in my chapter on *Anna Karenina*, rather than take up space exploring this third analogy again. I also discussed 'understanding others' and 'knowledge of persons' in the chapters on *The Brothers Karamazov* and *A la recherche du temps perdu*.

To understand a person involves not only judging his behaviour to consist of actions that are purposeful and pointful, but grasping their point, and perhaps seeing grounds for their appropriateness in the context. To understand a person is to know how to respond to him, and to know how he would respond in given circumstances—it involves knowing that something is the case, knowing how to respond and what to do. It is not to predict that there may be no surprises, since people change or reveal unexpected traits in unexpected situations. And although it is often said that understanding involves sympathy, in some sense of that term, it does not involve liking the person. To understand a person involves not so much the capacity to control him, for this would not differentiate persons from things; rather, it involves the capacity to control oneself in respect and with respect to the other person. We speak of complete understanding not only when a person is judged uncomplicated (notice the recurrence of 'judging' or 'estimating') but in complex cases when there has been considerable intimacy, usually over a long period of time and in a variety of contexts. It is sometimes thought to be to a man's credit if his complexity denies others complete understanding of him.

To understand another person, as I have very incompletely sketched it—and much depends, of course, on the notion of a 'person'—involves self-consciousness, reflection upon the other person, and intentional action in a chosen direction; that is, action which is both intended, and thought-directed towards certain ends. Understanding a novel involves assuming that the work is purposive, is the product of human agency (with all that that involves); and this assumption delimits the range of concepts we regard as appropriate in talking about the work. In addition to the assumption of purposiveness we assume that anyone who creates a work of art in a language, both knows and intends this language-use to be open to interpretation and understanding. The assumption of purposiveness, however, does not commit us to a search for the *actual* purposes that informed the work. Some writers have claimed that complexity, rather than simplicity, is a necessary condition for both understanding and favourable evaluation; and others have argued that our understanding of great novels is necessarily always incomplete. They have argued for this view not on the muddled ground that our critical comments, like all empirical claims, are only ever conditionally true against possible falsification; but on the ground that novels are continually being seen in a new light.

As well as its similarities to understanding a person, understanding a novel is in some ways like understanding an argument, where 'argument' is recognized as covering both a purposive human process and a product. In the cases of both novels and arguments a man must particularize what he claims not to understand before relevantly remedial action can be taken. A man may be mistaken both in a claim to understand and in a claim not to understand an argument; for, when understanding is taken to imply that an argument is correct, a man who failed to detect errors would be wrong to claim that he understood; and where there are no errors he would be wrong to claim that he understood if there was nothing he could do to show his understanding. A man may claim not to understand precisely because he has detected a mistake or a contradiction. But a concern for the truth of an argument may be only one of the factors behind a man's claim not to understand an argument, and his needs for remedial action on our part vary with these factors. He may need paraphrase, explanation, or straight repetition; he may need illustration or clarification; he may be puzzled by the meaning, truth, or logic of an argument, or about the evidence for it. Here we must remember, once more, that although the speaker's intentions are relevant to determining what he meant to say, the arguer has no special rights over the public conventions of the language he has used nor over the independent phenomena to which his argument refers.

The analogy between understanding-a-novel and understanding-an-argument rests largely on the notion of intentions, and further brief discussion of that notion is therefore necessary. Historically-oriented critics have detected a difficulty in talking about the work to which they are attending. Although there are many descriptions of differing generality of many pieces of behaviour, there are not author-intentions corresponding to each of them; therefore not all descriptions of what has been done describe the successful fulfilment of intentions. This being so, it is helpful to distinguish between 'what the author did' and 'what has been done'; we can then refer to what has been done as 'X' without implying that 'X' was what the author actually wanted, intended or tried to do. In the context of art intentions are sought or postulated for the purposes of determining what has been done, and how to take it; the aim, usually, is not to distribute moral responsibility, but to provide a coherent account, akin to a reasoned justification, and thereby help to explain why the work is as it is claimed to be. Many descriptions, especially those using action verbs (e.g. to telephone) presuppose that the agent is performing intentionally—even if there have been no prior or accompanying states that may be called 'intentions'. It is not even necessary to interpret a man's avowals of intention, which are unreliable in any case, as referring to such mental states or events; for their quotation is aimed at making some action coherent to an observer, and thereby explaining or justifying it. When we are interested in a man's prior plans and wishes, however, we often have to ascribe these to him by means of inferences from particular descriptions of the performance we are examining.

Miss Anscombe has claimed that a man's intended actions are specified by 'the description under which' he saw himself as acting, and some critics have sought for intention-ascribing descriptions of the work which they felt would have been acceptable to the artist himself. Although such descriptions often specifically refer to antecedently formulated goals they need not do so. In most contexts 'In order to solve the problem of P, he did Q' would be an intention-ascribing description, whereas 'By doing Q, he solved the problem of P' would not, for the latter describes what was done as the solution to a problem without implying the author's own consciousness of it. Even so, both descriptions assume that what was done is purposive in the sense that coherence may be found in it. It is important to recognize, further, that not all intentions, seen as mental events, leave a trace on their execution; so that an intention-ascribing description of a process may not be acceptable as a description of the work itself. Takings are sought and assessed, of course, in relation to desired ends and purposes: 'That is not the way to look at it if you want to do X (e.g. to see it in the historical, social context of its creation); this way of taking it is valuable if you want to do Y (e.g. to see what it can offer to a reader today).' Critics too often forget that readers have different interests in reading texts, that such interests change, and that they govern the range of questions a reader asks a text.

It is often mistakenly assumed that since an author did not change what is evident in the work, he must have found it acceptable; and that what he accepted is to be identified with what he formerly wanted or intended to do. Critics often invoke reference to prior intentions in contexts already described as problem-solving, that is, in contexts where the author is assumed to have chosen between consciously considered alternatives. But the author need not have been conscious of everything plausibly described as 'in' the work. Further, intended effects can come about by accident and this fact is not necessarily detectable in the work itself; and precise effects may not be foreseen, nor their attainment precisely planned by one particular means rather than by others. And artists perform habitual and mechanical activities which are yet 'intended'.

If we confront a living author with an interpretation of his text that he had not himself previously envisaged, we would not withdraw it simply because he had not thought of it. The author is one judge among others and, further, he is likely to confuse comment upon what has been done with comment upon what he remembers he was doing or trying to do. His refusal even to consider our interpretation would shake our confidence in him as a serious critic, and possibly, in the end, in our own attitude towards at least the work in question; a great deal would depend on the context, and upon exactly how the author reacted. An artist who believed that there was only one interpretation of his work, namely the one he had in some sense thought of himself, would be insensitive not only to the variety of contexts in which people (including himself at later times) would approach his work, but also to the undeniable fact that products of the past, *a fortiori* works of art, are continually reinterpreted.

Let us take our bearings in the discussion so far.

Our understanding of a person and of a novel may grow in depth and in breadth; the intimacy of our relations with a person or a novel depends on our capacity to control ourselves and to refrain also from merely passive reaction to them. In both cases we are concerned to suggest or discover coherence in what we observe; but because of the different contexts in which, and the different interests with which, we approach them, the coherence we find or create alters. In addition to the traits we display are those that are drawn out of us; our behaviour is mutually dependent on that of others. Similarly the significance of a work and the knowledge of a reader are mutually interdependent; in this way a man's understanding of a novel may constantly change. Novels also resemble arguments, in that they may be taken either as actual or as possible episodes. By appearing in different contexts the 'same' argument may represent different purposes and have different significance; listeners who disregard the actual contextual background of an argument are, as it were, prizing it from its proponent, and using it for themselves. Similarly, readers of texts who disregard the author's contextual purposes, are, in the sense I have outlined, using it for the creation of their own interpretations. To classify a text as a novel—or, more generally, a work of art—is to legitimize the freedom they claim for their creative interpretation. We sometimes claim this freedom in every day discourse. Another factor about art may be noted. In everyday discourse there is often a practical need for speakers to reach agreement on the interpretation of given utterances. In the realm of art there is often no practical need to reach such agreement; indeed, when we wish to preserve our freedom to interpret, agreement of the practical sort is accorded a low priority. On the other hand we should recognize that the practical need to do something does occur in criticism; for a critic who needs to say something may, in effect, invent something to say, and in so doing lay the foundation for a convention for speaking in that way. A number of these features are brought out in the following fable; after its telling I shall draw attention to specific aspects of it.

Two friends, Ernest and Gilbert, have no liking or appreciation for, and no enjoyment of, the novels in particular, or the works of art in general praised by their friends. But aware of the cachet in their community of being thought to have Taste [*sic*], they carefully observe their friends' conversation and other behaviour. They note, among other things, the consistent praise and absence of dispraise of certain works, and the application of certain terms to particular works. But Ernest fails to find rules or criteria for the application of these terms, and he can hardly ask; he is always in doubt what to say when confronted with a new case, with a novel he has not encountered before, or upon which he has heard no one else's comment. He gives up the unequal struggle, and refers to every novel with which he is confronted, like the Countess Gemini (in *The Portrait of a Lady*) as 'interesting'. But now everyone knows what he knows: that he has neither judgement nor understanding—and no Taste. He knows, both from their withholding these accolades from him, and from his own absence of any discernible inner feeling that might be correlatable with the award of the accolade. He says what others say—but only after they have said it. No one speaks of his understanding particular novels or ranges of works. Now Gilbert finds no rules, either, for the application of the terms his friends use, but when confronted with new cases he makes guesses as to what others might say; he bases his guesses on his memory of what others have said of novels which in at least one identifiable respect resemble the novel in question. In any case, the vocabulary of apparently crucial (recurrent) terms is not all that large, much of it is indeterminate, if not vague, and, in addition, he often knows the names of the novelists before he has to comment upon their work. When his guesses coincide with, or approximate to, what others say, no one notices. When they do not, others either remark upon his errant taste, or praise him for brilliant and thought-provoking criticism. Gilbert becomes a famous critic, and others, nervous as he once was, now await his every utterance. For he is known not only to understand particular novels, but to understand about novels, and to understand art. But Gilbert himself still has no enjoyment from the novels about which he talks, nor any interest in them apart from the motive to be judged favourably on his talk; he believes his reputation depends entirely upon what he says, not upon what he feels, nor upon the features of the work he talks about. He believes that what counts as understanding a particular novel is what is said or done, and is found acceptable, sometimes without reflection or reason, within a particular group at a particular time.

Several features of this fable should be noted, apart from the question whether it is logically possible for anyone, including Gilbert, to tell the story. The fable implies a distinction between first-person and third-person recognition that a man understands a given novel; it implies that 'he exhibits understanding-behaviour but yet does not understand the novel' is not self-contradictory; nevertheless, it implies that a man's behaviour justifies others in *saying* 'He understands'; it implies that if we accept Gilbert's critical judgements and his disclaimer to have any relevantly discernible internal state correlatable with his judgements or the works they are about, then no such state is necessary; it implies that critics have an interest in saying something unusual, and that they may have many motives for attending to works of art; it implies that entirely contingent factors about the context of the utterance may determine whether banalities are ignored or positively rejected, and whether originalities are dismissed as aberrations or adopted as thought-provoking; the social context in which these matters take place reveal the intimate connection between the evaluations and critical comment found acceptable; the fable raises the question of whether a man may pretend to understand a particular novel, and implies that if Gilbert has no grasp of what constitutes understanding any work at all, he could not tell the story in terms of his own pretending. There is a further implication of the fable: although it is logically possible for a man to understand a given work, in some sense of 'understand', while yet being unable, contingently, to show that he did, it would be logically impossible actually to pick out such a case; nevertheless it would be a case in which the third-person judgement 'He does not understand' would be mistaken.

In so far as understanding, in its various senses, is an achievement concept, a man who achieves understanding possesses a power which he may decide to exercise or not. A man's behaviour is the evidence to others that he understands, and his behaviour is the only way in which that understanding can be defined. A man's understanding does not *consist* in his behaviour, however, nor is his own behaviour evidence to *him*, or his justification for a claim to understand. There is no contradiction in his revealing understanding-behaviour but yet not understanding; and it may be a measure of his understanding of a context to keep his understanding to himself. In any case, the possibility that our third-person judgements of him may be wrong in a given instance, does nothing to diminish our rational reliance on the probability that in most instances we are right. But decisions whether a man's behaviour is counted by others as evidence of understanding are matters largely of agreement and convention about the type of context; and these are contingent matters.

A man who is content with his understanding of a novel is content with the way he takes it, and one who regrets his partial or incomplete understanding is not satisfied with the way he takes it. The implication of possession in the expression 'Now I've got it', which might characterize a satisfied man's response, is not incompatible with the notion of creative interpretation; for it refers to seeing what can be done with a work, and to what behaviour towards the work is found appropriate. Although we may try to reach a satisfactory interpretation of a novel by various means, for example by adopting different viewpoints of it or selecting different aspects of it, the 'taking' we adopt cannot be antecedently characterized; it is something of which we can be aware only after we have reached it. In this respect understanding shares features of what are called, in the classical terminology, activities and passivities. Claims to understand a novel may be provisional in two respects: first, a man may always discover something about the work that he did not previously know, and which he wishes to incorporate in his interpretation in some way; secondly, he may at any time cease to be satisfied with the significance he has created, or his interests may change so that he derives no satisfaction from taking it in that way, or, indeed, from attending to it at all.

In conclusion some important points must be stressed. I have said that to classify something as art is to confer some degree of freedom on an interpreter; but I emphasized that this is only one feature of the concept of art, and in no way captures the complexity of it. There is, of course, a host of other features that would need examination in a thorough analysis of the concept, such as the role of the artist's thought and emotion, technical skill and medium, tradition and genre, the interaction and condensation of diverse intentions, aims, and purposes, and so on. The classification of a particular text as 'a novel' may well carry implications about any or all of these features. I have not been concerned to discuss these matters, although I have indicated that an interest in them may guide a particular reader's interpretation of a given text. It is important to remember, however, that the concept of art undergoes constant modification itself, and, with changes in the concept and thus in the range of phenomena that fall under it, go changes in discourse and attitudes. It is thus impossible for a single theory to account for a set of aesthetic problems for all time, even if it solves them for a given time. It is also impossible for a single theory to account for all the aesthetic problems at any one time, because these problems reflect different stages of constantly changing thought about art and art criticism. Some problems, therefore, will be legacies of views already being superseded, others will be harbingers of as yet half-developed views. My theory of interpretation does not illuminate evenly all the problems on which I claimed it shed some light, because those problems embody different elements of different assumptions and theories. It is worth reflecting on why my theory seems to work better for some novels than for others, and what the features are of those works to which it seems not to apply at all. Since the theory can apply outside art, it cannot by itself completely explain those problems it illuminates within the realm of art. But the notion of creative interpretation serves to stress continuities between what is, and what is not, classified as art; and it also sheds some light on the view that artists can make artists of us all. By reflecting on the importance of creative interpretation one may even come to the view that the possibility of art, in some of its forms, rests on the possibility of creative interpretation; and only spectators can determine whether a particular case realizes such a possibility.

I have quite deliberately painted my claims in broad outline, and I reserve for another occasion consideration of related but peripheral issues. I have given no formal criteria for identifying a text, an interpretation, significance, the use of a text, or the legitimacy of such a use in a given instance. I have not considered what critical assumptions would enable a reader to accept my interpretations of the novels and reject what I have said in this chapter. I must stress again that many works can be taken to operate on different levels, and that different kinds of criticism reflect different questions posed and different purposes. In practice, I believe, the legitimacy of a given use of a text is assessed only after the event, in the light of its returns; in this field, the ends often justify the means. One feature of these means should be noted: the rhetoric of their presentation. Just as philosophical argument is rarely linear in form, after the manner of a syllogism, so creative interpretation is often not overtly inferential, but immediate—in the sense explained above. In point of method, there are no sharp boundaries between the novels themselves, my interpretations of them, and the philosophical reflections in the present chapter. And this suggests that a study of certain kinds of literature may well be a fruitful way of pursuing philosophical enquiry.

SELECT BIBLIOGRAPHY

I have compiled a brief list of books which, after I had reached my own conclusions, I have found provoking or instructive. They nearly all contain further bibliographies for an interested reader.

MIDDLEMARCH; AND THE PHILOSOPHY OF GEORGE ELIOT

BOURL'HONNE, P., *George Eliot. Essai de biographie et morale*. Paris, 1933.

HAIGHT, Gordon S., *George Eliot. A Biography*. London, 1968.

—— ed., *A Century of George Eliot Criticism*. New York, 1965.

HARDY, Barbara, *The Novels of George Eliot*. London, 1959.

——, ed., *Middlemarch. Critical Approaches to the Novel*. London, 1967.

HARVEY, W. J., *The Art of George Eliot*. London, 1963.

HOLLOWAY, John, *The Victorian Sage*. London, 1953.

HOUGHTON, W. E., *The Victorian Frame of Mind 1830–1870*. New Haven, 1957.

KNOEPFLMACHER, U. C., *Religious Humanism and the Victorian Novel*. Princeton, 1965.

PARIS, B. J., *Experiments in Life. George Eliot's Quest for Value*. Detroit, 1965.

STEPHEN, Leslie, *George Eliot*. London, 1902.

ANNA KARENINA

BAYLEY, John, *Tolstoy and the Novel*. London, 1968.

CHRISTIAN, R. F., *Tolstoy. A Critical Introduction*. Cambridge, 1969.

MANN, Thomas, *Essays of Three Decades*. London, 1947.

MATLAW, Ralph E., ed., *Tolstoy. A Collection of Critical Essays*. Englewood Cliffs, N.J. 1967.

STEINER, George, *Tolstoy or Dostoevsky*. New York, 1959.

TROYAT, Henri, *Tolstoy*. London. 1968.

THE BROTHERS KARAMAZOV

BELKNAP, Robert L., *The Structure of The Brothers Karamazov*. The Hague, 1967.

COULSON, Jessie, *Dostoevsky. A Self-portrait*. London, 1962.

IVANOV, V., *Freedom and the Tragic Life*. New York, 1957.

JACKSON, R. L., *Dostoevsky's Quest for Form*. Yale, 1966.

MATLAW, Ralph E., *The Brothers Karamazov. Novelistic Technique*. The Hague, 1947.

MOCHULSKY, K., *Dostoevsky*. Princeton, 1967.

WASIOLEK, E., *Dostoevsky. The Major Fiction*. Cambridge, Mass. 1964.

WELLEK, Rene, ed., *Dostoevsky. A Collection of Critical Essays*. Englewood Cliffs, N.J. 1962.

A LA RECHERCHE DU TEMPS PERDU

BERSANI, Leo, *Marcel Proust. The Fictions of Life and of Art*. New York, 1965.

BRÉE, Germaine, *Marcel Proust and Deliverance from Time*. London, 1956.

CHERNOWITZ, Maurice E., *Proust and Painting*. New York, 1945.

MOSS, Howard, *The Magic Lantern of Marcel Proust*. London, 1963.

PAINTER, George D., *Marcel Proust. A Biography*. London, Vol. I, 1959; Vol. 2, 1965.

SHATTUCK, Roger, *Proust's Binoculars. A Study of memory, time and recognition in A la recherche du temps perdu*. London, 1964.

STRAUSS, Walter A., *Proust and Literature. The Novelist as Critic*. Cambridge, Mass. 1957.

CHAPTER 5

Good discussions of matters I raise in this chapter may be found in:

ALSTON, William P., *Philosophy of Language*. Englewood Cliffs, N.J. 1964.

HOSPERS, John, *Meaning and Truth in the Arts*. Hamden, Conn. 1964.

MARGOLIS, Joseph, *The Language of Art and Art Criticism*. Detroit, 1965.

WEITZ, Morris, *Hamlet and the Philosophy of Literary Criticism*. London, 1965.

WOLLHEIM, Richard, *Art and Its Objects*. New York, 1968; London, (Penguin Books) 1970.

References to Wittgenstein have been to:

WITTGENSTEIN, L., *Philosophical Investigations*. Oxford, 1953.

Among numerous commentaries on Wittgenstein's work may be mentioned:

FANN, K. T., *Wittgenstein's Conception of Philosophy*. Oxford, 1969.

PITCHER, George, ed., *Wittgenstein. The Philosophical Investigations*. New York, 1966.

SPECHT, E. K., *The Foundations of Wittgenstein's Late Philosophy*. Manchester, 1969.

INDEX

Index

fear: of consequences, 44–5, 54, 116, 144–5; and egoism, 45, 54

feeling(s): basis of knowledge, 10, 42, 46, 166; expression of, 81; 'impressions' or, 149, 152, 153–4, 163–9, 171, 176–9; indulgence in, 127; known with certainty, 92–3; thinking and, 74, 89–90, 95, 98, 163; unexpected, 119–20; *see also* experience, expression, impressions, inner states, knowledge

Feuerbach, L., 51, 52, 65

'form of life', 185

Fortnightly Review, 63

freedom: absence of, 113; in *Brothers Karamazov*, 6; conscience and, 107–8; desire and, 116–17; duties and, 87–8; egoism and, 85–8; experiment and, 159; in interpretation of the novel, 8, 182, 185, 186, 188–90, 195, 201, 204; in love, 87–8; how much, 31, 107; from past, 3–4, 18, 47; proof and, 124; result of understanding, 42; self-identity and, 86–7; self-punishment and, 130–1; unconditioned, 142, 144–5; views of Bray, Mill, Spinoza on, 52

Freedom of the Will, 52

Freud, S., 188–9

Galileo Galilei, 63

God: conscience and, 140–1; faith in, 113, 114, 117, 118, 124, 144–5; life and, 117, 138–9, 142; intelligibility of, 124–5

Goethe, J. W. von, 59

habit in *A la recherche du temps perdu*, 157, 162, 169, 176, 178

Hamilton, A., 63

hands as expressive, 98–9

Hegel, G. W. F., 60

historical setting in interpretation, 184–5

Hobbes, T., 64

Horne, R., 61

Hume, D., 9, 25, 49, 51, 52, 61, 63, 65, 67, 165n.

ideals: constructed by imagination, 150–1, 159, 162, 176–7; love for, 150

illusion: knowledge and, 163–8

imagination: in *A la recherche du temps perdu*, 7–8, 149, 150, 151, 154–6, 178; Anna Karenina's failure in, 87–8, 91; Blackwood's report, 59–60; cause and, 18, 25, 31; concepts and, 18; constructive, 17–19, 21–5, 27, 29–32, 47–8; desire and, 4, 35; Eliot's view, 58–9; experience and, 18–19, 29, 46–7, 49; ideals constructed by, 150–1, 159, 162.

175; interpretation requires, 18–19, 21–5, 27; interpretive function of, 18–19, 21–6, 27–31, 32; inventiveness of, 122–3; knowledge and, 9, 66–7; Lewes's view, 62–5; in *Middlemarch*, 3–4, 9–10, 13, 14, 15; morality and, 4, 10, 19–20; past conditions, 154; perception presupposes, 3–4, 17–18, 21–2, 25–7, 47; possibilities as proper objects of, 18, 33–5, 154–6; supplements experience, 19; sympathy and, 30–1; three functions of, 17–20, 47–9; used by Casaubon and Lydgate, 27–30

immediacy: in interpretation, 2, 183, 186, 205; *see also* conviction

implications, *see* inferences

import, *see* significance

impressions: in *A la recherche du temps perdu*, 7–8, 149, 152, 153, 163–9, 170–1, 176–80; *see also* feeling(s)

inferences: from behaviour, 17, 45–8, 77, 104–6, 126; in interpretation of the novel, 2, 182, 187, 192–3, 194

inner states: ascription to others of, 41–2; expression and, 14, 20–1, 71, 84, 96–101, 105–6, 119–20, 129; inexpressible, 96–9; inferred from behaviour, 17, 45–8, 77, 104–6, 126; in *Middlemarch*, 3–4; tension caused by, 77, 84, 97–8; unchallengeable claims about, 74; *see also* expression, feeling(s)

Inquiry concerning Human Understanding, 165n.

Inquiry into the Human Mind, 163n.

intellect: in *A la recherche du temps perdu*, 149, 156–60, 163–9, 176, 178–80; desire and, 143; emotion and, 63; feeling and morality, 54–5, 67; influenced by passions, 16; interpretation and, 163–6; in service of morality, 6, 143

intelligibility: assent and truth, 188; of God, 124–5; intentions and, 198–9; interpretation and, 182; purposiveness and, 186; and unintelligibility, 136, 144–5; *see also* meaning, significance, understanding

intentions: and actions, 121; of authors, 2, 10, 50, 68–9, 198–200; descriptions and, 198–9; intelligibility and, 198–9

interpretation of the novel: author's, 183–5, 189–90, 198–200; competence presupposed in, 186; constraints on, 184–5, 190–1; creative, 186–7, 189–91; dispensable, 192; extremities in, 184–5; freedom in, 8, 182, 185, 186, 189, 195, 201, 204; immediacy of, 2, 183, 186, 205; inferences and, 2, 182, 186–